P9-DHM-046

Stereotypes as Explanations

Stereotyping is one of the biggest single issues in social psychology but relatively little is known about how and why stereotypes form. *Stereotypes as Explanations* is the first book to explore the process of stereotype formation, the way that people develop impressions and views of social groups. Conventional approaches to stereotyping assume that stereotypes are based on erroneous and distorted processes, but the authors of this book take a very different view; namely that stereotypes form in order to explain aspects of social groups and in particular to explain relationships between groups. In developing this view, the authors explore classic and contemporary approaches to stereotype formation and advance new ideas about such topics as the importance of category formation, essentialism, illusory correlation, interdependence, social reality and stereotype consensus. They conclude that stereotypes are indeed explanations but they are nevertheless highly selective, variable and frequently contested explanations.

CRAIG MCGARTY is Reader in Psychology at the Australian National University. He is author of *Categorization and Social Psychology* (1999), co-author with Alex Haslam of *Doing Psychology* (1998), and editor of *The Message of Social Psychology* (1997).

VINCENT Y. YZERBYT is Professor of Social Psychology at the Catholic University of Louvain, Louvain-la-Neuve, Belgium. He is co-author, with Jacques-Philippe Leyens and Georges Schadron, of *Stereotypes and Social Cognition* (1994), and co-editor, with Guy Lories and Benoit Dardenne, of *Metacognition: Cognitive and Social Dimensions* (1998).

RUSSELL SPEARS is Professor of Social Psychology at the University of Amsterdam. He is co-editor, with Penny Oakes, Naomi Ellemers and Alex Haslam, of *The Social Psychology of Stereotyping and Group Life* (1997) and, with Naomi Ellemers and Bertjan Doosje, of *Social Identity: Context, Commitment, Content* (1999).

Stereotypes as Explanations

The formation of meaningful beliefs about social groups

Craig McGarty, Vincent Y. Yzerbyt
and Russell Spears

CAMBRIDGE
UNIVERSITY PRESS

PUBLISHED BY THE PRESS SYNDICATE OF THE UNIVERSITY OF CAMBRIDGE
The Pitt Building, Trumpington Street, Cambridge, United Kingdom

CAMBRIDGE UNIVERSITY PRESS
The Edinburgh Building, Cambridge CB2 2RU, UK
40 West 20th Street, New York, NY 10011-4211, USA
477 Williamstown Road, Port Melbourne, VIC 3207, Australia
Ruiz de Alarcón 13, 28014 Madrid, Spain
Dock House, The Waterfront, Cape Town 8001, South Africa

http://www.cambridge.org

© Cambridge University Press 2002

This book is in copyright. Subject to statutory exception
and to the provisions of relevant collective licensing agreements,
no reproduction of any part may take place without
the written permission of Cambridge University Press.

First published 2002

Printed in the United Kingdom at the University Press, Cambridge

Typeface Plantin 10/12 pt   *System* LaTeX 2$_\varepsilon$ [TB]

A catalogue record for this book is available from the British Library

ISBN 0 521 80047 1 hardback
ISBN 0 521 80482 5 paperback

Contents

Figures

Contributors

MARIËTTE BERNDSEN *University of Amsterdam*

PATRICIA M. BROWN *University of Canberra*

OLIVIER CORNEILLE *Catholic University of Louvain at Louvain-la-Neuve and the Belgian National Foundation of Scientific Research*

BERTJAN DOOSJE *University of Amsterdam*

S. ALEXANDER HASLAM *University of Exeter*

CRAIG McGARTY *The Australian National University*

STEVE ROCHER *Catholic University of Louvain at Louvain-la-Neuve and the Belgian National Foundation of Scientific Research*

PENELOPE J. OAKES *The Australian National University*

KATHERINE J. REYNOLDS *The Australian National University*

RUSSELL SPEARS *University of Amsterdam*

JOHN C. TURNER *The Australian National University*

JOOP VAN DER PLIGT *University of Amsterdam*

VINCENT Y. YZERBYT *Catholic University of Louvain at Louvain-la-Neuve*

Preface

This book developed from a series of interactions between social psychologists at the Australian National University, the Catholic University at Louvain-la-Neuve and the University of Amsterdam. In fact, all of the contributors to the current volume were doing research at one or other of those institutions during the 1990s.

All of the contributors to the volume were motivated by a desire to get beyond some of the ideas about stereotyping that had so dominated work in the 1970s and 1980s and were showing remarkable powers of recovery in the 1990s. In doing this work several of us saw that despite differences in theoretical perspectives and/or our geographical location there were common threads in our work.

Many of the common ideas related to a view of stereotype formation as a search for meaning on the part of the perceiver. We used different terms for this search for meaning, such as explanation, understanding, deriving differentiated meaning, but the commonalities in what we were doing were obvious to us. The key ideas were consistent with the classic work of Bruner and had figured prominently in social psychology in work inspired by self-categorization theory and by social judgeability theory, which made the point about the link between stereotyping and meaning in a more general way.

It was perhaps in the domain of stereotype formation that the idea of sense-making had the most to offer. Stereotype formation seemed to be covered in every introductory social psychology textbook, but work in the field had very little to say about why stereotypes were formed, except under quite unusual (albeit interesting) circumstances. In our different ways, we have sought to apply the idea that people form stereotypes in order to make sense of their world, and this book is really a progress report on what we have discovered so far.

Many of our colleagues are contributors to this volume and their contributions will be readily apparent as you read this book. As editors we extend our sincere thanks to all of them, in their different ways they have all taught us a lot about stereotype formation. However, we would like to thank those numerous other colleagues who are not directly involved in the current project but who have been involved in related work or with whom we have discussed some of the current ideas. These include Ana-Maria Bliuc, Amaly Khalaf, Girish Lala and Mark Nolan at ANU. At the Research Group of the Social Psychology Division at the Catholic University of Louvain at Louvain-la-Neuve we would like to thank particularly Jacques-Philippe Leyens, Emanuele Castano, Alastair Coull, Muriel Dumont and Anouk Rogier. Of the people who have been involved in related work in the Netherlands Russell Spears would like to thank Ap Dijksterhuis, Ernestine Gordijn, Naomi Ellemers, Jolanda Jetten, Tony Manstead and Daan Scheepers. Vincent Yzerbyt would like to thank the Belgian National Fund for Scientific Research for their financial support allowing him to travel to Australia and his university for giving him academic and financial support during his sabbatical semester. Our thoughts go primarily though to our families, and in particular to Craig's partner Fiona and their son Aidan and to Vincent's wife, Isabelle, and their three kids, Simon, Mathilde and Lucas, for their constant support.

Finally we would like to thank Sarah Caro at Cambridge University Press for her assistance and her enormous forbearance given the unanticipated delays with this book, and Sara Barnes for her meticulous copyediting.

CRAIG McGARTY, VINCENT YZERBYT
AND RUSSELL SPEARS

1   Social, cultural and cognitive factors in stereotype formation

Craig McGarty, Vincent Y. Yzerbyt and Russell Spears

The purpose of this book

Imagine for a moment a busy city intersection with a police officer controlling traffic. All of the users of that street are individuals, but they are also members of society and, like the police officer they are members of groups that help us to explain why those people act in the way they do at particular times. Indeed, individuals and groups can be said to be the central facts of society. Without individuals there could be no society, but unless individuals also perceive themselves to belong to groups, that is, to share characteristics, circumstances, values and beliefs with other people, then society would be without structure or order. These perceptions of groups are called stereotypes.

If we accept that perceptions of groups are so important for people to understand the social world, then understanding those stereotypes is also extremely important for social psychology. Social psychologists such as Asch (1952) have argued that understanding the relationship between individuals and groups is the master problem for social psychology. In addressing this problem we need to recognize though, that individuals and groups tend to have their effects on each other through their psychological representation within individual minds. That is, social objects affect us through the way they are perceived rather than through the application of physical force.

Think again of the police officer controlling traffic at a busy intersection. The police officer does not (normally) need to physically restrain the traffic from passing through the intersection. He or she can signal to drivers to wait and, because they accept that the police officer has that responsibility, or because they believe there will be a risk of an accident or fine if they proceed through the intersection (or for any one of a myriad of other reasons) they do in fact stop when signalled. Our perception of the authority of the police officer rests on our perception of the membership of that police officer in the police service. Interpretations of that police officer's actions are largely shaped by our understanding of the role of the police service. Drivers will respond to a police officer's signals in one way, but would respond in a completely different way to someone they *believed* to be a prankster dressed as a police officer.

Thus, interactions with other people are powerfully constrained by group memberships and these are usually effective through the psychological representation of those groups. We say 'usually effective' because there are obvious circumstances where social interactions do involve physical forces. If the truck in front obeys the police officer's signal to halt then our car will stop as well, regardless of our psychological representation of the situation: either because we apply our brakes or because we have run into the back of the truck.

If it is true, though, that groups and individuals have their effects on us through their psychological representation, and in particular the representation of individuals as members of groups, then a particular and important problem emerges that needs to be solved in order for social psychology to progress. How do people represent groups and how do these representations form? These are precisely the questions that we propose to address in this book.

Such representations or impressions of groups (such as the impressions of police in the example above) are called *stereotypes*. These are psychological representations of the characteristics of people that belong to particular groups.

What are stereotypes?

To understand what stereotypes are it is useful to consider three principles which guide work on the social psychology of stereotyping. No perspective shares all principles to the same degree, rather different perspectives sample from each of the principles to greater or lesser degrees. Nevertheless the three guiding principles we can identify are as follows: (a) stereotypes are aids to explanation, (b) stereotypes are energy-saving devices, and (c) stereotypes are shared group beliefs. The first of these implies that stereotypes should form so as to help the perceiver make sense of a situation, the second implies that stereotypes should form to reduce effort on the part of the perceiver, and the third implies that stereotypes should be formed in line with the accepted views or norms of social groups that the perceiver belongs to.

Guiding principle 1: stereotypes are aids to explanation

A widely accepted view in social psychology stemming from the work of Tajfel (1969, 1981a; Tajfel & Wilkes, 1963) is that stereotyping is an instantiation of the categorization process. We cannot have an impression of a group unless we can tell the difference between that group and some other group. Categorization is the cognitive process by which we detect those differences and similarities.

In Tajfel's analysis (aspects of which are prefigured in the work of Allport, 1954; Campbell, 1956; Bruner, 1957a) categorization is the process by which categories become coherently separable and clear through the detection and accentuation of relevant similarities and differences. This accentuation can be seen as a means of crystallizing important regularities amongst the stimuli so that they can be recognized, remembered and responded to.

Bruner (1957a) argued that perception proceeded on the basis of the fit between category specifications and the readiness of the perceiver to use those categories. This argument is echoed in the stereotype formation literature: stereotype formation involves the perception or encoding of new information but it also enlists prior knowledge. Rarely is the mind a blank slate on which a fresh stereotype can be inscribed, but, continuing the analogy, its surface is marked with many well-worn grooves that make certain stereotypes more likely to appear.

Sense-making approaches to social stereotyping are extremely numerous (for a review see McGarty, 1999). They include self-categorization theory (Oakes, Haslam & Turner, 1994; Turner, Hogg, Oakes, Reicher & Wetherell, 1987), social judgeability theory (Leyens, Yzerbyt & Schadron, 1992, 1994) the exemplar model of social judgement (Smith & Zárate, 1992) and a variety of approaches based on processes of assimilation and contrast (e.g., Biernat, Vescio & Manis, 1998). Many aspects of these approaches are considered in the chapters to come.

Although most social psychologists pay lip service to the idea that stereotypes involve sense-making or knowledge creation in practical terms this emphasis is often reduced to a very simple idea. In an environment that contains too much information the most adaptive response by the perceiver is to attempt to reduce this information overload by filtering out or ignoring much of it (see Medin, 1988; Oakes & Turner, 1990, for critical discussions from different perspectives). This idea is pursued in the next sub-section.

Guiding principle 2: stereotypes are energy saving devices

If stereotypes are devices which people form in order to help understand the world, why do they take the particular form they do and how do they achieve this explanatory function? The most common answer in social psychology is that stereotypes aid explanation by saving time and effort.

In particular, treating people as group members saves energy because it means that we can ignore all of the diverse and detailed information that is associated with individuals.

This idea, which was first clearly articulated by Allport (1954), became the cornerstone of the cognitive approach to social stereotyping in the 1970s (the key publication is the book edited by Hamilton, 1981a). The key ideas can be summarised as follows (see McGarty, 1999). Individual people have limited capacities to perform cognitive tasks such as processing information. Nevertheless they exist in a complex, multi-faceted world that places enormous demands on that limited capacity. This complexity is certainly true of the social environment, and the resulting overload of human information processing capacity leads people to take shortcuts and to adopt biased and erroneous perceptions of the world. Stereotypes are simply one example of the biases that can develop.

Over time this negative view of stereotypes has become the received wisdom. Stereotypes are not so much aids to understanding but aids to misunderstanding. Stereotypes have received such a bad press in social psychology for a very long time. As Asch (1952) noted 'The term stereotype has come to symbolise nearly all that is deficient in popular thinking' (p. 232). In particular, stereotypes have often been seen as rigid and distorted mental structures that lead people to make serious errors. The negative view has been rekindled in the last thirty years by the rise of social cognition in social psychology. For a variety of reasons that we will not explore here (but see Oakes et al., 1994; Oakes & Turner, 1990; Spears, Oakes, Ellemers & Haslam, 1997), social cognition has tended to focus on the limitations of human cognition, that is, it has tended to focus on what is defective, flawed or irrational in the way people think. The stereotype has been of interest because it has been understood to be the form of representation where defective thinking reaches its nadir. That is, researchers suggest that what seems most wrong about human thinking is encapsulated in the stereotype, to the point that some authors have argued that stereotypes are even held to be wrong (and are therefore unwanted) by the people who hold them (Bodenhausen & Macrae, 1998).

This view of the falsity of stereotypes creates a tension in terms of the master problem of social psychology that we have already touched upon. If stereotyping is so central to our understanding of the world how plausible is it that the process could be so deficient? It also creates an enormous tension in relation to the first guiding principle. How can stereotypes assist with explanation if they produce falsehoods and distortions (i.e., misunderstandings not understandings)?

The ubiquitous nature of the negative stance on stereotypes can be seen by the fact that it is sometimes adopted by writers who explicitly disavow it. In Hilton and von Hippel's (1996) review of stereotypes in the *Annual Review of Psychology* the authors commit themselves to the position that the functions of stereotypes are context-dependent, and that stereotypes may reflect existing group differences, but when addressing stereotype formation their discussion is restricted entirely to an 'attempt to identify those processes that cause stereotypes to emerge, *independent of preexisting differences among groups.*' (p. 244, emphasis added). In other words, the possibility of processes by which stereotypes could form on some basis that was not largely erroneous is excluded from consideration as part of the topic in a general review of the field. The need to explore the alternatives, including the possibility that stereotypes can form on the basis of valid information, provides much of the motivation for this book.

We will provide a much more detailed exposition of the falsity of stereotypes and a range of arguments against this position later (see also Oakes et al., 1994; Oakes & Reynolds, 1997; and for a slightly different view see McGarty, 1999), but before we can go further we must settle a definitional problem. We use the term stereotype for any impression of groups held by anybody regardless of whether the accuracy of that belief is disputed. Stereotypes are impressions of groups held by people. The accuracy of those beliefs may be important in its own right, but it should play no part in the definition of stereotypes (Judd & Park, 1993). It may be tempting to describe our own views as accurate and logically justified (after all why would we believe something we knew to be wrong or illogical) and those of others with whom we disagree as stereotypes, but this is no more than name-calling and not a substitute for a scientific definition (see Oakes et al., 1994; Spears et al., 1997).

Guiding principle 3: stereotypes are shared group beliefs

Stereotypes attract little attention when they are not shared by many people. If every individual had a very different stereotype of some group then those stereotypes would be of little interest. Shared stereotypes, for example, are useful for predicting and understanding the behaviour of members of one group to another. If stereotypes are primarily interesting because they are shared it becomes important to understand why they are shared and how they come to be shared.

When we observe that many different people have similar stereotypes of the same group then we can offer a number of qualitatively different explanations for that state of affairs. One obvious explanation is the effect of coincidental processes operating on individual minds. There are two key variants on this view: one is that a common environment provides similar stimulus experience to different people and therefore similar stereotypes emerge.

In simple terms this first version is not all that plausible. There is plenty of evidence of shared stereotypes where there is no direct stimulus experience (Katz & Braly, 1933, make this point, see also Haslam, 1997).

The second variant is a better suggestion. This is the idea that there is a shared cultural pool of knowledge, social representations, ideology or culture from which different people sample and it is this which produces the commonality of views. However, this idea in turn ignores the reality that people's views become similar to each other through mutual social influence: people systematically become more similar to or more different from each other. Indeed McGarty (1999) argues that increasing similarity and difference is a ubiquitous but not unique key marker of social organization. Green peas in a pod may be very similar to each other in relevant ways and very different from (say) snow peas. Unlike members of a human social group though, the peas do not become more similar to each other. Members of human groups therefore have the power to become more similar and different, and stereotyping needs to be able to capture this dynamism.

Thus, the most interesting way in which stereotypes can become shared relates to the argument that stereotypes are normative beliefs just like other beliefs. They are shared by members of groups not just through the coincidence of common experience or the existence of shared knowledge within society, but because the members of groups act to coordinate their behaviour. The processes by which this occurs are relatively well-understood. Group members engage in processes of differentiation to make their groups distinctive from other groups, but they also engage in processes of social influence within groups so that their members become more similar to each other on relevant dimensions. There is no reason to believe that impressions of groups will be less dependent on these processes than other phenomena. Indeed if we argue that stereotypes can entail behavioural outcomes such as (positive and negative) discrimination it would be remarkable if such behaviour were not guided by consensualized norms. In practice some of the most consensual behaviours performed within any group relate to the treatment of outgroups, and this is especially so in intergroup conflict (including the extreme case of war or other forms of intergroup violence).

Stereotypes as psychological constructs

The cornerstone beliefs that we have addressed so far suggest some of the central concerns in the field and point to aspects of the character of stereotypes. They may be less directly informative about the psychological nature of stereotypes. That is, they do not tell us much about stereotypes as psychological constructs. Here we discuss two possibilities briefly.

The first is that a stereotype is a set of associated beliefs. That is, the stereotype can be thought of as a relatively enduring system of interrelated concepts that inform perceptions of members of certain groups. The large number of variants of this view make it the most popular within the field (Stangor & Lange, 1994, provide one such detailed statement but there are many other possibilities).

The second possibility is that the term stereotype is reserved to refer to a specific representation of a particular group at a particular time. The difference between these views is analogous to the difference between knowledge and perception. To see the difference consider whether you would term a statement like 'the unemployed are lazy' as a stereotype or see the stereotype as something deeper and more complex which contributes to the expression of statements such as the one given in the example, but is not exactly the same as those expressions. Clearly this definitional issue is important for the study of stereotype formation. We need to know whether we are dealing with the formation of individual beliefs that can be readily expressed (and hence measured). Generally speaking our approach is in line with the customary practice in the field: we assume individual stereotypical statements and beliefs are related to the expressions of underlying systems.

Why do stereotypes form?

Several possible motivations have been suggested for the process of stereotype formation. As we have seen, many authors suggest that the accentuation of differences between groups serves to clarify or make sense of reality by selectively crystallizing important differences from the current vantage point of the perceiver (Oakes et al., 1994; Spears et al., 1997) or by simplifying the overwhelming environment which confronts the perceiver (Brewer, 1988; Fiske & Neuberg, 1990).

Other motivations include self-enhancement, that is, accentuating or magnifying differences on relevant dimensions may serve to underscore the positive features of some ingroup with respect to outgroup members thereby contributing to a positive social identity (Tajfel & Turner, 1979; see also Doise, Csepeli, Gouge, Larsen & Ostell, 1972; Schaller & Maass, 1989). Other authors make the rather different argument that distortions are self-enhancing because they reflect self-serving biases.

A more multi-faceted motivational account is provided by social judgeability theorists such as Leyens et al. (1994), who, however, have suggested that stereotyping serves pragmatic functions by producing judgements which are adequate at a number of different levels. The aim of each of these levels is to provide a useful fit with reality rather than an exact match with reality, and in particular, to allow people to interact with other people. The cultural level of adequacy reflects people's propensity to follow the social rules within a particular culture at a particular time. An example of such a social rule that is immediately relevant to this discussion (and is introduced by Leyens et al., 1994, pp. 5–6; for empirical work on this topic see Yzerbyt, Schadron, Leyens & Rocher, 1994) is that in many Western societies it is seen as wrong to treat people at the categorical level (i.e., to stereotype them) without paying attention to individuating information.

The integrity level relates to the personal and social integrity of the judge. The suggestion is therefore that people avoid applying categorizations which would threaten the identity of themselves as individuals or of groups to which they belong. Thus, a supporter of a political party may resist forming an impression of their leader as corrupt, despite evidence of dubious deals, because that impression would have negative consequences for the party, the supporter's self-esteem and so on.

The theoretical level of adequacy relates to the degree to which the judgement explains the relationships between the information that is to be integrated. Under this view a judgement should comprise an *enlightening gestalt* that gives meaning to the world and allows communication. These ideas closely correspond to the ideas of Medin and colleagues that the naïve theory of *psychological essentialism* underpins categorization behaviour (Medin, 1989; and as applied to social categories by Rothbart & Taylor, 1992) and in particular that some categories have essences. Put simply, theoretical integrity refers to the perceived correspondence between a judgement and some theory of the world.

Yet another rationale is suggested by the argument of Tajfel (1981b, for a somewhat different view see Jost & Banaji, 1994) about the system-justifying role of stereotypes. That is, stereotypes can serve to maintain the status quo. The stereotype that Blacks are less intelligent than Whites might serve to justify the maintenance of limited programmes for educational advancement by Blacks.

How do stereotypes form?

So far we have dealt with some very broad introductory questions. We now tighten our focus to deal with the more specific mechanisms by which stereotypes could form. For historical reasons the discussion of these mechanisms centres around the idea of the development of perceived erroneous relationships between group membership and behaviour. That is, stereotype formation has largely been understood as being about coming to see relationships which (a) involve behaviours and (b) are not based on objective evidence (i.e., the relationships do not actually exist). The analysis which emerged in terms of these ideas provided one of the clearest examples of the cognitive approach to social psychology.

Distinctiveness and expectancy-based illusory correlations

The work of Hamilton and colleagues in the late 1970s and early 1980s made the distinction between stereotyping as the encoding of new information and the application of existing knowledge clear. These authors focused on the formation of new stereotypes in terms of *distinctiveness-based illusory correlation* (Hamilton & Gifford, 1976) and on the application of existing knowledge through *expectancy-based illusory correlation* (Hamilton & Rose, 1980).

The particular attraction of the illusory correlation effect was as an explanation of the formation and development of stereotypes of minorities. A distinctiveness-based illusory correlation is generally defined as the erroneous perception of the co-occurrence of rare characteristics. Normally, in social psychological usage, the effect is concerned with a perceived linkage between minority group membership and rare (usually undesirable) behaviours.

The details of the illusory correlation effect (ICE) and paradigm used by Hamilton and Gifford (1976) are well-known in social psychology and are discussed in several of the chapters to follow. For the time being we will just note that participants are exposed to a number of statements describing either positive or negative behaviours about members of Group A and Group B. Two thirds of the behaviours performed by members of each group are desirable and one third are undesirable. Participants are then normally asked to recall the group membership associated with each statement and to make judgements about the two groups. As there is no association between group membership and desirability of behaviour in the actual stimulus set then any observed association is said to be illusory.

The original explanation of the effect was Hamilton and Gifford's distinctiveness-based account. The cognitive process underlying ICE is as follows. The co-occurrence of two relatively infrequent events is especially noticeable or *distinctive*: it automatically triggers the observer's attention. These jointly infrequent events are hence better encoded, and more accessible to retrieval. Following Tversky and Kahneman's (1973) *availability heuristic*, the more easily they are retrieved, the more the subject perceives them as numerous, and therefore overestimates their frequency.

Hamilton and Gifford (1976, p. 405) do not 'deny, or even question, the importance of socially learned or culturally transmitted bases of stereotypes'. However, their core argument is that 'cognitive factors alone can be sufficient to produce differential perceptions of social groups'.

The illusory correlation phenomenon has been borne out by a number of studies (see the meta-analytic review by Mullen & Johnson, 1990). At the end of the 1980s almost all social psychology textbooks reported illusory correlation as a well established phenomenon that was best explained in terms of a universal cognitive bias (in the early 1990s, however, a range of explanations for the effect were proposed). (Fiedler, 1991; McGarty, Haslam, Turner & Oakes, 1993; Smith, 1991.)

The effect of this work on the field was two-fold. The first was that most discussions of stereotype formation were focused on stereotype formation as being a process by which erroneous views formed. The second was that the emphasis in the field became fixed on the formation of stereotypes of minorities. While this matched certain preoccupations in the societies within which the research was conducted, it meant that analyses of stereotype formation were necessarily incomplete.

At about the same time expectancy-based illusory correlation was demonstrated by Hamilton and Rose (1980). These authors showed that illusory correlation could be detected not just when people saw stimulus information but when people relied on expectations about the differences between social groups. That is, for meaningful social groups, expectations about those groups could serve as a basis for the perception of stereotypical differences.

There are two principal suggestions as to the ways in which stereotypes can emerge from expectancies. Both of these are contained in the work of Jussim (1991; Madon et al., 1998) and colleagues. The first is that stereotypes may emerge from actual differences between groups. This is the famous *kernel of truth* hypothesis (for a review see Oakes et al., 1994). Actual differences between groups may be detected and then become accentuated or magnified.

The second possibility is that stereotypes may actually be self-fulfilling prophecies (Snyder, 1981). Stereotypes may affect the ways that members of one group treat another and that in turn may lead to changes in behaviour of the stereotyped group. Perceiving the members of some group as violent and dangerous may, for example, lead to hostile treatment of that group which may in turn lead to a violent response from the stereotyped group.

In recent times there has been a range of new developments in the study of stereotype formation. These include fresh attempts to integrate distinctiveness and expectancy-based illusory correlation into the study of stereotype formation, and heightened attention to the importance of explanation in stereotyping.

Integrating distinctiveness and expectancy-based illusory correlation through the idea of differentiated meaning

McGarty et al. (1993) obtained results which were inconsistent with the prevailing explanations of the illusory correlation effect in terms of *biased encoding of stimulus information* (Hamilton & Gifford, 1976; McConnell, Sherman & Hamilton, 1994a) or *information loss* (Fiedler, 1991; Fiedler, Russer & Gramm, 1993; Smith, 1991). These authors showed that the illusory correlation effect could occur in the absence of stimulus information. This finding was problematic for the existing explanations because it implied that the effect was not essentially related to the processing or retrieval of the stimulus information.

The alternative explanation developed by McGarty and colleagues (Haslam, McGarty & Brown, 1996; McGarty et al., 1993; McGarty & de la Haye, 1997) was that illusory correlation was a reflection of processes of differentiation between social groups (what de la Haye and colleagues refer to as evaluative contrast). That is, when people are asked to find the differences between two groups, and are given information about the positions of group members on a dimension that might serve to distinguish between those groups they make certain assumptions. In particular they presume that the groups are different in some way and therefore look for some interpretation of the stimulus information that shows that the groups are different (given that the logic of the experimental setting, see Bless, Schwarz & Strack, 1993, implies that the groups are different a failure to detect these differences would be a failure to perform the required task).

When faced with this situation McGarty et al. believe participants engage in a process of reinterpretation whereby they seek to find some way in which the groups differ. This process is referred to as deriving differentiated meaning. It can be shown that there are at least two bases in the standard information for perceiving the groups to be different and in line with the suggestions of Fiedler (1991, 1996) and Smith (1991) these relate to sensitivities to group size. Furthermore, as Haslam et al. (1996) show, when participants know that the groups are not different on the underlying evaluative dimension (e.g., when considering left handed vs. right handed people) the illusory correlation effect disappears entirely. These ideas are wholly consistent with the work of Leyens, Yzerbyt and Schadron (1994) where pragmatic arguments are used to elucidate stereotyping effects such as the dilution effect.

Berndsen and colleagues have done much to validate and develop this explanation. They have shown that the stimulus information that people process in the illusory correlation paradigm actually changes in meaning as people differentiate between the groups. For example, positive behaviours performed by a minority are considered to be less positive and negative behaviours performed by the majority are seen to be less negative following the process of social categorization which participants perform. In other words, the stimulus information does not have a constant meaning but rather it varies in response to differentiation.

More generally, Berndsen, Spears, McGarty and van der Pligt (1998) have shown that stereotype formation is a dynamic process whereby the perception of the entitativity (Campbell, 1958, the extent to which the group is seen to have the quality of being a real thing) of the group impacts upon stereotype formation. Their work suggests that stereotype formation is a cyclical process whereby perceptions of similarity are a precursor to the perception of the coherence of the group and these perceptions are reinforced by the process of categorization.

This approach is fully consistent with recent work on the cognitive psychology of categorization which dispenses with the sharp distinction between theory-based and similarity-based perceptions (for a review see McGarty, 1999; this volume). Our impressions of categories rest on our understanding of the features that lead those categories to hang together but those understandings are in turn modified by impressions.

The renaissance of explanation in stereotyping

Allied with this reinterpretation of the illusory correlation paradigm in terms of meaningful differentiation between social groups has been a reemergence of the importance of explanation in stereotyping. Some of this work stems from the self-categorization and social judgeability traditions referred to earlier but this is only a small proportion of the total amount of work in these areas. Much of the work also stems from developments in cognitive psychology (see McGarty, this volume). Authors such as Kunda (1990; Kunda & Thagard, 1996) and Wittenbrink (e.g., Wittenbrink, Gist & Hilton, 1997) have made advances in relation to motivated reasoning, parallel constraint satisfaction and the use of mental models in stereotyping. There has also been a profusion of work on the perception of group entitativity (Brewer & Harasty, 1996; Hamilton & Sherman, 1996; McGarty, Haslam, Hutchinson & Grace, 1995; Yzerbyt, Rocher & Schadron, 1997). The main aim of this book is to move beyond the previous preoccupations of the field with limited information processing capacity to applying the lessons of the current wave of work on explanation in order to explicate stereotype formation.

An overview of the chapters to come

Our ideas can be explicated by reference to an example of a widely-held stereotype in many societies. This is the stereotype that unemployed people are lazy. Importantly, for our perspective, the belief that unemployed people are lazy helps to explain unemployment from the perspective of the stereotyper but it does much, much more. The stereotype also justifies an unsympathetic treatment of the unemployed. These points are well-understood in the social psychological literature (e.g., Allport, 1954; Augoustinos & Walker, 1996; Jost & Banaji, 1994; Tajfel, 1981b), but a range of fresh insights into this pervasive phenomenon are possible.

McGarty (Chapter 2 this volume; see also McGarty, 1999) argues that there is a fine distinction between the processes of explanation and justification (see Kunda & Oleson, 1995). The first relates to the more or less implicit (automatic) detection of covariation and mechanism-based information whereas the second relates to the production of vivid, symbolic representations which people can communicate to other people, or at least tell them about these representations. We might not have the ability or the desire to articulate our stereotype of some group but we may still talk about that stereotype in ways which convey it. Implicit and explicit processes tend to be associated so that through the actual exchange of explicit justifications implicit background knowledge can also become constrained to be similar. In this way stereotypes become shared explanations. Under this view, implicit expectations that the members of the category *unemployed* tend to have the characteristic *laziness*, as well as explicit references to groups in ways which justify social conditions or explain social relations (such as 'the unemployed don't have jobs because they are lazy') are all properly considered to be part of the stereotyping process.

Yzerbyt and Rocher (Chapter 3; Yzerbyt et al., 1997; Yzerbyt, Rogier & Fiske, 1998) argue that the formation of a stereotype of the unemployed is most likely to develop under conditions where unemployed people are perceived to share an underlying essence. The perception of a group as being entitative leads to the belief that, although group members have similarities and differences on the surface, they all share the same underlying core attributes. People will then tend to think of these inherent features as causing the observable behaviours. For instance, laziness would appear as an essential characteristic explaining why unemployed people are what they are.

Brown and Turner (Chapter 4) argue that the stereotype of the unemployed as lazy reflects a certain type of theory or explanation about unemployment rather than simply a fixed representation. A social categorization, such as unemployed, may or may not contain the trait 'lazy' depending on the accessible explanation perceivers hold for the causes of unemployment. In addition they argue that many theories encompass explanations that are broader than the actions of any one group. This means that stereotypes about the unemployed may also reflect widely shared ideologies about individualism versus collectivism.

Berndsen and colleagues (Chapter 5; see Berndsen & Spears, 1997; Berndsen et al., 1998) argue that the development of the stereotype of the unemployed would depend on whether perceivers expected differences between unemployed and employed people enabling them to differentiate and to create coherent groups on relevant dimensions. This would proceed through the development, testing and revision of hypotheses about the relative laziness of unemployed people. The idea of relative laziness is very important here because Berndsen's research suggests that meanings can be changed through a process of categorical contrast. That is, what it means to be lazy could be affected by the comparison that is being made.

Corneille and Yzerbyt (Chapter 6) provide a timely reminder that group perceptions are powerfully constrained by interdependence between group members. Although much recent research has focused on what Tajfel and Turner (1979) called 'subjective' conflicts between groups, objective conflicts of interest remain crucial and stereotype formation may be driven in part by such conflicts. Stereotyping the unemployed as lazy justifies social relations of disadvantage, and in particular explains why taxes and charity should not be used to support this group.

Work by Spears (Chapter 7) argues that the traditional cognitive information processing approach is ill-prepared for dealing with the full gamut of stereotype formation. Instead he argues it is necessary to bear in mind a series of key principles drawn from the social identity/self-categorization approach. These are the *meaning* principle, the *distinctiveness* principle, the *enhancement* principle and the *reality* principle. He applies these principles to stereotype formation under conditions ranging from information rich environments (where there is a great deal of activated stereotype knowledge) and information poor conditions (where there are no clear differences between the groups). Spears's principles are readily applied to the unemployment example. The reality principle dictates that the objective economic disadvantage of the unemployed exists. The meaning principle suggests that this difference must be made sense of in some way, and the distinctiveness and enhancement principles suggest that to the extent to which employed people think in group terms they will tend to see the unemployed as different from the employed but to see the employed positively (perhaps in terms of being diligent, and charitable to the deserving needy, or withholding charity from those who are undeserving).

Finally, work by Haslam and colleagues (Haslam, Turner, Oakes, Reynolds & Doosje, this volume; Haslam, 1997; Haslam, Oakes, McGarty, Turner, Reynolds & Eggins, 1996; Haslam, Oakes, Turner, McGarty & Reynolds, 1998; see also Reicher, Hopkins & Condor, 1997) implies that what is most interesting about stereotypes, but is often neglected in stereotyping research, is that stereotypes are consensual. That is, if the view that the unemployed are lazy were held only by isolated individuals it would receive little attention. On the contrary, the fact that the stereotype is an explanation which is shared by many other people is what makes it important. Beliefs about groups are also beliefs which can be shared by groups and to understand how they form we need to understand the process by which they come to be shared (consensualization). These beliefs represent a necessary precondition for collective action such as protest as well as for regulation and law enforcement. Their argument is that stereotypes form to enable action. They are political weapons that are used in the attempt to achieve and resist social change.

To begin the process of exploring these ideas in the chapters to come it is appropriate first to consider some of the foundational ideas touched upon in this chapter about the role of cognition in stereotype formation. This is the focus of Chapter 2.

2   Stereotype formation as category formation

Craig McGarty

In this chapter I explore the contribution of research on category formation to the study of stereotype formation. The rationale for this is fairly straightforward. Stereotypes are based on or rely on categories, and in particular they rely on categories of people. If we accept the additional point that stereotypes are explanations then we are left with an important question: how does categorization contribute to the explanatory power of stereotypes?

As we will see in this chapter the explanatory nature of categories has been acknowledged for a long time. This is seen most clearly when we consider that the use of the term *concept* in cognitive psychology has been almost indistinguishable from the use of the term *category*. The term 'concept' is synonymous with the assignment of meaning or the development of understanding. If stereotypes are inextricably bound to categories then it should also be the case that stereotypes involve gaining or developing understanding as was argued in Chapter 1. It follows that the cognitive psychological work on category and concept formation should repay a close look.

The path I will follow is first to discuss how that approach that I term the *constraint relations formulation* helps us to understand treatments of categorization in cognitive and social psychology. I use this formulation to arrive at a summary of some key implications of the categorization process for understanding stereotype formation. These implications centre around the idea that the explanatory potential of categories is realized in the form of relatively enduring understandings of the differences between social groups. These understandings in turn provide bases for developing and communicating perceptions so that stereotypes come to be shared with other people.

After completing this review I then consider two important distinctions drawn from other work on explanation that helps us to understand stereotype formation. The first distinction is between explanation (which tends to be implicit) and justification (which tends to be explicitly available to consciousness and therefore in a communicable form). This distinction is drawn from an analysis of attempts to model connectionist accounts of explanation. The second distinction is between mechanism and covariation-based knowledge. I argue that stereotypes can be used for explanatory and justificatory purposes depending on the current cognitive needs of the perceiver and that they rely on a mix of both mechanism-based and covariational knowledge. I conclude by pointing to the need to distinguish between impressions of groups and social categories.

In discussing stereotype formation the idea of *formation* itself needs some explication. What does it mean to say that a stereotype is formed? Are entire stereotypes created afresh when a perceiver encounters some social group, or are previously stored stereotypes reactivated (see Spears, this volume)? Another way of framing these questions is to ask whether there is any important difference between stereotype formation and activation. It seems that there must be an important difference because one of the most important and interesting features of stereotypes is their propensity to be shared across a large number of people. If stereotypes are utterly fleeting and are always formed anew as a response to the specific situation then they can only be shared by different people when those different people are in the same psychological situation. If stereotypes are actually transmitted between people then they must be able to be stored (or at least retained) and reactivated in some form for later use and transmission.

To make progress in this discussion, however, I first need to say something about the structure and nature of categories based on the social psychological and cognitive work in this field. This is the topic of the first section.

Social and cognitive psychological approaches to category formation

I reviewed the social and psychological traditions of research on category formation in my 1999 book *Categorization in social psychology*. A key distinction in recent cognitive research on category formation is between category formation on the basis of similarity and category formation on the basis of theory or prior knowledge.

To understand the difference between these two it is helpful to discuss the notions of categories and categorization in some detail. The term 'category' is best used to describe a perception that two or more things are the same in some way and different from other things. Such perceptions can involve the current explicit recognition that two things are equivalent (as might be observed when the same label is explicitly applied to both of them) or implicit and background knowledge about commonality or connections between things. Each of these needs to be distinguished from the perception that two things are similar in some way with or without sharing some categorical identity from the vantage point of the perceiver in that instance.

It is for the purposes of both distinguishing between category labelling, perceiving equivalence and background knowledge, and also to show their relatedness that I proposed the constraint relations formulation (McGarty, 1999). Its application to stereotyping and stereotype formation is direct. The psychological instantiation of a stereotype is not simply (a) the application of a group label, or (b) the perception that members of some group are very similar to each other or very different from members of some other group, or (c) an accumulation of knowledge about the members of those groups. Rather it is a combination of those things in a way that serves two key purposes. First of all, it makes sense of aspects of some group. I use 'makes sense of' here as a shorthand for a variety of psychological processes related to developing understandings. The term therefore subsumes justification and explanation, each of which demands attention in its own right (see the next section). Secondly, and equally importantly, stereotypes tend to combine perceived equivalence, background knowledge and category labels in ways which are readily transmitted to other members of society, especially those who hold the same values and (especially) group memberships as the perceiver.

These are complex ideas that need to be teased out. To take an example, a perceiver's stereotype of librarians is obviously more than the mere application of the label 'librarian' to a collection of people who share the same job description. It is also clearly more than a store of knowledge about libraries and the people who work in them. Is the stereotype also more than a specific perception of some group? Such a perception might be that librarians are seen to be more similar to each other on characteristics such as being literate and introverted than are people in general. The answer seems to be that the stereotype must be more than just a perception of some group. Informally, we might say that the statement 'Librarians are bookish and quiet' is a stereotype (or 'just a stereotype'), but it seems wiser to preserve the technical term stereotype for something broader and deeper than this. In my preferred terminology such a statement about a group is referred to as a *stereotypical depiction*. The stereotype itself is the set of relations between knowledge, labels and perceived equivalences. An example of a way of representing such a stereotype is shown in Figure 2.1.

We can use the constraint relations formulation to help us address a series of important questions. The most relevant question for us to ask

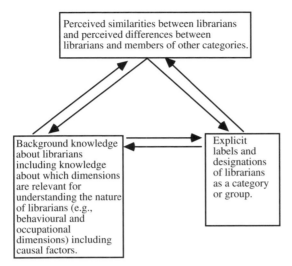

Figure 2.1 A representation of the aspects of a stereotype from the constraint relations perspective.

is, how do stereotypes form? More elaborately, what does it mean to say that a stereotype has formed?

In line with the previous discussion, stereotype formation must refer to more than just the development of a stereotypical depiction. Rather, it must refer to the development of a set of constraint relations between background knowledge, perceived equivalence and group labels. These must be capable of generating stereotypical depictions that can inform behaviour towards the members of the stereotyped group and facilitate communication between members of currently relevant groups to which the perceiver belongs. A person searching for romance through a dating service might use the profession of librarian as a cue to the personality of possible partners, but s/he might also seek to use a supposedly consensual stereotype about 'librarians' to explain to the dating service the sort of person that s/he is or is not looking for.

If this is what a stereotype is, then we need to think of them as explanatory systems that have the potential to be relatively enduring. Stereotypes are associated with stereotypical depictions which are themselves necessarily immediate, transitory and fleeting. Nevertheless these depictions have the potential to be incorporated into mental structures which are much less ephemeral through the capacity of the human mind to store previous representations and the power of communicative acts to convey these representations to other people. Under conditions that can be specified reasonably precisely then, stereotypes can become long lasting because people can make them concrete thereby potentially creating lasting traces of elements of these stereotypes in their own minds, and also to communicate them in symbolic form to other people. To paraphrase Wittgenstein: that which we *can* speak of we need not pass over in silence.

Having defined what it means for a stereotype to be formed the constraint relations formulation is helpful for discussing the key distinction in cognitive work on category formation and use: whether category formation is widely understood to be similarity or theory-based.

This is an old question in cognition. In order for a concept to exist it needs to be *about* some set of things. In order for the concept to be about those things the set needs to be constrained in some way and similarity is one plausible way of constraining that set (i.e., on the basis of perceived equivalence as shown in Figure 2.1 above). Thus, the stereotype about librarians might be based on the collection of perceived similarities amongst people who work in libraries. Over time it will have become necessary to come up with a label 'librarian' which captures the similarities that are perceived to exist amongst those workers. As Brown and Turner (this volume) explain, such a label is itself a theoretical proposition that serves to explain similarities and differences. This idea is easy to capture in constraint relations terms: category labels and background knowledge constrain each other.

Following the work of Murphy, Medin (e.g., Murphy & Medin, 1985; Medin, Goldstone & Gentner, 1993) and others it is now readily apparent that similarity is not of itself a sufficient source of constraints for categories. With the exception of some psychophysical phenomena which have little relevance for social psychological discussions there does not appear to be any basis for similarity to exist in a pure or primitive form. When we say two things are similar we always explicitly or implicitly carry with that statement a set of conditions which make them similar. That is, Thing A and Thing B can never be said to just be similar, they can only be similar in certain respects.

This is not to say that similarity is irrelevant or that it is never a precondition for establishing category membership (indeed both causal directions are shown in Figure 2.1), but rather that similarity and category membership are mutually enabling conditions. We see things to be similar to the extent to which they share a category membership, but we also see things to share category memberships to the degree to which they are similar (see also Berndsen et al., 1998).

The rationale for this position is derived from two broad and continuing traditions that are well-known within cognitive and social psychology. The earlier social psychological tradition develops directly out of work on stereotyping associated with Allport, Campbell and especially Tajfel, and is carried on in work on accentuation by Eiser and on self-categorization by Turner and others. The clearest contemporary statement is probably that contained within self-categorization theory:

> Category formation (categorization) depends upon the comparison of stimuli and follows the *principle of meta-contrast*: that is, within any given frame of reference (in any situation comprising some definite pool of psychologically significant stimuli), any collection of stimuli is more likely to be categorized as an entity (i.e., grouped as identical) to the degree that the differences between those stimuli on relevant dimensions of comparison (intraclass differences) are perceived as less than the differences between that collection and other stimuli (interclass differences). Turner et al. (1987, p. 47).

A key concept here is the idea of a *relevant* dimension of comparison. Relevant dimensions are those dimensions which are *known* to distinguish stimuli in a given context. Obviously the relevance of particular dimensions changes from context to context. That aside, the primary implication of this argument to category formation is then that similarity is derived from the categorical identity of the stimuli. Two things are seen to be similar if they currently share a category membership, and they are seen to be different if they currently belong to different categories.

The idea here is that categorization leads to the accentuation of perceived differences between groups and of perceived similarities within groups. In the terms originally envisaged by Tajfel and others this involved a distortion of reality. This idea of distortion has remained prominent in treatments of social categorization to this day (Claire & Fiske, 1998; Krueger & Clement, 1994; Judd & Park, 1993) but it has also been challenged by another approach which has treated the effects of categorization on judgement not as distortions but as selective crystallisations of reality from the current vantage point of the perceiver. SCT in particular champions this view (Turner et al., 1987; Turner, Oakes, Haslam & McGarty, 1994). Self-categorization theorists have argued, for example, that prominent stereotyping effects such as outgroup homogeneity (Haslam, Oakes, Turner & McGarty, 1995, 1996), ingroup bias (McGarty, 1999; and in particular the positive-negative asymmetry effect, Reynolds, Turner & Haslam, 2000), accentuation effects (Haslam & Turner, 1992, 1995; McGarty & Turner, 1992) and illusory correlation (Haslam, McGarty & Brown, 1996; McGarty & de la Haye, 1997; McGarty et al., 1993, for reviews see McGarty, 1999; Oakes et al., 1994) do not reflect distortions of reality but are accurate reflections of the facts from the point of view of the perceiver (for rather different approaches to this point see Chapter 11 by McGarty, 1999; and Oakes & Reynolds, 1997).

Roughly parallel with these developments in social psychology has been the rise of theory-based categorization in cognitive psychology. This work starts with the idea that similarity is an insufficient principle to constrain categorization and that therefore other principles need to be invoked. To take a famous example, Rips and Handte (cited by Medin & Smith, 1984) showed that a 12 cm disk was more likely to be categorized as a pizza rather than a coin even though it was equally different from the typical sizes of both coins and pizzas. The argument here was that coins are *known* to be limited by law and custom to particular size ranges, whereas it is *known to be possible* for pizzas to be as small as 12cm even though this is unlikely. Somewhat later Tversky (1977) showed that in comparisons of countries made by US college students Mexico was seen as similar to the USA and Poland to Russia, but that the USA was not seen as being like Mexico, and Russia was not like Poland. In other words, similarity was not a stable feature that could be used to determine comparisons rather it was *determined by comparison.*

A wide variety of principles have been invoked to deal with the insufficiency of mere similarity. These include theories (Murphy & Medin, 1985; Wisniewski & Medin, 1994), goal-directed categorization (Barsalou, 1991), the compatibility of linear separability with activated knowledge (Wattenmaker, 1995), structural alignment (Gentner, 1983; Gentner & Medina, 1998), psychological essentialism (Medin, 1989; Medin & Ortony, 1989) and thematic integration (Medin & Bassok, 1997). The key idea in each case is that knowledge of the relations between things is necessary to define those things to be similar.

This point has also been taken on board in various social psychological treatments such as Rothbart and Taylor's (1992) application of Medin's concept of psychological essentialism (but see N. Haslam, Rothschild & Ernst, 2000). Recent discussions of normative fit by self-categorization theorists, for example, need to be read closely with the work on the constraining role of theory (see Brown & Turner, this volume). At the same time, Yzerbyt and colleagues (Yzerbyt, Rocher & Schadron, 1997; Yzerbyt, Rogier & Fiske, 1998; see Yzerbyt & Rocher, and Corneille & Yzerbyt, this volume) have argued that the existence of underlying inherent characteristics which serve to explain observable similarities and differences binds together stereotypes. Indeed the ability to bind together observations in this way provides the basis for such a subjective essentialist conception of stereotypes.

The consensus has developed (for a review see Sloman & Rips, 1998) that categorization is based on both similarity and abstract rule-based processes but there has been a response to the idea of theory-constraints in cognitive psychology. In particular, in rather different ways Jones and

Smith (1993) and Goldstone and Barsalou (1998) have affirmed the prime importance of perception for categorization. Jones and Smith argue that categorization involves task-specific assemblies of knowledge that are not tightly constrained by long-term higher order knowledge but by lower-level perceptual memories. Goldstone and Barsalou (1998) argue that conceptual and perceptual processing are closely allied and that the mechanisms of conceptual processing are drawn from perception, and come close to endorsing the view that all knowledge is perceptual.

Similar views can be found in social psychology. Brewer's (1988) impression formation model and Carlston's (1994) associated systems theory both emphasize the importance of visual knowledge in representations of persons and groups, and the very idea that particular categories like race, sex, and age may be primary or central to certain forms of stereotyping (see Fiske & Neuberg's, 1990, continuum model) rests on the early and easy detection of these categories by visual means.

This short summary suggests that there is a rich tradition of work that points to important functioning interrelationships between knowledge and theory. Overall the work suggests that to understand category formation we need to understand how long-term knowledge about things interplays with the specific instantiation of categories at some instant. Exactly the same argument should apply to stereotypes. As we have already noted, either the specific impression that one has of a group at one instant, or the long-term knowledge about the group, may be called a stereotype, but to understand the process of stereotyping we need to understand how relatively long-term knowledge about those groups serves to underpin those specific instantiations. For ease of exposition I refer to the instantiation of the stereotype as the *stereotypical depiction* or *group impression* and refer to the long-term knowledge as *stereotypical knowledge*.

Stereotypical knowledge can then be assumed to have the following characteristics:

1. Stereotypical knowledge is explanatory. That is, it serves to help the perceiver to understand aspects of groups and their members and may also help to explain relations between groups. For example, the view that unemployed people are lazy serves to explain any perceived lack of activity on the part of unemployed people (individual or contextual factors are inevitably available to explain counterexamples), but in this case it also explains how people came to be unemployed in the first place. Jost and Banaji (1994) discuss how stereotypes also serve to maintain relations within societies by providing ideological justification for socio-political systems. In this case believing that the unemployed are lazy (and have brought their condition on themselves) also justifies a relatively harsh treatment of them.

2. Stereotypical knowledge should serve to make certain stereotypical depictions more or less likely across a range of contexts (but importantly, always in interaction with that context). Understanding laziness as the cause of unemployment should serve to increase the likelihood that particular unemployed individuals are perceived to be lazy but it should also make it more likely that someone will express agreement with that stereotype at particular times. In self-categorization theory terms, this effect of stereotypical knowledge can be understood as the effect of background knowledge on perceiver readiness. Perceivers are more likely to perceive some thing in terms of previously understood categories.

3. Stereotypical knowledge should provide an account of similarities and differences (see Brown & Turner, this volume; Oakes, Turner & Haslam, 1991). In other words, the knowledge associated with the classification system should be able to be reconciled with observed similarities and differences, but that body of knowledge should also be able to explain or rationalize observed similarities and differences or be updated to take account of those similarities and differences. Thus, the belief that the unemployed are lazy could serve to explain some observed differences in activity between the employed and unemployed, but it might also be used to explain differences in terms of other behaviour or characteristics (e.g., if unemployment is associated with particular ethnic, age and socio-economic groups it may be intuited that these groups contain many lazy people).

4. Stereotypical knowledge should contain explicit and implicit aspects. In the terms formalized by Higgins (e.g., 1996) we are talking about the range of knowledge available to be *activated* (which itself will vary in the ease with which it can be activated or its *accessibility*). Some knowledge will be available in a non-conscious, possibly sub-symbolic form while other knowledge will be symbolic and readily communicable. One important distinction that I will explore below is that between mechanism and covariation-based knowledge (after Ahn et al., 1995). Following on from evidence that covariation-based knowledge is often difficult to articulate I assume that the explicit-implicit distinction is slightly correlated with the mechanism-covariation distinction.

5. Stereotypical knowledge must incorporate knowledge of categories. This is a logical point. While a number of authors in cognitive and social psychology have emphasized the spontaneous ad hoc nature of categories that are assembled online for particular cognitive tasks in specific situations there must also be a capacity of the cognitive system to store these products. If the mind could not do this there could be

no stereotypical knowledge: we cannot store knowledge about what some thing is like unless we also store knowledge about what makes this thing different from other things. This necessarily means storing categorical knowledge. In other words, we must imbue our knowledge *about* things with differentiated meaning (McGarty & Turner, 1992), in order to understand the ways in which things are clearly different to each other.

6. Stereotypical knowledge must provide a basis for inferences in the form that people actually make them. This more or less rules out knowledge structures of a strictly hierarchical form as there is substantial evidence that people rarely make inferences to category membership on the basis of hierarchies despite the logical advantages that hierarchies would confer if they were used (see Sloman, 1998). Stereotypical knowledge also needs to be able to deal with conditions where categories overlap, or are wholly or partially contained or included in some other category.

Stereotypes for explanation, justification and rationalization

I (McGarty, 1999) endorse the distinction between explanation and justification that appears in the work of Kunda and Oleson (1995) and others. This endorsement is based partly on an analysis of attempts to model causal reasoning based on various connectionist models (see van Overwalle, 1998).

These connectionist models provide metaphors for describing the way the mind works. They normally involve writing computer programs that simulate the mathematical rules that the mind might follow when making decisions about information received from the environment. Normally, these systems involve the simulation of the processing of large amounts of information, or repeated sampling of the same information. The connections refer to connections between information received and the conclusions reached and to the connection between the nodes or units of the system that process the information. Connectionist models of causal reasoning involve the simulation of the processing of event information to arrive at conclusions about the causes of these events.

The key insight provided by van Overwalle was that models (such as the parallel-constraint-satisfaction model adopted by Read & Marcus-Newhall, 1993; Read & Miller, 1993; and also Kunda & Thagard, 1996, in the stereotyping domain) which did not include a particular learning rule were unable to detect covariation between stimuli. This was held to be an important advantage for another class of model, the feedforward model. Despite this advantage, the feedforward performed no better in modelling the actual performance of human participants.

This result raises two important possibilities: either human reasoning could be unrelated to the processes specified in either formulation, or the two formulations may each specify separate processes, each of which is important for reasoning. Given that the models performed tolerably well in modelling actual causal reasoning the latter idea appeared more intriguing.

The details of the two formulations are well outside the scope of this book (see Kunda & Thagard, 1996; McGarty, 1999; Read & Miller, 1993; and van Overwalle, 1998) but I want to provide a glimpse of the central elements of each here. The feedforward model involves patterns of activated nodes that flow from input nodes to output nodes, where the inputs are explanations and the outputs are events. Over time the system learns through changes in the strength of the connections between particular inputs and outputs. The output is then tested against evidence and adjusted so that it closely matches that evidence.

The system therefore identifies causes as those input nodes that are most strongly associated with particular events. Thus the sort of answer that the system is assumed to generate to questions of the form 'Why did Event X occur?' are of the form 'Because of Explanation Y [the explanation with the highest connection strength to Event X]'.

Importantly, the input nodes need not be explanations that can be expressed in symbolic terms. The inputs can be assumed to be distributed networks that defy expression in any form other than a computer simulation (and thereby are assumed to be patterns of neural activity within the brain at some instant).

On the other hand, recent instantiations of parallel-constraint-satisfaction models in social psychology have examined reasoning as the interaction between nodes which have a symbolic meaning. These nodes can be thought of as ideas or percepts that involve either evidence or explanations. These nodes can be mutually excitatory or inhibitory: thinking one thing at a particular time can make other related thoughts more or less likely and thinking those related thoughts can further serve to sustain or change the other line of thinking. The success of a particular explanation is represented by high levels of activation of particular explanatory nodes. Thus, the assumed answers to questions such as 'Why did Event X occur?' are of the form 'Because of Event Y [the most highly activated explanatory node in the system]'.

Both models have attractive features but they may be better seen as complementary rather than opposed formulations. The feedforward model with its ability to model the detection of covariation may provide a better model of the process of explanation, a process by which explanations often emerge implicitly without any obvious intrusions into consciousness. The dynamic and competing processes incorporated into the parallel constraint satisfaction system in symbolic terms may more closely match the explicit process of justification, where the outputs of cognition are available to consciousness and, through their representation in symbolic terms, are also available for communication to other people. Thus we have two correlated processes, explanation which includes covariation detection and which proceeds relatively automatically (see Bargh, 1996) and justification which works on a more explicit level with the outputs of the explanatory process. Thus, explanation deals with why we come to believe that 'Y is the cause of X' and justification deals with why we may think and say that 'Y is the cause of X'.

The explanation/justification distinction is as important for stereotype formation as for other forms of reasoning. The long-term knowledge about some group can be expected to be accumulated from a wide variety of sources. This will include a myriad of previous interactions with, or reactions to, members of that group which may no longer be available to conscious recall (and perhaps never were perceived at a more than subliminal level in the first place) but which retain some trace in memory. At particular times that long-term knowledge will be instantiated in current perceptions of a group or of group members. Thus, when the perceiver who believes that the unemployed are lazy sees John, an unemployed person, refuse a job offer, then their stereotype may provide the explanation for the observed event. This may result in a perception of the following form:

> John refused the job offer because he is unemployed
> AND the unemployed are lazy.

The effect of this may therefore be to apply the stereotype to John and also to reaffirm this stereotype. However, the process by which this explanation and even the role of the stereotype in the explanation, may be unavailable to the perceiver at any time. Importantly though, the explanation given in verbal form (what I call the justification) may be of a different form such as:

> John refused the job offer because he is lazy.

In this case the stereotype may have affected the judgement automatically and without the perceiver even being aware of its formal role. This is not to say that stereotypes figure less prominently in explicit justifications, rather the point is that stereotypical beliefs can be prominent in both automatically generated explanations and explicit justifications, there is every reason to believe that these usages will be correlated but they need not be perfectly correlated.

The implication of these ideas for stereotype formation is that we need to distinguish the more or less automatic process of the development of stereotypical knowledge as relatively enduring explanations (that can be more or less strongly activated at particular times) from the dynamic creation of instantaneous justifications or current understandings that will tend to implicate currently active stereotypical knowledge, but are not synonymous with that knowledge (and indeed need involve no consciously available reference to that knowledge). In a limited sense stereotype formation can be understood as either the creation of the enduring explanation or the instantaneous justification but this misses the point. Stereotype formation is to do with both the creation of the enduring knowledge which underpins current understandings and those current understandings and the relations between these two, and this is the idea that is encapsulated in Figure 2.1.

One key danger in focusing on only long-term knowledge *or* the current stereotypical depiction is that we also risk losing sight of the constraining effect of the latter on the former. Justifications/depictions exist in a symbolic form which presumably facilitates the storage of some trace of that explicit thought in memory and which will serve to prime and thereby aid the retrieval of related memories which will in turn help retrieve the original thought. In that sense explicit thinking should serve to sustain implicit knowledge, but this is really only part of the social psychological process.

Explicit thoughts which exist in a symbolic form have the potential to be communicated in natural language in a way that sub-symbolic or distributed knowledge cannot be. In other words, symbolic communication with other people can affect the contents of their long-term knowledge. As was noted in Chapter 1, perhaps the most fascinating aspect of stereotypes is the fact that they come to be shared with (but also contested by) other people (see Haslam et al., this volume). Indeed, if everybody had different stereotypes then they would be of rather less interest.

The process by which current stereotypical depictions come to be consensual are reasonably well-understood as aspects of social influence. The work of Haslam and colleagues (Haslam, 1997; Haslam, Oakes, McGarty et al., 1996; Haslam et al., 1998) on consensualization explains how members of social groups can come to agree on stereotypical depictions of certain groups by identifying the normative positions of their own groups and shifting to those positions. The deeper and less tractable problem is the investigation of how the longer-term knowledge which helps to produce the stereotypical depictions in the first place is modified so that different people agree at the level of that knowledge. I say this problem is deeper and less tractable because that longer-term knowledge is not directly exchangeable between individuals. We cannot share our understandings with some other person, all we can do is seek to help them understand. Despite this limitation human cognition enables us to share remarkably common understandings of things we struggle to communicate about. We can all laugh at the same joke but nevertheless struggle to explain what is funny about it.

In much of this section we have dealt with the idea of covariation detection. This is widely acknowledged to underpin explanations. It is very important to consider covariation in more detail though. Is the idea of covariation sufficient to provide an account of the way that people make sense of their environments?

Covariation and mechanism-based knowledge

Most social psychologists are familiar with the idea of perceived covariation as it underlies attribution theory (e.g., Kelley's, 1967, ANOVA model of causal attribution). The basic idea is that the mind can abstract cause from statistical regularities, an idea which was first formalized by Hume. The chief idea is that people can learn that where one event tends to occur before another event that the first event is the cause for the second event. According to Kelley's attribution theory everyday explanations of other people's responses to stimuli can be understood in terms of the characteristics of the person, the stimulus or the occasion on which the stimulus was encountered. If a perceiver sees the same person respond in the same way on many occasions they will tend to attribute the behaviour to the person. If, however, many people respond in the same way on a particular occasion then they will tend to attribute the behaviour to the stimulus or occasion.

The key problem with this and other popular covariational approaches is that they do not address the problem that some other factor which is correlated with a preceding event may be the true cause of that event. Look at the example used by Cheng (1997) and others where a rooster may always crow before sunrise (and only before the sunrise), but crowing is never the cause of the sun to rise.

The solution to this problem has been to use the major alternative to the covariational approach which is to posit the existence of causal powers. This relates to perceivers' knowledge of mechanisms that would allow some preceding event to cause a later event. Given that no mechanism is known to exist that would allow crowing to cause the sun to rise thus crowing could not be the cause.

Ahn et al. (1995) develop a distinction between covariation and mechanism-based knowledge that subsumes the preceding distinction. They assume that both are necessary for causal reasoning but that reasoners tend to have a clear preference for mechanism-based knowledge and that this form of knowledge has a stronger influence on reasoning than covariation knowledge. There are two key reasons for this. Firstly, covariational information may not be available in everyday situations. This is because certain events do not ever occur or there are confounding factors. Secondly, mechanism-based information is easier to express in natural language. For many purposes a covariational account can never be fully satisfactory until it provides or implies a mechanism. If we were to ask why some event occurred and received a thoroughly covariational answer along the lines of 'Well that's the way it has always happened' then we are entitled to feel that we have received no explanation at all.

Ahn et al. (1995) suggest that the difference between mechanism and covariation information maps onto the theory/similarity distinction. This argument can be extended to make the stronger claim that causal reasoning is a special case of categorization (in that it deals with categories of events), but that categorization has the same form as causal reasoning. In general, categorization involves identifying covariation between relevant features (i.e., similarities and differences) and mechanisms which account for such covariation.

The same is true of stereotyping. Stereotypes include information about relevant similarities and differences but they also include explanations of the way those similarities and differences have come about. Two different people could accept that there was a level of lethargy amongst unemployed people that they might agree to call laziness. They might dispute, however, the degree to which that condition was a cause or an effect of unemployment. That is, laziness could be a mechanism that explained unemployment or unemployment could be a mechanism that explained laziness (i.e., the isolation and socio-economic disadvantages experienced by unemployed people reduce their motivation). If the latter explanation is invoked then some further principle, such as economic conditions, must also be invoked to explain unemployment but this also can be part of the stereotype.

The principal implication of this discussion for stereotype formation is that stereotypical knowledge should include knowledge about both covariation and mechanisms. Known covariations between features provide the framework to create categories, but these become more psychologically prepotent when they are linked to causal mechanisms which explain that covariation.

Using the covariation–mechanism distinction: defining stereotypes in more detail

The covariation–mechanism distinction puts us in a position to define stereotypes in considerable detail. Essentially a stereotype is a set of associations between people and features, and between features and features. Some of the latter associations are in turn associated with knowledge about mechanisms which serve to explain how some associations came into existence. This knowledge structure need not be bounded in any strict sense and it need not have all of its aspects activated at any one time (indeed all aspects may never be activated). Activation of the stereotype itself must be understood in terms of the generally implicit process of explanation and the more explicit, symbolic process of justification. The extent to which stereotypical thinking is more in the implicit or explicit form will reflect the states and needs of the cognitive system at the time. Under conditions of normal everyday interaction with members of some group, stereotypical thinking will probably tend to reflect implicit stereotyping, but under conditions where perceivers need to give an impression of some group (perhaps to communicate the stereotypical impression to an ingroup member or to justify a particular form of treatment of the outgroup) or where the category label of the group has been invoked, stereotypical thinking will tend to take an explicit form.

To return to the example discussed earlier, an individual's stereotypical knowledge about the unemployed might be a set of associations between particular people and the feature 'unemployed' and other associations between unemployment and other attributes such as laziness (which may be seen as a causal factor in producing the association of particular people with the attribute unemployment). At any particular point of time specific associations may be dormant and therefore are unavailable to influence explicit or implicit psychological processes. At other times the same process may be highly activated and may be strongly influencing explicit perceptions and statements or implicit expectations about unemployed people. In general, explicit social self-categorization or even mere symbolic reference by self or relevant others to category labels (like 'the unemployed') which are consistent with activated knowledge will tend to amplify the degree to which persons are seen in categorical terms. This will be reflected in the coordination of justifications for behavioural treatment and attitudes towards the outgroup as well as expectancies about the future behaviour of the outgroup members and interpretation

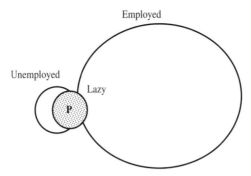

Figure 2.2 A schematic of one person's stereotypic knowledge about two social categories and their association with laziness, highlighted here as a possible causal factor. In this scheme laziness serves as a potential explanation for unemployment because both laziness and unemployment are relatively low frequency events. If laziness were perceived to be very common (and therefore strongly associated with both unemployed and employed people) it would cease to serve as a viable distinctive explanation.

of current and past behaviour. That is, under these conditions the unemployed person should be perceived in terms of their unemployed status rather than as a member of some alternative category or as an individual. Furthermore the person should be perceived to be lazy and laziness should be seen as the causal mechanism which has made that person unemployed. Under other conditions the explicit and implicit processes may be less correlated or even unrelated.

Such a system of stereotypical knowledge can be shown as a set of Venn diagrams as in Figure 2.2. The advantage of the Venn diagrams is that they show associations as overlap at a particular instant. At some other instant, say where the category 'unemployed' was not invoked, the effective degree of overlap may be close to zero.

As McGarty (1999) discusses, the overlap between categories is important for a variety of other reasons. These include the fact that it gives clues as to whether some attribute is a plausible cause. Laziness is a plausible sufficient cause of unemployment only so long as both laziness and unemployment are believed to be relatively infrequent. If laziness were believed to be much more common than unemployment it would need to be discounted as a cause unless some second factor were invoked. More clearly still, laziness could never be a plausible explanation of a high frequency category such as employment. The illusory correlation paradigm is instructive here: a majority tendency (such as a general tendency for most people to behave in socially desirable ways) can be explained in terms of a single majority group membership but not a single minority group membership.

Such stereotypical knowledge forms through learning associations and causal mechanisms and through the instantiation of stereotypical depictions which can then be stored or transmitted to other people. This transmission provides the basis for the development of both consensual and contested stereotypes.

It is worth contrasting the explanatory association model of stereotypical knowledge with another popular view in categorization research: the hierarchically organized mental model. This is the idea that categories are comprised of discrete sub-categories and that comparison between members of categories rests on a perceived equivalence at some higher level of a hierarchy. This is the idea that underpins the self-categorization theory treatment of the self-concept.

The particular problem is that few concepts in the world are readily understood in terms of hierarchies and even where there are available hierarchies (such as in the biological taxonomy of species) that the character of people's inferences does not reflect these hierarchies (Sloman, 1998). This is surprising because logically speaking hierarchies provide a very strong basis for inference. However, hierarchies are relatively poor at reflecting overlap, indeed hierarchical tree diagrams can be seen as special cases of Venn diagrams that do not allow overlap. This limitation is the principal reason why I prefer the Venn diagrammatic representation for reflecting stereotypical knowledge.

One final caveat is that stereotyping is a particularly useful process when applied to social groups. Social groups themselves obey processes of normalization and differentiation which are well described by the categorization process. The peas in a pod are very similar to each other in a number of respects, but there is no mechanism by which they *become* more similar to each other. Indeed if we did see peas becoming more similar to each other over time we would very likely attribute the increased similarity to some external force or agent rather than to some quality of the peas. Members of social groups, on the other hand, do tend to become more similar to each other and more different from members of alternative groups when they act collectively. That is, where psychological group formation is validly attributed to other people it should provide an excellent basis for the formation of stereotypes which can be applied reliably to members of those groups. The symmetry is provided by the fact that the group is most likely to be stereotyped when its members are themselves thinking and acting in stereotypical terms, that is, when their self-perception is depersonalized. For the most significant intergroup encounters, such as those involving threat or actual conflict, the stereotyping process will tend to capitalize on tendencies that the outgroup will display that are not true of categories of inanimate objects. An opposing outgroup will be expected to behave in highly consistent ways (e.g., in ways which are consistently hostile to the ingroup), and due to processes of social influence and differentiation within the group these expectations tend to be accurate. Paradoxically, rather than being stuck in rigidities stereotyping should actually help perceivers to keep track of the dynamics of social groups.

The vital point here is that where there is no perceived group formation, that is, where the outgroup members are not believed to be self-categorizing then these dynamics do not exist to be capitalized upon. Unless group-formation occurs (and, in principle, any category could provide the basis for such psychological group formation) the members of a category such as red-headed men may share behavioural characteristics in exactly the same way as members of a breed of dog may be perceived to share a characteristic. However, there should be no stronger basis for the regulation of behaviour within the category than there would be for the dogs. Redheads do not currently comprise a group and have no norms or social organization that underpin their internal similarities or external differences (though they could use the social categorization to form a group at any time).

A strong implication of this idea is that if people are sensitive to outgroup formation (and there is no way that people could develop accurate and useful perceptions of the social world without people being able to detect this) then the process of categorization should have very different effects on occasions when people are perceiving members of some social category and occasions where the social category is perceived to be a social group. That is, the same process of categorization should apply in each case but the process should be applied in ways which are much more sensitive to the intercategory context when group formation is perceived to exist. Members of a category cannot organize to compete or cooperate until group formation occurs (see also Abelson et al., 1998). They cannot act collectively to reinforce or contest stereotypes.

Khalaf (forthcoming) argues that this sort of distinction is especially relevant to cases such as perceptions of categories of mental illness. For example, schizophrenic people may be perceived to be violent, unpredictable and unmotivated, but perceivers are probably not imputing this perceived commonality in schizophrenic behaviour to the social regulation of behaviour by group processes. An almost identical negative stereotype could exist in relation to some ethnic or racial group but in this latter case the stereotype is much more likely to reflect social and political relations between the perceivers' own group and that outgroup.

This distinction between an impression of a category and an impression of a social group needs to be clarified in a number of ways. The first is that the term stereotyping is probably best reserved for impressions where group formation is inferred or is at least plausible. We prefer the term *typecasting* for impressions of categories where these are based on a type, that is a category without inferred group formation.

The second implication is that the type-group distinction is quite different to the individual-group distinction. Groups do not need to be more or less abstract than categories or types, they simply need to be believed to exist.

Thirdly, the distinction is independent of the essence/entitativity distinction (N. Haslam, Ernst & Rothschild, 2000). A racial and a mental illness category could be seen to have equally strong essences (they would both be biologically based for example) but the racial group could provide a strong basis for stereotyping or typecasting whereas the mental illness category would only provide a strong basis for typecasting.

Fourthly, the distinction has strong implications for stereotype change: dispersed disconfirming information about category members should provide a strong argument against typecasting, when perceiving social groups, however, disconfirming evidence can be rationalized in different ways. Disconfirming information can be attributed to coordinated action on the part of the group (e.g., to have pretended to have changed their ways) or to the formation of organized sub-groups.

Fifthly, the distinction refers to the phenomenology of the outgroup or perceived category and not directly to actual social groups or organization. One can perceive the mentally ill to be a group or a type but that perception may be variously mapped onto the actual self-categorizations of the people perceived. Having said that, the collective behaviour which tends to result from self-categorization will tend to have sharp consequences for the contents of the perceptions we can develop of those groups (see McGarty, 1999, Chapter 11).

Sixthly, the distinction is a matter of degree not kind. Are gay men best considered as a group or a category? Clearly, the answer one gives should depend on beliefs about current self-perception and long-term identification with the group amongst the particular gay men being considered. Some of these issues are being explored by Girish Lala, who, in addressing these issues has examined virtual communities (i.e., communities which form via computer-mediated communication without necessarily having physical contact between members). In particular, members of social groups can vary in terms of their orientations to specific groups and categories at a specific time. A person who is highly committed to a category will probably tend to have a social movement orientation towards that category and will often see specific groups or institutions as vehicles for achieving goals that are consistent with the needs of the category. For gay men with such a social movement orientation to this category, the category of gay men will tend to function as an institution or group. For others it may be no more than a mere biographical detail.

The seventh implication is that some groups form on attitudinal or ideological bases. As Ana-Maria Bliuc (forthcoming) argues in her PhD research, one basis for the formation of such opinion-based groups will be the certainty with which some defining ideological issue is held. It is easier to form a group of people who are certain about whether abortion is right or wrong than to form a group from people who are not sure. Much of this certainty may reflect influence processes occurring after group formation but the initial decision to join or the final decision to leave will often be structured by perceptions of issue certainty.

Finally, categories always provide a potential basis for self-categorization. Mental illness categories may not be associated with institutions but they nevertheless provide a basis for the formation of support/action groups which might seek to change stereotypes for example.

Conclusion

This chapter contains a strong statement about the consequences of the categorization process for the explanation of stereotype formation. This rests on the idea that the formation of long-term stereotypical knowledge must be distinguished from the formation of current stereotypical depictions or impressions of social groups. This allowed me to propose a definition of the stereotype as a set of constraints between knowledge about a group, the explicit use of labels about group members, and perceived equivalence of group members. Stereotype formation is therefore the process by which the constraints between these elements develop. Nevertheless both long-term knowledge and current impressions reflect attempts on the part of the perceiver to understand or explain aspects of the social world. Some of these efforts after understanding are realized in explicit (and normally) symbolic form with reference to category labels in a form that is available to conscious experience and these can largely be subsumed within the process of justification. Others are realized in an implicit form that is less readily available as conscious experience which I refer to as explanation.

Allied with the explanation-justification distinction is the distinction between those aspects of stereotypic knowledge and its current instantiations which entail covariation between features and those aspects of stereotypic knowledge which reflect mechanisms that create, maintain or prevent covariations. Importantly in the case of stereotyping these known or hypothesized causal mechanisms will include mechanisms which explain why groups have particular features and why other groups do not.

All of this then suggests a refinement of the definition of stereotype that was suggested above. Stereotypic knowledge involves the development of both covariational and mechanism-based knowledge, in particular, where it is crucially important to recognize the existence of knowledge of the mechanisms which explain the collective and organized behaviour of real social groups. It is this sort of mechanism-based knowledge which, put simply, breathes group life into social categories.

3   Subjective essentialism and the emergence of stereotypes

Vincent Yzerbyt and Steve Rocher

Being able to make sense of the surrounding social environment is no doubt one of the major wonders of our cognitive apparatus. In most instances, perceivers encounter no difficulty in assigning people to social categories (Bodenhausen & Macrae, 1998; Fiske, 1998, 2000; Leyens, Yzerbyt & Schadron, 1994; Oakes, Haslam & Turner, 1994). According to one strand of research, such an achievement stems from people's ability to recognize regularities and patterns that are available in the social setting. From this perspective, social categories impose themselves upon observers. An alternative perspective holds that perceivers play quite an active role in the representation of the social world. Specifically, observers are thought to rely on abstract knowledge in order to organize the incoming information.

The distinction between these two approaches is a key issue whenever we ask ourselves the question of the origin of stereotypes. After all, are those beliefs that social psychologists and lay people alike call stereotypes the mere reflection of the environment in what could be seen as rather passive perceivers? In contrast, should they be seen as the product of a more active, yet partly unconscious, process that builds upon perceivers' naïve theories? In line with an impressive body of evidence, the present contribution takes it that the second viewpoint provides a more faithful description of the processes involved in the acquisition of social knowledge. That is, beliefs about a social group tend to emerge because perceivers construe the group in terms of some a priori theoretical knowledge.

In the present chapter, we would like to build a case for the crucial role of essentialist theories in the emergence of stereotypic beliefs. In agreement with the extant literature on the social psychology of stereotyping and intergroup relations (Allport, 1954; Fiske, 1998; Leyens, Yzerbyt & Schadron, 1994; Oakes, Haslam & Turner, 1994; Spears, Haslam, Ellemers & Oakes, 1997; Sedikides, Schopler & Insko, 1998), we hold that stereotypes refer to the features that are thought to be associated with a particular group. According to our subjective essentialist view (Yzerbyt, Rocher & Schadron, 1997), however, stereotypes are likely to be a bit

38

more than that. Stereotypes also evoke a particular explanation for the co-occurrence of a specific set of attributes (for a similar point, see Wittenbrink, Gist & Hilton, 1997; Wittenbrink, Hilton & Gist, 1998). Indeed, we propose that stereotypic beliefs allude to the underlying reason that, at least subjectively, accounts for the unique association between a series of characteristics and a target group.

We devote the first section of our chapter to a quick overview of the basic tenets of subjective essentialism. We examine the role of the perception of entitativity on the emergence of essentialist beliefs. We also discuss recent efforts in cognitive, social, and personality psychology that aim at uncovering the potential impact of essentialist beliefs on social perception. The next three sections are devoted to a selection of studies carried out in our laboratory. What these empirical efforts have in common is that they isolate the specific impact of essentialist beliefs in the emergence of stereotypic beliefs. In the final section, we examine various factors that may affect the tendency to rely on essentialist beliefs in the formation of stereotypic beliefs.

The essence of subjective essentialism

Why do people come up with certain categories and not with others? A quarter of a century ago, Rosch and colleagues' (1975, 1976) answer to this crucial question was that perceivers happen to be sensitive to the regularities that exist 'out there': Because certain attributes tend to co-occur in the environment, perceivers end up noticing them. People become aware of the clusters of features and cut the surrounding world accordingly. The net result is that perceivers build up a knowledge base that is organized both vertically (people's world knowledge is making up a hierarchy where some categories are included in other, superordinate, categories) and horizontally (certain members, called prototypes, embody a high number of features that are diagnostic of the category). Social psychologists embraced the Roschian view of concept and categories with amazing enthusiasm (Brewer, Dull & Lui, 1981; Cantor & Mischel 1979; for a review, see Fiske & Taylor, 1991).

Clearly, the Roschian view represented a major breakthrough in the way researchers approached category formation. Still, it quickly became apparent that an alternative conception, namely the exemplar view, could also provide a satisfactory account of the way people organize their conceptual knowledge (Medin & Schaffer, 1978; for a review, see Smith & Medin, 1981). Social psychologists were quick to see the possible advantages of adopting an exemplar view in the context of social judgement (Smith, 1990; Smith & Zárate, 1990).

After a decade of sovereignty, the prototype and the exemplar views began to show the first signs of weakness (Barsalou, 1985; Smith & Medin, 1981). The most serious critique was launched by Murphy and Medin (1985). The thrust of the argument was that the prototype and exemplar views offered no satisfactory account of the selection of the particular features that make up a specific category nor, for that matter, a clear indication of the rules governing the computation of similarity (Medin, 1989; Medin & Ortony, 1989; Medin, Goldstone & Gentner, 1993; Wisniewski & Medin, 1994). Indeed, what is it that allows perceivers to select certain characteristics over others? If one is to provide a satisfactory account of the origin of the categories, there must be a mechanism that points to the critical characteristics making up a category. For Medin and colleagues, perceivers are in fact guided by their naïve knowledge of the world in general and by their beliefs regarding the deep nature of things (see also, Gelman & Wellman, 1991; Keil, 1989; Malt, 1994). Such knowledge regarding the 'genotypic' (i.e., underlying) commonality of objects then guides the search for the 'phenotypic' (i.e., the surface) similarity. To be sure, certain surface features likely hint at the existence of an underlying shared nature. In other words, Medin and colleagues (Medin, 1989; Medin & Ortony, 1989) advocated that there is a constant dialogue between the observable features and the deep characteristics.

Within social psychology, the message launched by Medin and colleagues did not go unnoticed. As a case in point, self-categorization theorists (SCT, e.g., Oakes, Turner & Haslam, 1991) stressed the joint participation of immediate data and background knowledge in the construction of social categories (for a review, see Oakes, Haslam & Turner, 1994). Whereas the actual data contribute to what SCT calls comparative fit, background knowledge plays a crucial role in the appraisal of what is labelled normative fit (see Brown & Turner, this volume). Comparative and normative fit both shape the content of categories. In a very similar way, social judgeability theorists (for reviews, see Leyens, Yzerbyt & Schadron, 1994; Yzerbyt, Dardenne & Leyens, 1998) emphasized the combined influence of theories and data in the production of social judgements. Although social judgeability also stresses the impact of additional factors such as ego or group-defensive concerns, the key message is that social judgements will only make sense if they take into account both the hard evidence and people's naïve theories of the world. These developments notwithstanding, Rothbart and Taylor (1992) must be credited with being the first to apply psychological essentialism in a straightforward way to the issue of stereotyping and intergroup relations. Relying on findings in cognitive and developmental psychology, these authors proposed that social observers may well mistake social categories to be natural categories. Natural categories (e.g., tigers, birds, etc.) are established on the basis of some underlying characteristic that is assumed to be common to all members of the category. In contrast, Rothbart and Taylor (1992) argued, perceivers should be approaching social categories as simple arte-facts. Categories of artefacts (i.e., chairs, cars, etc.) are structured around sets of surface features. At no point is there an assumption that some deep reality may account for the observed similarities.

Building upon these empirical and theoretical efforts, we proposed a subjective essentialist view of stereotyping (Rogier & Yzerbyt, 1999; Yzerbyt, Corneille & Estrada, 2001; Yzerbyt, Rocher & Schadron, 1997; Yzerbyt & Rogier, 2001; Yzerbyt, Rogier & Rocher, 1998). We argued that a social stereotype should be seen as a set of interconnected features that builds upon some underlying deep characteristic (for a related view, see Brown & Turner, this volume). Moreover, we proposed that perceivers not only rely on observable associations to infer the presence of some profound reality common to all group members, but also use their naïve theories about the inherent nature of people to generate surface links among the members. In a nutshell, the surface characteristics that are associated with the group members are both the antecedent and the result of the beliefs that people entertain about any given social group. We used the notion of entitativity (Campbell, 1958) to refer to the various forms of observable connections between people, be it under the form of similarity (proximity, appearance, etc.) or interdependence (organization, common fate, etc.). We noted that observers are generally aware of the influence of entitativity on their search for deep communality among group members. In contrast, they typically overlook the impact of their naïve beliefs about the nature of people on the creation of entitativity. The link between strong essentialist beliefs and perceived entitativity should thus be seen as a two-way street (Martin & Parker, 1995; see Yzerbyt, Corneille & Estrada, 2001).

In an initial test of our subjective essentialist account (Yzerbyt, Rogier & Fiske, 1998), we wanted to see whether observers confronted with en-titativity would assume the presence of some essence. Specifically, we wanted to show that the perception of people as forming a homogeneous group is likely to foster social attribution (i.e., the interpretation of be-haviour in terms of enduring dispositions common to all group members, Deschamps, 1973–1974; Oakes, Turner & S. A. Haslam, 1991). We therefore adapted Ross, Amabile and Steinmetz' (1977) quiz paradigm to a group situation. In the original study, three participants come to the laboratory and learn that they are going to take part in a quiz. The exper-imenter then randomly assigns one participant to the role of questioner, one to the role of answerer, and one to the role of observer. After a short period of time during which the questioner is asked to come up with a series of questions, the game takes place. At the end of the game, all three participants rate the intelligence and knowledge of both the questioner and the answerer. A clear fundamental attribution error (FAE) pattern of findings emerges in the ratings made by the answerer and the observer, such that both evaluate the questioner as being more intelligent and knowledgeable than the answerer. Apparently, the questioner seems to be the only one who is aware of the obvious advantage associated with the task of asking questions.

In our group version of the experiment, groups of at least seven students were called into the laboratory in order to take part in a game in which two teams of three people were opposed. Assignment to the team of questioners, the team of answerers and the role of observer was made on an explicitly random basis. The study was carried out at the University of Massachusetts at Amherst, allowing us to take advantage of the proximity of several other colleges for our manipulation of homogeneity. The participants believed that the students in their session belonged to one of several institutions. In reality, they all came from the University of Massachusetts. Whereas some students learned that the group of questioners all came from the same school so that they constituted an entity, others were informed that they came from three different institutions so that they formed an aggregate. Similarly, whereas half of the participants learned that the group of answerers comprised students from the same school, the remaining participants were informed that they came from three different schools. The participants then played the quiz game for approximately 10 minutes. Questions about sports and entertainment were selected, because pilot research had revealed that there were no stereotypes linking these topics to the various institutions. At the end of the game, we collected observers' ratings regarding the competence and the general knowledge of the questioners and the answerers, both individually and as groups. We hypothesized that, overall, observers would see questioners as being more competent than answerers. The random assignment of the participants to the roles of questioners and answerers suggests that any systematic difference in the evaluation of these two groups of participants is likely to be a bias. Moreover, we predicted that the effect would be more pronounced as a function of the homogeneity of these groups. Finally, we expected the effect to emerge not only for the group ratings but also for the individual ratings, thereby confirming the prediction that each target person would indeed be perceived differently depending on the degree of homogeneity of his or her group.

Our data confirmed the presence of a global FAE. In other words, answerers were generally rated less positively than questioners (see Figure 3.1). As expected, however, the difference between the two categories of participants was not constant across all four experimental

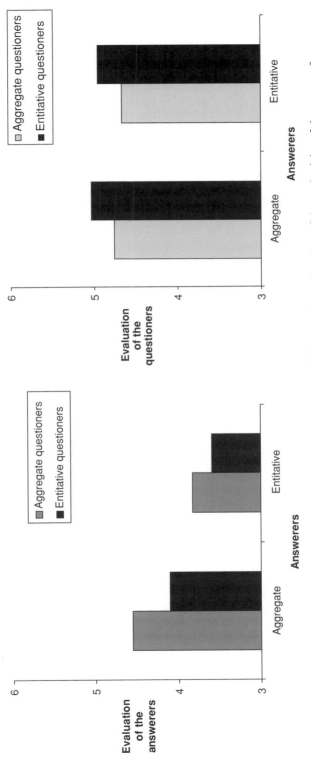

Figure 3.1 Evaluation of the answerers (left panel) and of the questioners (right panel) as a function of the entitativity of the group of answerers and the group of questioners.

conditions. In line with our prediction that homogeneity would affect the emergence of the FAE, the difference between the group of answerers and the group of questioners was largest (*Mean difference* = 1.36) when they both formed a homogeneous whole (i.e. an entity), lowest (*Mean difference* = 0.20) when the two groups were aggregates, and intermediate (*Mean differences* = 0.94 and 0.84) when one group was an entity and the other an aggregate. These data go a long way to support the idea that entitativity incites perceivers to infer the presence of some essence, a shared disposition, that accounts for the behaviour of the members of the group and obscures the influence of the situational constraints.

Rogier and Yzerbyt (1999) recently conducted a conceptual replication of Yzerbyt et al.'s study by relying on the well-known attitude attribution paradigm first proposed by Jones and Harris (1967). Contrary to what took place in the original study, participants were asked to infer the true attitude not of one but of three speakers who had allegedly been forced to defend a particular viewpoint on a controversial topic. Moreover, depending on conditions, the three people who were shown on a video excerpt had been presented as belonging to the same versus a different major. Although pilot study had indicated that there was no a priori relationship between any of the majors and the topic under discussion, observers made significantly more dispositional inferences when they had been confronted with the speakers belonging to the same major that when the speakers were said to belong to different majors.

The above demonstrations mainly concerned the perception of a group 'out there'. As it happens, a similar reasoning can be applied as far as an ingroup is concerned. Building upon a vast number of studies, Yzerbyt, Castano, Leyens and Paladino (2000) recently argued that the perception that the ingroup is more or less entitative may indeed have a dramatic impact on the extent to which group members identify with the group (Castano, Yzerbyt & Bourguignon, 2000). According to Yzerbyt and colleagues (2000), group members tend to identify more with an entitative ingroup because the similarity of its members and/or its organization makes clear that some unique feature characterizes all the members of the group. Said otherwise, entitativity suggests the existence of a deep underlying essence that defines group membership.

Although Hoffman and Hurst (1990) were not interested in essentialism per se, they conducted a study that speaks to the issue of the impact of essentialist views on the emergence of stereotypic beliefs. These authors gave their participants descriptions of a series of members of two fictional categories living on a distant planet, the Ackmians and the Orynthians, one group consisting of a majority of 'cityworkers' and a minority of 'childraisers', and vice versa. Importantly, the members of the two groups did not differ at all in personality traits. The goal of the study was to show that gender stereotypes may well arise in order to justify the differences in social roles (men are more likely to be breadwinners and women homemakers). This hypothesis was supported. In other words, the strict equivalence of the individual profiles did not prevent participants from forming role-based category stereotypes. From the present perspective, other findings deserve a special mention. Indeed, additional manipulations revealed that the effects were especially strong when the categories were biologically defined and when the participants had to think of an explanation for the category-role correlation. That is, perceivers' *a priori* theories and their explanatory goals seem to have jointly contributed to the emergence of stereotypic judgements.

In our view, research by Dweck and her colleagues is also highly relevant here insofar as it focused on individual differences in essentialist beliefs (Chiu, Hong & Dweck, 1997; Dweck, Hong & Chiu, 1993). According to these researchers, some people, referred to as 'entity theorists', believe that traits are fixed whereas others, called 'incremental theorists', believe that traits are malleable. In a series of studies, Levy, Stroessner and Dweck (1998) confirmed that people's implicit theories about the fixedness versus the malleability of human beings predict differences in degree of social stereotyping. For instance, participants holding an entity theory were more confident that the stereotypic traits of various ethnic and occupational groups were accurate descriptions of the groups and formed more extreme judgements of new groups than participants holding an incremental theory. Levy and her colleagues (1998) also found that entity theorists attributed stereotyped traits to inborn group qualities more than incremental theorists and that incremental theorists attributed stereotyped traits to environmental factors more than entity theorists. Thus, people who believe that other people's behaviour can be explained in terms of enduring deep characteristics are more prone to stereotype any given group and to see it as a coherent whole.

Finally, Nick Haslam (1998; Haslam, Rothschild & Ernst, 2000) examined the organization and structure of essentialist beliefs, arguing that the concept of essentialism contains several distinct elements. Building on the work conducted by social psychologists (McGarty, S.A. Haslam, Hutchinson & Grace, 1995; Rothbart & Taylor, 1992; Yzerbyt, Rocher & Schadron, 1997) as well as on research efforts by anthropologists (e.g., Hirschfeld, 1996), Haslam (1998) listed a series of characteristics that have been mentioned to accompany essentialist beliefs. In a most informative study, Haslam et al. (2000) then asked their participants to use these belief elements to rate forty social categories. Two distinct dimensions emerged from the ratings of the various categories. One dimension closely corresponds to the concept of 'natural kind' and entails beliefs that the category has sharp boundaries, necessary features, immutable membership and is historically invariant. The other dimension corresponds to the notion of 'entitativity' and involves beliefs that the category has an underlying inherent basis, is homogeneous, affords many inferences about its members, and excludes its members from other categories. Clearly, the entitativity dimension stresses the extent to which a group is seen as a meaningful unit with deep commonalties which define the group members' social identity (see also Yzerbyt et al., 2000).

In sum, several lines of research suggest that essentialist and stereotypic beliefs are linked. Whereas some studies reveal that the confrontation with an entitative group facilitates the evocation of an essence as being at the heart of group membership (Castano et al., 2000; Rogier & Yzerbyt, 1999; Yzerbyt et al., 1998; Yzerbyt et al., 2000), others stress the potential role of essentialist beliefs in the emergence of stereotypes (Hoffman & Hurst, 1990; Levy, Stroessner & Dweck, 1998). Although such preliminary evidence is indicative of the role of essentialism in intergroup relations and stereotyping, we think that more work is needed to fully understand the impact of naïve theories in general and essentialist beliefs in particular in the creation of social stereotypes. The remainder of this chapter is devoted to a series of studies conducted in our laboratory showing the impact of essentialism on the creation of coherence (i.e., entitativity) in a variety of settings.

Subjective essentialism and the accentuation of accentuation

Our first illustration of the role of essentialist theories in the emergence of stereotype beliefs builds upon the well-known accentuation effect (Corneille & Judd, 1999; Eiser & Stroebe, 1972; Krueger, 1992; McGarty & Penny, 1988; Tajfel & Wilkes, 1963). Accentuation is seen as the direct consequence of the addition of a categorical label to a continuous dimension. The correlation between categorical membership and the standing on the continuous dimension leads perceivers to exacerbate the similarities among the members of a given category and the differences between the members of different categories. The question that we set out to examine is whether essentialist beliefs could in fact play a role in the accentuation effect. In line with a strict interpretation of the theory, initial demonstrations of the accentuation effect relied on the presentation of trivial category labels (Tajfel & Wilkes, 1963). As it happens, the findings, though significant, were also associated with modest effect sizes. Subsequent studies were more successful in their attempt to evidence the presence of stronger within-group similarity and between-group difference (McGarty & Penny, 1988). Interestingly enough, the more recent research has confronted participants with meaningful category labels. For instance, Krueger and Clement (1994) reasoned that the calendar superimposes arbitrary intermonth boundaries on day-to-day variations in temperature. They thus asked their participants to estimate the average temperatures of forty-eight days distributed through one calendar year. In line with predictions, differences between estimates for two days belonging to neighbouring months were greater and difference between estimates for two days belong to the same month were smaller than the actual differences. These findings confirm that participants displayed assimilation for the days that belonged to the same month and contrast for membership to a different month. From the present perspective, one could argue that people's naïve knowledge about the weather guided them in increasing the similarities between days of the same month and the differences between days of different months.

In light of our suspicion that naïve beliefs about the categories may play a role in the emergence of accentuation effects by possibly accentuating the phenomenon, our initial step was thus to compare the impact of the presence of a trivial category label to that of a more meaningful category label. Specifically, we wanted to see whether the confrontation with a category label that suggested the existence of some essential basis for the surface characteristics would lead perceivers to see the two groups as more different from one another and the members of the same groups as more similar to one another. Our hope was thus that a category label that referred to some underlying essence would outperform the trivial label in that the accentuation effect would be significantly stronger. These conjectures were tested in a series of two studies (Yzerbyt & Buidin, 1998).

In order to secure the materials for the studies, we asked a variety of people to write a one-page description of themselves in the context of a social setting. A final set of ten descriptions was selected on the basis of the richness and the length of the text. These texts were then typewritten and presented on separate sheets. Each description was followed by one page comprising ten rating scales. These scales had been selected so that two scales would concern each one of the five dimensions of the Big Five (Norman, 1963; for a similar approach, see Park, DeKay & Kraus, 1994). A consistent finding over the various groups of participants, though, is that seven of the ten scales were highly inter-correlated and could be interpreted as concerning sociability. Hence, we used the seven scales to compute a sociability index.

In a first study (Yzerbyt & Buidin, 1998, Exp. 1), we distributed the ten descriptions in two groups of five before we handed them out to the participants. The participants' task was to read the first group of five descriptions and form an idea of the first group. They were then to come back to the first person, rate the first person on the ten traits, read the second description and rate the second person on the ten traits, and so on. When the five members of the first group were evaluated, participants were instructed to rate the group as a whole again using the ten traits. These steps were repeated for the second group of five members. Finally, participants were fully debriefed, thanked and dismissed. The presentation of one of two random distributions of the descriptions constituted the first experimental manipulation. The key independent variable of the study however was the rationale given to the participants for the two groups. Whereas half of the participants were told that the two groups of five people corresponded to two sets of people waiting for a different bus, the remaining participants learned that the two groups were made of people sharing the same genetic marker.

The ratings allowed to compute a variety of indices of central tendency and variability. First, we recorded the evaluation of each group by computing the evaluation index on the group ratings. Second, we also computed a target-based evaluation of each group. To this end, we averaged the sociability index for the five members of each group. We thus secured two group-based evaluations and two target-based evaluations for each participant. As for the measure of variability, we computed the standard deviation of the sociability index within each group of five targets. We thus had two standard deviation scores for each participant. Confirming the random nature of the distribution of the ten descriptions in two groups of five, this first study revealed no difference in the mean evaluations of the groups, be it at the level of the target or at the level of the group. More importantly, and in line with our hypotheses, we found that the within-group standard deviations varied significantly as a function of the availability of a naïve theory stressing the essential nature of the two groups. As predicted, the standard deviation was much lower, thereby revealing the presence of a higher level of internal coherence in the groups, when the participants were led to think that the groups revolved around different genetic markers than when they thought that they comprised people waiting for different buses.

In a second study (Yzerbyt & Buidin, 1998, Exp. 2), we used the same scenario with the important exception that the descriptions were first ranked on the basis of the mean evaluations given in the bus condition of the first study. Whereas one group comprised the five most sociable targets, the other was made of the five least sociable targets. The five descriptions were then randomly presented within each group. Participants were confronted with one of two orders of presentation depending on whether the more social group was presented first or second. The crucial experimental manipulation however concerned the information regarding the nature of the two groups. In the bus condition, the two groups were said to be constituted of sets of people waiting for a different bus. Participants in the gene condition learned that the two groups comprised people with different genetic markers. For the rest, the steps involved in data collection were the same as in the first study. A first set of findings concerns the within-group standard deviation. As expected, the nature of the beliefs influenced the perceived coherence of the groups. Participants rated the sociability of the five group members to be more similar when they thought that the members of a given group shared the same genetic marker than when they were informed that the groups comprised people waiting for a different bus.

We also looked at the evaluations of the members of the groups. To have an idea of the baseline evaluation, we also added a third condition in which ten participants were simply informed that they would be confronted with descriptions of different people. A highly significant group main effect confirmed the built-in difference between the more sociable ($M = 5.72$) and the less sociable group ($M = 4.19$). A significant main effect of the a priori beliefs about the target groups indicated that the way people evaluated the two groups was slightly affected by the information that was given to the participants about the composition of the groups. More importantly, the data revealed the presence of a very significant interaction between condition and the a priori sociability of the groups. The mention of an explicit category label referring to the existence of some essential feature underlying group membership led to the perception of a stronger difference between the two groups (*Difference* = 2.02) than when participants thought that the descriptions originated from one group of ten people (*Difference* = 1.37) or when the two groups were said to comprise five people waiting for a different bus (*Difference* = 1.16).

As a set, these data reveal that the provision of a meaningful category label contributed to exacerbate the similarity among the various members of the category. Although the presence of a group label that is correlated with a continuous dimension may well affect the extent to which group members resemble one another, the suggestion that the label refers to some underlying essence increases the magnitude of the effect. Needless to say, findings such as these suggest that the availability of essentialist beliefs facilitates and amplifies the tendency to create stereotypic expectations about social groups. As such, this phenomenon is likely to contribute to the creation of stereotypes. Having ascertained the potential impact of essentialist beliefs in the context of the accentuation effect, we now turn our attention to another phenomenon generally thought to be responsible for the emergence of stereotypic beliefs namely the illusory correlation effect.

Subjective essentialism and the amplification of illusory correlation

The illusory correlation phenomenon corresponds to the fact that an association between two variables is perceived although none exists. Numerous versions of the effect have been studied in the psychological literature but the best-known example is the manifestation of an illusory correlation in the context of the formation of stereotypes (Hamilton & Gifford, 1976). The paradigm consists in showing a series of behaviours of two groups. These behaviours vary on one dimension which is usually likeability. Whereas one group constitutes the majority (for example, participants read about the behaviours of twenty-six individuals), the other group forms a minority (for example, participants read about the behaviours of thirteen individuals). Moreover, the majority of the behaviours are located on one pole of the dimension (for example, twenty-seven of the thirty-nine behaviours are likeable) and the minority on the other pole (in this case, twelve behaviours are unlikeable). The key feature of the distribution of the behaviours is that the proportion of likeable and unlikeable behaviours is the same in the two groups (in the present example, eighteen likeable behaviours are attributed to the largest group). As a result of the equal proportional presence of likeable versus unlikeable behaviours in each group, there is no relation between likeability of the behaviours and group membership.

Despite the absence of a correlation in the materials presented to the participants, the findings reveal the existence of a systematic tendency to associate the minority group to the less frequent behaviours (in the example used here, the smallest group is seen to be significantly less positive than the largest group). According to Hamilton and Gifford (1976), the illusory correlation paradigm is realistic in the sense that we generally have much more contact with the members of our own group than with members of other groups. Besides, some behaviours, usually the negative ones, are much less frequent than others. The effect is known to be extremely robust (Mullen & Johnson, 1990) even if a multitude of factors have been found to moderate the effect (Hamilton, 1981b; McGarty & de la Haye, 1997).

The earliest explanation of the effect points to the causal role of a perceptual bias: perceivers' attention would automatically be directed toward infrequent events rather than toward frequent events (Hamilton & Gifford, 1976; for a fresh version of the same argument, see McConnell, Sherman & Hamilton, 1994a). According to this distinctiveness account, the co-occurrence of rare events would be particularly salient and would facilitate an association in memory. In the illusory correlation paradigm, the behaviours of the minority are less frequent than those of the majority and the unlikeable behaviours are less numerous than the likeable behaviours. The unlikeable behaviours of the minority are thus likely to attract perceivers' attention and to be memorized.

A number of alternative explanations have been proposed. According to Fiedler (Fiedler, 1991; Fiedler & Armbruster, 1994; Fiedler, Russer & Gramm, 1993) and Smith (1991), the illusory correlation effect emerges because participants selectively lose information in such a way as to suggest that one group is better than the other. Smith (1991) notes that the identical proportion of positive and negative information in the two groups does not take away the fact that the absolute difference between the positive and the negative information is different in the two groups (in our example, the absolute difference is $18 - 8 = 10$ for the positive behaviours and $9 - 4 = 5$ for the negative behaviours). Fiedler (1991) stresses the importance of information loss in a context that is bound to create some degree of memory load. Information loss leads to a regression towards less unbalanced proportions of positive and negative behaviours. Still, this phenomenon does not affect the majority and the minority to the same extent. Given that there is more information about the majority, it is rather easy to notice the overwhelming presence of positive information. The scarcity of information about the minority group renders the actual proportion much more difficult to perceive. Fiedler's argument thus holds that, although rare events are seen to be less prevalent than frequent events, the perceived frequency of rare events is overestimated and that of frequent events is underestimated.

The approaches based on distinctiveness, memory and information loss all rest on mechanisms that implicate the content of the stimulus information. Adopting a much broader perspective, McGarty and his colleagues (Haslam, McGarty & Brown, 1996; McGarty & de la Haye, 1997; McGarty, Haslam, Turner & Oakes, 1993) argued that participants' expectations about the nature of the task and the groups presented in the experimental setting play a major role in the emergence of the illusory correlation effect. The starting point of this research programme is a very simple manipulation in which participants were asked to observe a series of behaviours. This was done without providing participants with information about the group membership of the individuals. Next, participants had to assign these behaviours to one of two groups.

The only piece of information given to the participants is that one group is more numerous than the other. The findings are quite simple: participants attribute the less frequent behaviours to the minority. This is all the more surprising given that no association whatsoever had been presented to the participants.

For McGarty et al. (1993), these results show that participants understand the task as one that requires them to find a difference between the two groups (Berndsen, Spears, McGarty & van der Pligt, 1998; Berndsen, van der Pligt, Spears & McGarty, 1996). In other words, when people learn that behaviours have been performed by members of two different groups, they initiate a series of mechanisms that help them to clearly differentiate between these two social entities. Note that this interpretation is very interesting in light of the work on conversational norms (Grice, 1975, see also Bless, Strack & Schwarz, 1993). Indeed, as far as the illusory correlation paradigm is concerned, it is quite clear that the experimenter violates the most elementary norms of cooperation. Here is a person who gives participants information about two distinct groups, goes as far as to label the groups differently, and asks them to evaluate these two groups in spite of the fact that there is no actual difference between the behaviours performed by the members of these two groups. Given the fact that one group is more numerous than the other and that some behaviours are more frequent than others, the distribution that maximizes the difference between the two groups is the one that assigns the frequent behaviours to the majority and the rare behaviours to the minority. Not surprisingly, this is the strategy adopted by McGarty et al.'s (1993) participants.

The differentiation approach proposed by McGarty et al. (1993) suggests that the illusory correlation effect should emerge to the extent that participants have a good reason to believe that there are indeed true differences between the two groups. A clever experiment by S. A. Haslam, McGarty and Brown (1996) aimed at testing this conjecture. Half of the participants took part in a classic illusory correlation experiment. The remaining participants also learned that the majority group were in fact right-handed people and the minority were left-handed people. As in most illusory correlation studies, the behaviours presented to the participants concerned the dimension of likeability.

In light of the hypotheses, the selection of these particular labels had several advantages. For one thing, the presentation of right-handed and left-handed as, respectively, the majority and the minority fits quite well with prior expectations about the distribution of these two groups. More importantly, participants should not be led to think that one group is any better than the other. In contrast, the predominant belief among participants is that right-handed and left-handed people are strictly similar. In this particular condition, the information provided to the participants was able to eradicate the tendency to see an association between the dimension and the group. In other words, Haslam et al. (1996) found no evidence whatsoever for an illusory correlation effect. This finding is even more remarkable when taking into account the fact that participants were all right-handed. As a matter of fact, several researchers conducted studies showing that the illusory correlation effect is attenuated when participants are members of the minority but exacerbated when participants are members of the majority (McArthur & Friedman, 1980; Schaller & Maass, 1989; but see Spears, van der Pligt & Eiser, 1985). S. A. Haslam et al. (1996), however, found no trace of an ingroup bias: right-handed perceivers failed to derogate the minority of left-handed people.

The study conducted by S. A. Haslam and colleagues is quite elegant as the data neatly illustrate the way people's naïve theories about the nature of a category influence the perception of the characteristics associated with its members. Still, we see two major limitations to the study. Firstly, one should note that the experimental participants are confronted with two groups about which there exists a strong expectation, namely that the two groups *should not differ* on evaluative grounds. To put it another way, the ambient beliefs about right-handed and left-handed people remain entirely unrelated to the positivity or negativity of the behaviours of the two groups. In contrast to what happens for the control participants, experimental participants are thus not put in a situation where they learn information about two *new* groups. As a consequence, it would be most surprising if observers were to change their perception of the two groups after the confrontation with the various behaviours (for a similar argument, see Berndsen, Spears, van der Pligt & McGarty, 1999). The second limitation is empirical rather than methodological in nature. Indeed, S. A. Haslam et al. (1996) demonstrate that perceivers' naïve theories are in a position to counter the formation of illusory correlation. This is indeed a most important message. In our view, however, it remains to be shown that naïve theories may have a strong impact on the formation of new stereotypes. In other words, we would expect people to be inclined to create social beliefs with even more enthusiasm when they think that the groups are essentially different than when they have no information as to the basis of category membership. To address these issues, we decided to conduct a new study in which care was taken to manipulate the beliefs about the nature of the groups and the origin of the behaviours without providing information about the content of the stereotypes themselves (Yzerbyt, Rocher, McGarty & S. A. Haslam, 1997; see Berndsen, Spears, van der Pligt & McGarty, this volume).

Our experiment was modelled on the classic illusory correlation paradigm (Hamilton & Gifford, 1976). A total of seventy-two participants read thirty-nine sentences presented in a random order for 8s each. In line with the standard distribution of the information used to create the illusory correlation, eighteen positive behaviours and eight negative behaviours were associated with Group A and nine positive and four negative behaviours were associated with Group B. These behaviours had been carefully pre-tested so that their mean positivity and mean negativity was the same for the two groups. The participants' task was simply to memorize the behaviours as well as the group membership of their authors. The only experimental manipulation of the study concerned the information provided about the origin of the two groups. Experimental participants were informed that the two groups had been constituted either by a computer program or by clinical psychologists. Specifically, participants read that 'these groups have been formed by asking a panel of clinical psychologists (vs. a computer program) to assign one of two labels to the entire list of people. It happens to be case that the panel of clinical psychologists (vs. the computer program) assigned less people in group B than in group A. As a result, there are less sentences describing members of group B than sentences describing members of Group A'. A control group also took part in the study. These control participants were given the standard instructions in which no information is provided about the origin of two groups assumed to exist in real life (Hamilton & Gifford, 1976).

Our previous investigations had suggested that, in participants' eyes, clinical psychologists are experts in interpreting behaviour and classifying people in various groups. In contrast, the general suspicion is that computers are not capable of making subtle distinctions between people. As a consequence, our prediction was that participants would show a larger illusory correlation when a strong as opposed to a weak meaning is being attached to the constitution of the group. Specifically, the illusory correlation effect should be stronger in the clinical psychologists condition than in the control condition. Conversely, the illusory correlation effect should be weaker in the computer program condition than in the control condition.

After the presentation of the instructions and the thirty-nine behaviours, all participants were presented with a surprise recognition test. For each behaviour, participants were asked to indicate whether it had been performed by a member of Group A or a member of Group B. A phi coefficient was then computed such that the coefficient was positive if the illusory correlation favoured Group A and negative if the illusory correlation favoured Group B. As can be seen in the left panel of Figure 3.2,

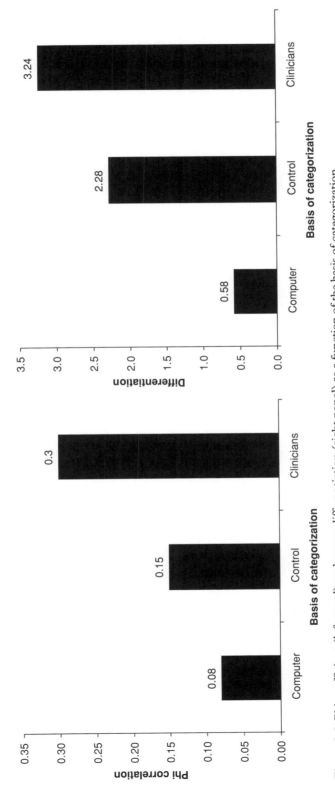

Figure 3.2 Phi coefficient (left panel) and group differentiation (right panel) as a function of the basis of categorization.

the mean phi coefficients observed in each one of the three conditions support our hypotheses. Participants who thought that the two groups had been created by a panel of clinical psychologists manifested a stronger illusory correlation than participants in the two other conditions (who did not differ from each other). Interestingly, whereas the illusory correlation was significantly different from zero in both the clinical psychologists, and control conditions, no significant illusory correlation was observed in the computer program condition. As it turns out, the magnitude of the phi coefficient in the clinical psychologist condition, .30, is particularly note-worthy. Mullen and Johnson's (1990) review would suggest that this is one of the larger correlations obtained in the illusory correlation paradigm.

After the recognition test, participants also evaluated the two groups on a series of four bipolar rating scales ranging from 0 to 11 (good-bad, unfriendly-friendly, unlikeable-likeable, dishonest-honest). These scales allowed an index of differentiation to be computed. The more positive the index of differentiation, the more participants express a bias in favour of Group A over Group B. As can be seen on the right panel of Figure 3.2, the pattern of the differentiation index parallels the one found for the phi coefficient. This time, the participants in the clinical psychologist and the control conditions did not differ from each other. However, participants in both these conditions expressed a stronger bias in favour of Group A than those in the computer program condition. Also, the clinical psychologist condition participants, and the control participants, but not the computer program participants, differed from the zero differentiation criterion.

The results of this study fully support our hypotheses. As we predicted, the illusory correlation was totally absent when the participants thought that the categories rested on the decision of a computer program. In sharp contrast, compared to what was observed in the control condition, illusory correlation was amplified when the groups were allegedly constructed by clinical psychologists. Whereas the absence of a mean-ingful rationale for the constitution of the two groups led participants to conclude that the two groups did not differ, the provision of a sen-sible reason for the existence of the two groups ended up in a more positive perception of Group A and a more negative perception of Group B. Clearly, this experiment shows the considerable impact of essentialist theories on the formation of group stereotypes. As a matter of fact, social perceivers process the information very differently when they are armed with a powerful theory concerning the existence of a target group than when they think that the observed people are not really members of a social entity. Our participants simply did not think that a computer pro-gram could validly assign people to meaningful social groups. Therefore, the categories that were created were not pointing at true differences between the group members and participants refrained from engaging in category differentiation.

One important feature of the accentuation paradigm discussed in the previous section and the illusory correlation paradigm examined here is that they remain limited to one dimension of differentiation. Depending on the subjective meaning of the criterion used to constitute the two groups, perceivers exacerbated or minimized the difference between the members of the two categories on the critical characteristic, namely likeability. Of course, the actual interactions between existing groups are much more complex. Whereas some behaviours may concern a dimension like intelligence, others may be related to a very different dimension such as sociability. As the work on the role of theories in categorization shows (Medin, 1989; Murphy, 1993; Murphy & Medin, 1985), a major problem of probabilistic accounts of categorization concerns the determination of the dimensions that turn out to be relevant for the construction of the categories (see also Corneille & Judd, 1999). Our subjective essentialist approach stresses the importance of perceivers' naïve theories on that front as well. This is the aspect we examine in the next section.

The emergence of group stereotypes in a multidimensional context

According to some researchers, the formation of stereotypes and the selection of the stereotypical dimensions rests on a direct comparison between the characteristics of the groups. Imagine two groups whose members are equally likeable. Assume further that one group comprises people who are more intelligent than the members of the other group. In a situation like this, observers will likely single out the intelligence of the group members and neglect their likeability. If, instead, both intellectual competence and social competence provide a means to distinguish the two groups (the members of one group are more intelligent but less sociable than the members of the other group), observers will select the dimension that best discriminates between the two groups. The idea here is that stereotypes are formed around those dimensions that allow us to make the clearest distinction between the groups. This view is a direct heritage of the probabilistic accounts of concept formation (Rosch & Mervis, 1975; see Corneille & Judd, 1999).

In their work on family resemblance, Rosch and colleagues (Rosch, Mervis, Grey, Johnson & Boyes-Braem, 1976; Rosch & Mervis, 1975) showed that those exemplars that become more strongly associated with the category label (e.g., apples) were the ones that shared the largest number of features with the other members of the category and the least features with members of other categories (e.g., oranges, pears, etc.). This similarity perspective can also be found in social psychological accounts. Building upon Festinger's (1954) notion of social comparison, Tajfel (1972) argued that the features of a group take on their meaning only by comparison with other groups (Turner, 1975). The Tajfelian tradition culminates with the idea of the meta-contrast ratio which, exactly like the principle of family resemblance proposed by Rosch and Mervis (1975), holds that the most typical member of a group is the one who shares the highest number of characteristics with the other members of the group and the lowest number of characteristics with members of other groups (Oakes, Haslam & Turner, 1994; Oakes & Turner, 1990; Turner, 1985; Turner et al., 1987). Other researchers also consider that the comparison between groups is a key aspect of group perception. For instance, McCauley, Stitt & Segal (1980) defined stereotypes by making an explicit reference to the issue of between-groups discrimination. For them, stereotypes are generalizations about a social group that distinguish them from other groups. These authors even developed a stereotype measure that includes the distinction from other groups as a component of the index. Research efforts in person perception similarly made a direct reference to the issue of family resemblance (Andersen & Klatzky, 1987; Cantor & Mischel, 1979).

Despite the wide availability of theories and models, there are only a few empirical demonstrations of the role of comparison and family resemblance principles in the formation of group stereotypes. As a case in point, Ford and Stangor (1992) showed that asking observers to describe two groups leads them to rely on those dimensions (intelligence or sociability depending on the experimental conditions) with the largest difference in means between the groups or with the smallest within-group variance when the mean differences on the two dimensions are equal. In other words, observers behaved as intuitive statisticians who seemed able to perform a series of analyses of variance or, more specifically, a stepwise discriminant analysis.

Without denying observers' ability to compute central tendencies on the various dimensions they are confronted with, we doubt that distributional features are the most relevant information that people can rely on in order to select dimensions in a given context (see Brown & Turner, this volume). The issue is not to know how people manage to compare groups on dimensions given a priori by the experimenter but to understand how they come to consider that one dimension is more useful than another. From a subjective essentialist viewpoint, we would argue that perceivers are likely to select those surface dimensions that naïve theories suggest are most related to the underlying causes of categorization. To test that idea, we conducted a study (Rocher & Yzerbyt, 1997) in which participants were given information about the attributes of group members on two different dimensions. Additionally, participants also received information that allowed them to infer that the deep basis for categorization was either climatic or genetic in nature.

Specifically, participants were asked to form an impression about two fictitious groups, group A and group B, on the basis of a series of behaviours allegedly performed by twelve different members of each group. These behaviours had been chosen on the basis of a pre-test that required students issued from the same population as the experimental participants to rate each one of 100 behaviours on a social competence scale ranging from 1 (= extremely asocial) to 11 (extremely sociable) and an intellectual competence scale ranging from 1 (= extremely unintelligent) to 11 (extremely intelligent). The behavioural descriptions used in the experiment proper disclosed information about the intelligence (in six of the behaviours) or the sociability (in the other six) of the individuals in each group. Importantly, each group was described as being more positive than the other group in one dimension and less positive than the other group in the other dimension. In other words, the members of group A were more sociable and less intelligent than the members of group B. Moreover, the behaviours presented to the participants were such that the difference in intelligence between the two groups was equal to the difference in sociability between the two groups. Finally, the within-group variance was the same for both groups and both dimensions.

Several reasons led us to select the dimensions of intellectual and social competence. For one thing, these dimensions have been shown to be largely orthogonal in implicit theories of personality and, as such, they seem to play a most important role in the perception of individuals and groups (Brown, 1986; Glick & Fiske, 2001; Peeters, 1986; Rosenberg & Sedlak, 1972; Wojciszke, 1994). One additional feature that concerned us here was that these dimensions are also accounted for by naïve theories that are largely independent of one another. Indeed, we asked students issued from the same population as our experimental participants to mention all those factors they could think of that could explain a series of personality factors like intelligence, sociability, honesty, optimism, altruism, etc. The explanations provided by the students were grouped into several categories such as environment, social and economical background, climate, genes, religion, etc.

Building upon the pattern emerging from this initial pre-test, another group of students issued from the same population was then confronted with a forced choice. Specifically, students were to indicate which factor, whether the climate or genes, best explained people's sociability and intelligence. The results were unambiguous as all students selected genes over climate as the factor causing intelligence and climate over genes as the factor explaining sociability. In other words, our pre-test work confirmed that genetic background was generally seen to be one of the major causes for a person's intelligence. In sharp contrast, the climate in which the individual lives was hardly seen as having any influence on the person's intellectual competence. Conversely, whereas climate was often thought to have an impact on people's sociability and warmth, intelligence was not believed to be affected much by climate.

Turning back to the experiment, a different basis of categorization was evoked depending on the experimental condition. In the climate condition, experimental participants were informed that the two groups about which they were to receive several pieces of information in order for them to form an impression had been initially observed by 'a researcher working on the impact of the climate on social groups'. These participants, we assumed, would be tempted to consider that the dimension of sociability was the critical dimension of comparison. To the remaining participants, the experimenter indicated that the behaviours had been collected 'by a researcher interested in the impact of genes on social groups'. With these instructions we hoped that our participants would rely on the members' intellectual competence to compare and contrast the two groups. It is important to note at this point that no reference whatsoever was made to the specific dimensions contained in the behavioural information. That is, we wanted to activate our naïve theories without mentioning the actual dimensions that differentiated between the groups. Our hypothesis was that the naïve theories would direct our participants toward the selection of one dimension at the expense of the other. As a consequence, the stereotypic representation of the two groups would be very different in the two experimental conditions although both groups of participants would be confronted with the same objective information about the social groups in the first place.

After participants had been provided with the instructions, the twenty-four behaviours were displayed on a computer screen one at a time in a random order. Once the impression formation task was completed, participants were given two minutes to write down 'any thoughts that came to their mind and that concerned the two groups'. In order to examine the strength of association between the representation of the groups and the descriptive dimensions, these thoughts were content analysed (Ford & Stangor, 1992). As a means to identify the most recurrent themes, two independent judges, blind to the experimental conditions, classified the ideas expressed by the participants in one of three categories depending on whether a reference was made to intelligence, sociability or another dimension (the latter category was excluded from the analysis of results given its low frequency and the lack of theoretical interest, see also Ford & Stangor, 1992). It is important to mention at this point that the valence of the thought was not taken into account. Indeed, a participant who indicates that the members of one group were rather distant is alluding to social competence as surely as another participant who praises the members of the other group for their warmth and sensitivity.

Our hypothesis was that participants would describe the two groups more in terms of intelligence when they thought that the behaviours had been collected by a researcher working on the influence of genes on social groups rather than on the impact of climate. Conversely, we expected participants to more readily characterize the groups in terms of sociability when they had been informed that the interest of the researcher was the impact of climate on social groups rather than the role of genes.

As can be seen on the left panel of Figure 3.3, the data fully support the predictions. In addition to a significant main effect of dimension, which indicated that participants generated more thoughts about social than about intellectual competence, we also found a significant interaction between the dimension and the theory underlying the categories. Further statistical analyses confirmed that the number of thoughts related to intelligence was more important when genes rather than no theory or climatic factors were the basis for the categorization of the groups, the latter two conditions not being different from each other. In contrast, there were more thoughts mentioning the sociability dimension when the groups had a climatic basis rather than when no theory or a genetic basis was mentioned, the latter two conditions being not different from each other. In other words, the availability of a naïve theory linking the constitution of the groups to a specific dimension made it more easy for participants to refer to this dimension to think and write about the groups.

After participants had spent two minutes writing about the groups, they were interrupted by the computer program and asked to rate the two groups on two rating scales. One scale evaluated social competence and ranged from 1 (= not at all sociable) to 11 (extremely sociable). The other scale concerned intellectual competence and ranged from 1(= not at all intelligent) to 11 (extremely intelligent). These raw judgements were then used to compute two stereotype scores, one for each dimension. Specifically, the difference between the sociability rating for Group A and Group B for each participant served as an index of differentiation on social competence. Similarly, the difference between the rating of intelligence of Group A and the rating of intelligence of Group B was used as an index of differentiation on intellectual competence. These scores

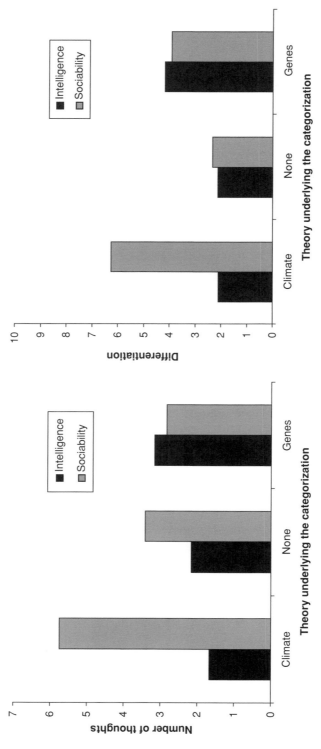

Figure 3.3 Number of thoughts generated about the groups (left panel) and differentiation between the groups (right panel) as a function of the theory underlying the categorization and the dimension.

meet the criterion of several definitions of stereotypes (McCauley et al., 1980; Tajfel, 1972; Turner, 1987b).

Once again, the data fully confirmed the hypotheses (see right panel of Figure 3.3). Participants differentiated the two groups more on intelligence when they believed the groups to be formed in order to study the impact of genes than when they thought that the climate was the focus of attention in the original study. Conversely, participants differentiated the two groups more in terms of their social competence when the instructions revealed that the interest for the impact of climate rather then genes had guided the constitution of the two groups.

Globally, this study provides strong evidence for the role of naïve theories in the formation of stereotypes. Knowing how the two groups were formed helped participants to make a decision about the relevance of the various dimensions. In turn, this information allowed participants to differentiate the two groups. The data pattern is all the more impressive given that participants were given information about the constitution of the two groups that was one step away from the content of the dimensions. In other words, we only activated a specific naïve theory and hoped that participants would make the connection themselves between the alleged basis for categorization and one of the two dimensions.

Two remarks are in order at this point. Firstly, it seems likely that there should be a priori differences between the various dimensions that can be used to characterize social groups. In fact, perceivers' naïve theories about social groups give us a hint as to which dimensions are more useful than others. So, for instance, it may generally be more important to know about the level of sociability or intelligence of group members than to determine their weight or height, except for certain very specific circumstances. As we said earlier, sociability and intelligence are aspects that perceivers seem to value quite a bit and there is no shortage of studies showing the privileged status of these two dimensions in impression formation. But even these two dimensions may not be strictly equivalent. Our data suggest that one dimension, namely sociability, may well attract more attention than the other, namely intelligence. The effect size on the two dependent measures used in the present study was systematically stronger for social competence than intellectual competence. As for the number of thoughts participants generated to describe the two groups, we found an advantage of the sociability dimension even when no rationale had been provided for the constitution of the two groups.

Several explanations can be offered in order to account for this differential 'attractiveness' of the two dimensions. For one thing, social desirability may be at work. Indeed, it may be more acceptable to express negative views about a person's or a group's sociability than about a person's or a group's intelligence. The same explanation can be used in the case of the number of thoughts generated by the participants. For another, social competence may hold some special status in the eyes of people in general and of our participants in particular (psychology students) for whom it may be more important to know about sociability than about intelligence (Reeder, Pryor & Wojciszke, 1992; Wojciszke, Bazinska & Jaworski, 1998). This idea is of course fully compatible with research showing the importance of what Peeters and Czapinski (1990) called other-profitable traits, (i.e., traits related to issues of social competence), as opposed to self-profitable traits, (i.e., traits related to issues of intellectual competence).

A second remark concerns the absence of inhibition effects. Although participants rely on the most relevant dimension, they do not seem to neglect the less appropriate dimension. Compared to the control condition, participants did not generate less thoughts related to intelligence when sociability was pertinent or, conversely, less thoughts related to sociability when intelligence was applicable. Similarly, compared to the control condition, participants still differentiated the two groups on sociability and intelligence when this dimension turned out to be less relevant in the experimental context. With respect to the genetic theory, the absence of inhibition on the sociability dimension is probably due to the theoretical status of the theory: even if genes offer a decent account for group differences in intelligence, they are not entirely silent as far as differences in sociability, or on any other trait for that matter, are concerned. This reaction may thus reflect the enormous explanatory potential of genetically-based theories. Interestingly, the absence of inhibition can also be observed on the intelligence dimension: groups are no less differentiated and the number of thoughts is not less important when the theory is climatic than when no theory is provided. Presumably, this indicates the insidious capacity of theories to explain most differences once they are sufficiently large to be noticed.

Conclusions

Social categorization allows perceivers to make sense of the surrounding world. According to our subjective essentialist theory of stereotypes (Yzerbyt, Rocher & Schadron, 1997), there is a strong relationship between perceivers' beliefs about the underlying essence shared by all group members and the features that are seen to characterize them (for a review, see Yzerbyt, Corneille & Estrada, 2001). Whenever the group is not seen as being accidental (i.e., its existence is not seen as purely the consequence of circumstances), perceivers may start to search for those deep features that come with group membership. By attributing the observed behaviours to some underlying characteristic that is common to all group members, stereotypic beliefs provide people with a subjectively valid understanding of the regularities encountered in the social environment (Yzerbyt & Rogier, 2001; Yzerbyt, Rogier & Fiske, 1998). Conversely, when some deep cause for membership is made salient, people feel tempted to impose order and meaning upon the incoming information. That is, people may want to engage in category differentiation only when the two groups are thought to have real significance. If perceivers possess a good rationale regarding the constitution of the groups, a theory that provides a strong justification for the existence of the two groups, then they will probably infer that the two groups must be different on a series of crucial dimensions. In sharp contrast, when group membership is thought to be arbitrary, there will be few reasons to engage in a search for differentiation.

The present chapter focused on the latter portion of the process namely the impact of an essentialist stance on the formation of stereotypes. We offered several empirical illustrations of the importance of such beliefs in the emergence of social beliefs. As we have seen, the accentuation of between-group differences and within-group similarities can be further accentuated when observers receive information that confirms the deep nature of the two categories. The same reasoning was helpful in the context of the illusory correlation paradigm (for a review of the illusory correlation paradigm, see McGarty, Yzerbyt & Spears, this volume; Berndsen et al., this volume). When people were confronted with two groups that were thought to be fundamentally different, participants set out to find ways to differentiate the groups. As the evaluative dimension proved to be the most practical, one group ended up being more positively evaluated than the other. Finally, we showed that the availability of a rationale for the constitution of the social groups helped participants to orient their perception of the difference between two groups (see Brown & Turner, this volume). Not only was there a stronger tendency to make a difference between the two groups, a pattern of accentuated accentuation, but the contrast between the two groups was relatively stronger along the lines implied by the naïve theory.

As we hope to have shown, the present set of findings can hardly be explained in terms of a simple probabilistic account of category formation. Instead, the relevance of the New Look approach is most obvious. For Bruner (1957b; Bruner, Goodnow & Austin, 1956), the true function of categories is to allow observers to make sense of the environment. Unfortunately, if the search for meaning is a laudable endeavour, the actual theories used by social observers may sometimes be quite problematic. The dangers are especially palpable in the social domain. Indeed, whereas the theories regarding the physical world may simply be wrong, in which case they will eventually be discarded, the consequences of certain theories in the social world may become dramatic when they are backed up by questionable motivations. Confirmation of hypotheses and self-fulfilling prophecies may do a great deal of harm by substantiating erroneous conceptions. More often than not, subjective essentialism and entitativity seem to serve the maintenance of the status quo, allowing dominant groups to perpetuate the existing social structure and justify the current treatment of minority groups (Jost & Banaji, 1994; Tajfel, 1981b; Yzerbyt & Schadron, 1994; Yzerbyt & Rogier, 2001; Yzerbyt et al., 1997).

In our opinion, however, naïve realist accounts of human nature need not by definition be associated with the perpetuation of a social system. As we have argued, people are extremely ingenious in their ability to find surface regularities that can be seen as expressions of deep underlying characteristics. The consequence is that they should be quite receptive to a multiplicity of ways of dividing up the social environment. Similarly, the propensity to imagine deep characteristics that may provide a decent rationale for the observed features should also contribute to facilitate the adoption of new modes of thinking about the surrounding world. The real challenge, we suspect, may come from the difficulty in rupturing the causal sequence that links observers' naïve theories and their social behaviour. History and social psychological work alike show that dramatic changes in the social relations between two groups indeed affect their stereotypic views of each other (Avigdor, 1953; Gilbert, 1951; Karlins, Coffman & Walters, 1969; Katz & Braly, 1933; Sherif, Harvey, White, Hood & Sherif, 1961). People simply forget the active role they play in pointing out the features that characterize the various social groups they are confronted with. As we hope to have shown, the existence of a priori theories constrains the vision of the surrounding world. Our preliminary work on these issues indicates that a better appraisal of the functional aspects of subjective essentialism should undoubtedly help us understand the conditions under which stereotypes are formed and, more generally, the mechanisms involved in the creation of social beliefs.

4   The role of theories in the formation of stereotype content

Patricia M. Brown and John C. Turner

Introduction

> ... groups differ in many ways. Some of the attributes that differentiate one group from other groups will become stereotypic of the group, whereas other such attributes will not. What determines which differences between groups will become central to the content of the stereotype? This is an important question but one that has been relatively neglected by social cognitive research.
>
> (Hamilton, Stroessner & Driscoll, 1994, p. 309)

In recent decades the emphasis of research into stereotype formation, and indeed stereotyping more generally, has tended to be on process rather than content. The rise of the social cognition approach within this field has shifted the focus of research towards an investigation of the cognitive processes involved in stereotyping. This is also true of approaches to stereotype formation, such as distinctiveness-based illusory correlation (Hamilton & Gifford, 1976). The actual content of stereotypes has appeared somewhat secondary in such accounts. However, recently we are witnessing something of a revival of interest in the content issue, with increased research into the functions served by stereotypes and an emphasis on stereotypes as 'aids to explanations' (see McGarty, Yzerbyt & Spears, this volume). Indeed, if one takes a 'meaning' based approach to stereotype formation, it would seem that the content of stereotypes should be highly significant to understanding stereotypes as explanations or sense-making devices.

In this chapter we take the formation of stereotype content as our focus. Importantly, however, we do not seek to separate content from process as has been done in many past accounts. It is not necessary to see these as two separate topics, and indeed we will argue that content and process are inextricably intertwined. We will be arguing that the formation of stereotype content is not separate from the formation of stereotypes and social categories – all are aspects of the same underlying process.

The account of stereotype content formation to be presented in this chapter focuses on the role of, and interaction between, theory and data (see also Yzerbyt & Rocher, this volume). When considering stereotype (and content) formation, three main possibilities arise. On the one hand, stereotypes may form to reflect our direct observations of a group's behaviour. On the other hand, stereotypes may reflect our expectations and broader theories about how we think that group should behave. Or perhaps stereotypes form to reflect some combination of our observations (data) and our expectations and knowledge (theory). This tension between the role of theory and data in determining content can be traced back to early accounts of stereotyping. For example, in the earliest studies of stereotype content (Katz & Braly, 1933, 1935) it was found that participants held stereotypes about groups with which they had little or no contact, prompting the authors to argue that stereotype content derived partly from direct contact with other groups, but that this contact was influenced by 'public attitudes' already held about those groups. However, early research also saw the genesis of the idea that stereotypes may contain a 'kernel of truth', that is they may form to reflect 'real' differences between groups, and it was argued that increased direct contact with groups may result in more accurate impressions of those groups (e.g., Prothro & Melikian, 1955; Triandis & Vassiliou, 1967).

Changes in the approach to stereotype formation and the switch in research emphasis away from content and toward process came about with the acceptance of the idea that stereotyping is linked to the categorization process. This idea largely originated in the work of Tajfel (e.g., Tajfel, 1969; Tajfel, 1981b; Tajfel & Wilkes, 1963). Tajfel argued that through personal and cultural experience personality dimensions become associated with classifications of people into groups. When a classification into social groups is correlated with a continuous dimension, such as a personality trait, there is a tendency to exaggerate differences on that dimension between classes and to minimize those differences within classes. Thus stereotypes, and stereotype content, reflect a correlation between personality attributes or traits and the division into social categories. However, while Tajfel's work emphasized the cognitive aspects of stereotyping, he also argued that to fully understand the content of stereotypes we need to take into account both the functions served by stereotypes and the dimensions on which stereotyping occurs (Tajfel, 1981b). The functions served by stereotypes, both individual and social, are important in determining which dimensions we select when differentiating between social groups. Tajfel argued that those dimensions selected and accentuated will be those which allow us to create clear value differentials between groups, allow us to make sense of and justify social relations between groups and allow us to make our group positively distinct from relevant outgroups (Tajfel, 1981b). Therefore, to understand the content of stereotypes we must take into account the nature of the dimensions on which differences between social groups are accentuated.

In this chapter we consider the dimensions on which we differentiate between groups and, in particular, the respective roles of theory and data in determining those dimensions. In particular, we will consider how theory and data are linked via fit, the perceived match between categories and content. We shall argue that fit is interpreted within a broader context of background knowledge and theories. We begin by considering accounts of stereotype formation and application from the social cognition perspective, and the relative importance of theory, data and fit in these accounts. Such accounts are contrasted with an account of stereotype (and content formation) based upon self-categorization theory (Turner, 1985; Turner, Hogg, Oakes, Reicher & Wetherell, 1987; Turner, Oakes, Haslam & McGarty, 1994) which emphasizes the importance of the categorization process and the role of comparative and normative fit in stereotype formation. We shall outline the results of empirical research which examined the influence of theories in interpreting the fit between categories and content, and in determining the content and 'meaning' of social stereotypes.

Data and theory in stereotype formation and stereotype application

Approaches to stereotyping, characterized by what has been termed the social cognition perspective (Devine, Hamilton & Ostrom, 1994), have tended to draw a distinction between stereotype formation and stereotype application. The role of bottom-up (or data-driven) and top-down (or theory-driven) processes are argued to be differentially important to each of these. Specifically, bottom-up processes are argued to dominate in stereotype formation whereas top-down processes dominate in stereotype application.

Stereotype formation

The majority of accounts of stereotype formation agree that stereotypes are initially based upon the *perception* of differences between groups, even though this perception may not always reflect *real* differences (see Campbell, 1967). Therefore, the categorization process is argued to play a crucial role in stereotype formation (Mackie, Hamilton, Susskind & Rosselli, 1996). The process of categorization may lead to the development of stereotype content based upon perceived intergroup differences; however these differences may be either real or perceived as the result of cognitive biases.

Arguably the most influential account of stereotype formation is distinctiveness-based illusory correlation (Hamilton & Gifford, 1976; see Berndsen, Spears, van der Pligt & McGarty, this volume; Yzerbyt & Rocher, this volume). According to this account, stereotypes can form even when no actual group differences exist. When two distinctive stimuli co-occur, they attract attention, become more available in memory and, thus, become cognitively correlated. Once a group becomes associated with a given behaviour, this becomes a meaningful category for the perceiver and may guide future perceptions of the group.

Other accounts of stereotype formation argue that, rather than resulting from cognitive biases, stereotypes may form to reflect *actual* observed differences between groups. For example, Eagly (1987; Eagly & Steffen, 1984, 1986) has argued that gender stereotypes reflect the observed social role-gender correlation in our society where women have traditionally been homemakers and men have been breadwinners. The traits associated with these roles, communion and agency, have come to be associated with women and men respectively. Jussim (1991) proposes that stereotypes may to some extent be based in accurate perception. His 'reflection-construction' model considers the relationship between perceivers' beliefs and expectancies about a target's attributes and behaviours, and the target's actual attributes and behaviours. Jussim argues that expectations may result in judgements which accurately reflect actual behaviour and attributes to the extent that those expectations are based on background information which itself accurately predicts behaviour and attributes (independently of the perceiver).

Ford and Stangor (1992) also argue that stereotype formation may be based upon the actual correlation between attributes and groups. They propose that in forming stereotypes perceivers take notice of those attributes that best differentiate between groups and these tend to become associated with the groups in memory. They instructed participants to form impressions of two groups that differed in terms of both intelligence and friendliness. In one condition, the differences in group means were larger for intelligence than friendliness while in the other condition this was reversed. Participants tended to stereotype groups more in terms of the more differentiating dimension.

All the accounts of stereotype formation outlined above suggest that to some extent stereotype content is based upon direct observation and experience with group members, whether that observation is accurate or filtered by cognitive biases. Stangor and Schaller (1996) suggest that there has tended to be a focus on 'bottom-up' determinants of stereotypes and stereotype content. These stereotypes, once formed, are assumed to be represented cognitively in a relatively fixed form, waiting to be activated (Stangor & Lange, 1994; Stangor & Schaller, 1996). Thus the activation and application of stereotypes and stereotype content are conceptualized as separate to their formation.

Stereotype application

In simple terms, the social cognitive approach argues that the activation and application of stored stereotype content to a judgement depends largely upon how a given stimulus is categorized. This, in turn, is determined by the perceived similarity or *fit* between features of the stimulus and the specifications or features of the stored category. However, there are biases in the encoding and recall of stimulus information that tend to favour a match with an activated category. Once a fit or a match between a stimulus and a stored category is deemed to exist, the content applied to judgements of that stimulus is derived from the stored category. Thus 'top-down' processes are argued to dominate stereotype application.

Influential impression formation models, such as those of Fiske and Neuberg (1990; Fiske, Lin & Neuberg, 1999) and Brewer (1988) assume that categories are abstract cognitive representations such as schemas or prototypes (other models argue that exemplars are more important than abstract knowledge, e.g., Smith & Zarate, 1992). Schemas act so as to guide perceivers toward relevant information and encourage them to resolve inconsistencies with the schema (Leyens & Fiske, 1994). Before a stereotype (and its content) or a schema can be applied, the stimulus in question must be categorized. The initial categorization of a stimulus may be a relatively automatic process and based upon well-established categories such as race, age or sex (Brewer, 1988; Devine, 1989; Fiske & Neuberg, 1990) or upon categories cued by distinctive cues or category labels (Fiske & Neuberg, 1990; Fiske, Neuberg, Beattie & Milberg, 1987). Likewise, categories which are used frequently or recently may be relatively more accessible (Higgins, 1996).

It is not entirely clear what role fit plays in initial categorization although it would seem that there must be some rudimentary match between features of the stimulus and the activated category at this stage, even if categorization is relatively automatic. Hamilton and Sherman (1994) suggest that when categorization is automatic 'the similarity matching process ... relies on a single salient cue rather than on resemblance to the group stereotype' (p. 18). Spears and Haslam (1997), discussing Fiske and Neuberg's continuum model, argue that it holds that categorization is separate from and prior to perceived fit, 'but may be undone by it' (p. 206).

Confirmation of an initial category is argued to depend upon the match or fit between this category and the features of the stimulus (Brewer, 1988; Fiske & Neuberg, 1990; Fiske et al., 1999). The initial categorization guides subsequent perception and is confirmed whenever possible (Leyens & Fiske, 1994). If a good fit is detected between category and stimulus, category-based or top-down processes are employed and the content associated with a stored representation is applied. If good fit is not achieved, recategorization or attribute-based perception may result.

While the activation and use of stored stereotype content is argued to be based on the fit between the stimulus and the category, there is considerable evidence to suggest that stereotypes tend to bias perception in favour of their own confirmation. For example, a number of studies have demonstrated that given social categorical information about a target person, we are more likely to recall information consistent with that category versus inconsistent (e.g., Cohen, 1981; Hamilton & Rose, 1980; Rothbart, Evans & Fulero, 1979). However, stereotype-disconfirming information can be more 'attention-grabbing' and two meta-analytic reviews of research in this area conclude that generally there is a recall advantage for inconsistent information (Rojahn & Pettigrew, 1992; Stangor & McMillan, 1992). This recall advantage for inconsistent information may be influenced by a number of factors (a) it is more likely to occur for individual versus group impression formation tasks (Stern, Marrs, Millar & Cole, 1984), (b) it is less likely to occur in studies using pre-existing stereotypes and expectancies (as opposed to lab-created ones – Hamilton & Sherman, 1994), (c) as cognitive load increases recall for consistent information has an advantage (Macrae, Hewstone & Griffiths, 1993). Importantly, regardless of the recall advantage of inconsistent information, a strong response bias has been found for consistent information (Fyock & Stangor, 1993; Rojahn & Pettigrew, 1992; Stangor & McMillan, 1992).

Summary

In social cognitive accounts of stereotyping a distinction is made between the formation and application of stereotypes (and by implication stereotype content). At the formation stage, data-driven processes tend to dominate. Stereotypes are based upon the perception of differences (real or otherwise) between groups. Once stereotypes are formed they are assumed to be stored as cognitive structures which have certain content associated with them (Stangor & Lange, 1994). The application of that content to a given judgement is controlled largely by top-down processes. Once a stimulus has been initially categorized perceivers then confirm its fit with this category. This fit appears to be based upon the perceived similarity between features of the stimulus and the stored representation of the category. If an adequate fit is found then judgements about the stimulus (and the stereotype content applied) will reflect the contents of the stored category (or stereotype). As categories tend to act in favour of their own confirmation, good fit will be found whenever possible. Stereotype content, in this view, derives largely from stored categories which are triggered by stimulus data.

The notion of fit is important in these models and indeed it is fit that determines whether judgements will be category-based or more attribute-based. However, the notion of what is 'fitting' or consistent (or typical) with a given category tends to be conceptualized as relatively fixed (deriving from the assumption that stereotypes are themselves relatively fixed cognitive structures). This assumption is also reflected in models of stereotype change, whereby change is brought about via disconfirming information that otherwise tends to fit well with, or be prototypical of, the initial category (e.g., Johnston & Hewstone, 1992; Johnston, Hewstone, Pendry & Frankish, 1994) and where 'goodness of fit' is seen as a match to a fixed category prototype (Rothbart & John, 1985).

Self-categorization theory and the formation of stereotype content

The relevance of self-categorization theory (Turner, 1985; Turner et al., 1987; Turner et al., 1994) to stereotype content derives from its application to stereotyping (e.g., Oakes, Haslam & Turner, 1994) and categorization (e.g., McGarty, 1999; Oakes, 1996; Oakes & Turner, 1990). We do not intend to provide a review of the theory here (see Turner, 1999, for a recent overview) but rather to outline briefly its account of the categorization process and how this may be applied to an understanding of the formation of stereotype content. In common with accounts discussed above, this approach sees the categorization process as being central to stereotyping and emphasises the role of fit in this process. However, some crucial differences exist in terms of how both categorization and fit are understood. We now turn to these.

Categorization, category formation and category salience

According to self-categorization theory all perception involves categorization (see Bruner, 1957a). Stereotyping is considered to be simply categorization at a given level of abstraction, namely intergroup (Oakes, 1996). That is, stereotyping is the categorical perception of groups. It is not argued that stereotyping involves top-down processing and individuation involves bottom-up processing. Rather, all impressions (all categorizations) reflect both top-down *and* bottom-up processes; that is all categorizations (including stereotypes) are based upon an *interaction* between stimulus data and stored background knowledge, plus the motives, goals and needs of the perceiver.

Crucially, for self-categorization theory, categorization is 'a dynamic, context-dependent process, determined by comparative relations within a given context' (Oakes, Haslam & Reynolds, 1999, p. 58). Categories form to reflect and maximize meta-contrast; that is, the ratio of inter- to intragroup differences (Turner, 1987b; see Ford & Stangor, 1992). Therefore, categorization is always relative to a frame of reference or context. Categorizations form to reflect actual but *relative* similarities and differences between groups. This perspective disagrees with accounts of stereotype formation such as illusory correlation. Indeed, the illusory correlation effect has been reinterpreted by self-categorization theory researchers as an outcome of the categorization process and as reflecting a search for comparative differences between groups (e.g., Berndsen, McGarty, van der Pligt & Spears, 2001; Berndsen, Spears, McGarty & van der Pligt, 1998; Haslam, McGarty & Brown, 1996; McGarty & de la Haye, 1997; McGarty, Haslam, Turner & Oakes, 1993: see also Berndsen et al., this volume; Yzerbyt & Rocher, this volume).

The comparative nature of categorization means that categories are not conceptualized as stored cognitive representations. This perspective rejects the idea of stereotypes as fixed prototypes or schemas waiting to be activated. Categories and their content are constructed 'on the spot' to reflect an interaction between theory and data. Considerable evidence has been found supporting the context-dependence of category prototypicality (e.g., Haslam, McGarty, Oakes, Turner & Onorato, 1995; Hogg, 1992; Hogg, Cooper-Shaw & Holzworth, 1993; Hogg, Turner & Davidson, 1990; McGarty, Turner, Hogg, Davidson & Wetherell, 1992; Oakes, Haslam & Reynolds, 1999; Oakes, Haslam & Turner, 1998). Given that categories are constructed 'on the spot', in this account no distinction is made between the formation and the application of content; rather both are part of the same process.

Fit is considered to be important in the categorization process. Two aspects of fit, comparative and normative fit, have been shown to be important in determining category salience (Oakes, 1987; Oakes, Turner & Haslam, 1991). Comparative fit concerns the comparative relations between stimuli as articulated by the principle of meta-contrast. Categories (and content) that form must fit with the comparative differences between groups. Therefore, the role of data is crucial in content formation; content reflects *real* comparative and contextual aspects of stimulus reality. However, the role of the perceiver is also important: because categorization and the search for similarity and difference are driven and guided by the perceiver's needs, motives and goals (perceiver readiness, Oakes et al., 1994; Turner et al., 1994) and because the perception and interpretation of similarity and difference depend on the perceiver's background knowledge and theories. Normative fit links background knowledge and theories to immediate data. Comparative differences between groups must *make sense* in terms of our knowledge and theories for us to make use of them in stereotyping. Therefore, comparative and normative fit operate in interaction to determine stereotype content. It has been demonstrated that category salience is greatest when comparative and normative fit are operating together (Oakes et al., 1991; van Knippenberg, van Twuyver & Pepels, 1994). Likewise, we argue that stereotype content forms to reflect comparative and normative fit operating together.

This perspective, in line with recent work from cognitive psychology (Medin, Goldstone & Gentner, 1993; Murphy & Medin, 1985) and other research on stereotyping (Yzerbyt, Rocher & Schadron, 1997), rejects similarity based accounts of categorization. Medin and colleagues argue that similarity is not a fixed feature of the stimulus. Alternatively they argue that perceptions of similarity are guided and constrained by both context (Medin et al., 1993) and by theories (Murphy & Medin, 1985). In self-categorization theory context and theories are broadly represented by comparative and normative fit. Thus the perception of stereotype content, of similarities within groups (and differences between groups) is driven by both the comparative frame of reference (meta-contrast) and by the perceiver's expectations and theories. The perception of similarity and difference is context- *and* theory-dependent.

There is considerable evidence for the context-dependence of content and perceived similarity. For example, it has been demonstrated that what is judged to be typical of a category (e.g., Americans: Haslam, Turner, Oakes, McGarty & Hayes, 1992; or psychology students: Doosje, Haslam, Spears, Oakes & Koomen, 1998) and perceived similarity of others to self (Haslam & Turner, 1992, 1995) both vary with changes in frame of reference. Likewise, other studies have shown that the content associated with a group (Haslam, Oakes, Turner & McGarty, 1995) and the content of self-stereotypes (Onorato & Turner, 1996, 1997; Turner & Onorato, 1999) both vary with intra- versus intergroup contexts. Stereotype change studies (Oakes et al., 1999) also demonstrate that what we judge to be confirming or disconfirming of a category varies with comparative context. Thus, perceived consistency or typicality of content with a category is context-dependent.

Linking fit and theories in the formation of stereotype content

We have outlined above how what is considered to be consistent with a category can vary with comparative context. However, the formation of categories and content also depend crucially upon normative fit. Comparative and normative fit are both vitally important to the categorization process (Oakes et al., 1994; Turner et al., 1994). Differences between groups must be meaningful ones, they must make sense in terms of our expectations, background knowledge and theories. In this section we elaborate upon the role of normative fit in the categorization process and in the formation of stereotype content, and in particular, the relationship between normative fit and theories.

There is considerable evidence pointing to the role of normative factors and expectations in stereotyping. Indeed, much of the evidence reviewed in this chapter suggests that stereotypes tend to confirm our expectations. However, many accounts of stereotyping tend to conceptualize fit, or the consistency between categories and content, in a rather fixed fashion. In contrast, we are arguing that normative fit is not simply connected with a fixed set of expectations and knowledge; rather the expectations and knowledge we draw upon are much broader and more flexible.

In articulating the role of these factors in categorization and stereotyping, self-categorization theorists have drawn upon work from cognitive psychology that has demonstrated that categorization is influenced and constrained by our background knowledge and theories (Oakes et al., 1994; Turner et al., 1994; Turner & Onorato, 1999). For example, Medin and colleagues have argued that our perception of similarities and differences, as well as being constrained by comparative context, is guided and constrained by our theories. Murphy and Medin (1985) argue that the lists of attributes that may be chosen to represent any concept are constrained by the theories and knowledge underlying the concept. Thus, on any given occasion in describing a category we would not list every possible attribute associated with that category – rather, we would list those relevant and diagnostic of our theory and knowledge.

Our theories and background knowledge guide us to look for certain similarities and differences between entities (or groups). A study by Medin and Wattenmaker (1987) presented participants with pictures of two sets of trains which were given different sets of labels. Participants had to devise rules for what features separated the two sets of trains. Although the actual trains were identical across conditions, different labels produced different rules. It appears that the labels given to the trains acted like (or made accessible) certain theories and these in turn made certain properties more salient. Similar findings emerged from a recent study reported by Wittenbrink, Hilton and Gist (1998). They presented participants with a set of drawings of persons ostensibly done by aliens (called Gnolkanians) of Earthlings. In one condition participants were told that the Gnolkanians' body surface was entirely covered with a vinyl-like substance and therefore they were surprised by the Earthlings' skin ('appearance' explanation). In the other condition they were told that for Gnolkanians it was a virtue to hide all emotions in public and therefore they were surprised by Earthlings' display of feelings ('inner state' explanation). All participants received the same set of twenty drawings and were instructed to sort them into groups of similar drawings as they saw appropriate. Results indicated that participants' background knowledge about the stimuli influenced how they sorted the drawings with different clusters of similarity formed across the two conditions.

The results of these studies suggests that categorization is based upon the perception of similarities (and differences) which make sense in terms of our theories and knowledge. Categorizing depends upon these theories which both guide the search for similarity and constrain it. Thus:

> ... the relationship between a concept and an example is analogous to the relation between theory and data. That is classification is not simply based on a direct matching of the concept with those in the example, but rather requires that the example have the right 'explanatory relationship' to the theory organising the concept. (Medin, 1989, p. 1474)

The concept of normative fit captures this relationship between theory and data. Importantly, normative fit is not a fixed expectation or category to which stimulus data is matched. What is considered fitting of a certain category will be guided by our background theories and knowledge. Our long-term knowledge about the world is not conceptualized as containing set categories but rather as containing information that can be flexibly applied to the categorization process.

Other recent work from social psychology is supportive of the idea that cognitive knowledge structures (or theories), that are broader than fixed representations of groups or schemas, influence the categorization process (cf. Oakes, 1987; Oakes et al., 1991; Tajfel, 1969). For example, the social judgeability theory of Leyens, Yzerbyt and Schadron (1994) argues for the importance of theories in interpreting data. They argue that 'people do not just rely on data and theories about data but also upon theories about judgements' (p. 7). Yzerbyt, Rocher and Schadron (1997; Yzerbyt, Corneille & Estrada, 2001; Yzerbyt, Rogier & Fiske, 1998; see

Yzerbyt & Rocher, this volume), building on the social judgeability perspective, argue that people may 'quite heavily rely on their naïve theories to organise incoming information' about target persons or groups (p. 27). They suggest that people may hold 'essentialist' theories such that surface attributes of individuals are believed to reflect deeper underlying dispositions (see also Medin & Ortony, 1989; Rothbart & Taylor, 1992). Employing such a theory is argued to result in the accentuation of observed differences between groups.

Work by Dweck and colleagues (Chiu, Hong & Dweck, 1997; Dweck, Hong & Chiu, 1993; Dweck, Chiu & Hong, 1995a, 1995b; Levy & Dweck, 1998; Levy, Stroessner & Dweck, 1998) demonstrates that people who hold *entity* versus *incremental* theories show differences in the ways they encode and organize incoming social information. Entity theorists believe traits are fixed dispositions, whereas incremental theorists believe traits are malleable and can be changed. Levy et al. (1998) found that entity theorists tended to endorse stereotypes more strongly than incremental theorists, to perceive groups to be more homogeneous and to draw more extreme trait judgements from limited information. Chiu et al. argue that while these implicit theories are rarely articulated 'they may set up an interpretative frame within which information is processed' (p. 19).

Recent work by Wittenbrink and colleagues (Wittenbrink, Gist & Hilton, 1997; Wittenbrink, Park & Judd, 1998; cf. Tajfel, 1969, 1981b) has also considered 'the role that higher order structural properties of stereotypic knowledge play in the processing of social information' (Wittenbrink et al., 1997, p. 526). They argue that our stereotypic knowledge does not just include the attributes of groups but also a causal structure concerning the links between those attributes and to the perceiver's wider knowledge about the world. Thus stereotypes serve as 'explanatory frameworks' which allow us to construe cause and effect relations.

Wittenbrink et al. (1997) sought to examine how stereotypic causal assumptions influence the encoding of stereotype-relevant information. In Experiment 1 they considered causal stereotypic assumptions regarding African Americans. They propose that there are two opposing causal models concerning white Americans' beliefs about African Americans – a 'perpetrator' model which holds that African Americans are 'individually responsible for economic failure and low social status' and a 'victim' model which holds that 'the lower social status and economic failure of African Americans is due to structural disadvantages' (p. 527). They screened white college students for their belief models concerning African Americans using the Modern Racism Scale (MRS: McConahay,

Hardee & Batts, 1981). Students identified as holding either a 'victim' model (low score on the MRS) or a 'perpetrator' model (high score on the MRS) participated in the next phase of the experiment. They read a trial summary which described a male basketball player (either African American or White) who was accused of assaulting one of his teammates (of the opposite race). Subjects' explanations for the events described were analysed for their explanatory structure. Subjects with different MRS scores tended to construct different causal explanations for the events with high MRS subjects more likely to blame an African American versus a White player for initiating the incident, and vice versa for the low MRS subjects.

In a second experiment they found that causal explanations or models from Experiment 1 could be applied to the interpretation of unrelated stimuli. There was a transfer of the original stereotypic construal to these stimuli, but these construal effects 'emerged only when the target episodes provided a potential match with the activated stereotype' (Wittenbrink et al., 1997, p. 539). That is, the 'models' were only applied to the stimuli when they provided a fit with the stimuli.

The research discussed above suggests that theories and knowledge can influence both the interpretation and categorization of stimuli. These theories, knowledge and expectations that influence the categorization and stereotyping process are conceived of as broader and more complex than, for example, simple category schemas. The implication for the content of categories is that it is not fixed but varies both with comparative context and with changes in the theories and knowledge being made use of in that context. Category or stereotype content is deployed in flexible ways as Oakes et al. (1994) observe:

The content of categories is selectively varied to match what is being represented in terms of our background theories and knowledge. It is therefore not a fixed category content being applied: the stereotype content is selectively constructed to describe, make sense of and rationalise the context-specific differences observed, to differentiate groups meaningfully in terms of the interplay between background knowledge and immediate data [p. 122]

This also implies that there is no fixed consistency between a given category and given content but that 'a given attribute could, in principle, match any number of categories' (Oakes et al., 1994, p. 122). Likewise, a given category could be meaningfully represented by any number of different attributes. The consistency or similarity between an attribute and a category varies with both comparative context, *and* with background theories.

Using theories to interpret fit

We have argued above that the fit between data and a category is not fixed. Rather, what is seen to be fitting of a given category may vary with both context and with theories. We have already reviewed evidence supportive of the idea that fit is context-dependent. The research to be reported here aimed to demonstrate that the fit between categories and data is interpreted in light of perceivers' relevant background theories.

Specifically a study (Brown & Turner, 2001b, Experiment 2) was performed which attempted to manipulate participants' background theories before they formed impressions of, and stereotyped, two target groups who differed in terms of the dimension 'friendliness'. Comparative context was held constant. Two different types of theories were employed – an 'individual-personality' theory and a 'social-variable' theory. These theories were based upon explanations that had been spontaneously generated by participants in a previous study (Experiment 1) to account for differences between groups. The 'individual-personality' theory explained behaviour in terms of individual personality and argued that individual behaviours are not related to group memberships. The 'social-variable' theory proposed that human behaviour is flexible and determined by social and contextual variables such as group memberships.

The types of theories manipulated in this study were somewhat similar to the types of implicit personality theories (entity versus incremental) that have been proposed by Dweck and colleagues (Chiu et al., 1997; Dweck et al., 1993; Dweck et al., 1995a, 1995b; Levy & Dweck, 1998; Levy et al., 1998). While this approach to theories has been presented as a model of individual differences (Dweck et al., 1995a) it is acknowledged that 'both theories may represent basic modes of thought that are at some level familiar to most individuals' (Chiu et al., 1997, p. 26). Thus, they suggest that either type of theory may be made accessible given the right circumstances (Dweck et al., 1995b; see also Anderson, 1995; Harackiewicz & Elliot, 1995). In previous studies it has been found that these types of theories can be successfully manipulated to produce different social judgemental outcomes (Chiu et al., 1997; Levy et al., 1998). We believed that the types of theories employed in our study are also both available to most people and therefore could be manipulated.[1]

The study manipulated two variables, the type of theory presented to participants and the category labels given to the two target groups. Participants (senior college students in the Australian Capital Territory) were told they would be completing a study about the relationship between people's personality and occupations. They were then presented with a theory – either 'fixed-personality' or 'variable-social' – or given no explicit theory. Next, all participants viewed a video describing behaviours performed by members of two groups, Group A and Group B. The video contained thirty-six statements – eighteen about each group, with twelve pertaining to friendliness and six being neutral. Group A was always presented as being more friendly than Group B (there was good comparative fit between the two categories and the dimension friendliness). In the consistent labels condition, participants were told that Group A were tour guides and Group B were chess players, with these labels reversed in the inconsistent labels condition.[2] After viewing the video, participants completed a number of dependent measures regarding the perceived friendliness of the two groups.

It was predicted that the type of theory made accessible to participants would influence how they interpreted the consistency (or fit) between the category labels and the presented differences between groups, and subsequently stereotyped the two groups. Specifically, it was expected that for those participants with no explicit theory more stereotyping would occur in the consistent labels versus inconsistent labels condition (i.e., more stereotyping where there is good fit between category labels and behaviours). A similar result was expected for those exposed to the 'fixed-personality' theory. This theory allows participants to 'make sense' of friendly tour guides and unfriendly chess players but not vice versa (e.g., if personality determines behaviour why would an unfriendly person become a tour guide?). However, it was expected that for those participants given a 'variable-social' theory, stereotyping (in terms of friendliness) would be equally high regardless of label-type. This was because this type of theory should allow participants to 'make sense' of both friendly tour guides and unfriendly chess players, *and* unfriendly tour guides and friendly chess players (e.g., if group and context determine behaviour then it must be something about being a tour guide which makes a person unfriendly).

A stereotyping measure was calculated which was the difference between ratings of Group A and Group B in terms of friendliness (i.e., how much participants differentiated between groups in terms of the relevant dimension). Results for this measure across conditions are presented in Figure 4.1. Planned orthogonal contrasts showed that participants demonstrated significantly more stereotyping in terms of friendliness when labels were consistent versus inconsistent, both when there was no theory and a 'fixed-personality' theory. There was no significant difference in stereotyping across label type in the 'variable-social' theory condition. In addition, when labels were inconsistent, more stereotyping occurred in the 'variable-social' versus the 'fixed-personality' condition.

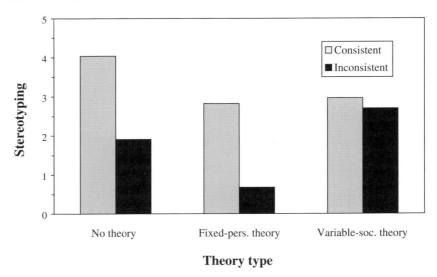

Figure 4.1 Friendliness stereotyping scores across theory-type and label-type.

Where category labels were consistent there were no significant differences across theory-type.

Therefore different results for label-type were found depending on what type of theory was made accessible to participants. Specifically, participants stereotyped more when there was good fit between categories and the dimension friendliness. It appears that the 'fixed-personality' theory allowed good fit between labels and behaviours when labels were consistent, but not when labels were inconsistent. When the 'variable-social' theory was made accessible, there were no effects for label-type. Regardless of whether labels were consistent or inconsistent, participants demonstrated stereotyping in this condition. Compared to the 'fixed-personality' theory condition, those in the 'variable-social' condition demonstrated more stereotyping when labels were inconsistent but the same amount of stereotyping when labels were consistent. Thus, it appears that this type of theory allowed for good fit between behaviours and labels, regardless of whether those labels might initially be thought of as consistent or inconsistent.

These results suggest that stereotyping will occur when there is good fit between stimulus data and a category. However, the 'category' is not conceptualized as a fixed cognitive structure that is cued by a category label. Rather, the category and the 'fit' between category labels and data appear to be generated within a broader framework of knowledge and theories which allow both the category itself and the fit between categories and data to be flexible. The 'consistency' between a personality attribute, such as 'friendliness', and a category label, such as 'tour guide', is not fixed and is dependent on the salient theoretical context. Importantly, these results suggest that the same category label can be interpreted as both 'consistent' and 'inconsistent' with the same set of intergroup differences, depending on the theoretical context. This goes against the idea that there is a 'fixed' relationship between category labels and attributes. Likewise, it challenges the notion that there is a *fixed* category, such as 'tour guide', with *fixed* contents, such as 'friendliness'. In this study, the category 'tour guide' was associated with both friendliness and unfriendliness when it made sense to do so. However, category labels may provide a low level theory that generates expectations about a category. Wisniewski and Medin (1994) argue that meaningful category labels are used to 'activate' theories, that labels activate prior knowledge or expectations about categories that are subsequently used in judgements. We argue that while these labels may generate a set of expectations, this is not to say that there is a *fixed* relationship between the category 'tour guides' and the attribute 'friendliness'. This relationship is interpreted within a broader theoretical context, and depending on what knowledge or 'explanatory system' is most accessible, may be interpreted as either consistent or inconsistent (or irrelevant).

It is important to note that the theories used in this study were not *directly* related to group behaviours or labels, or the relationship between the two. That is, the theory was not simply a matter of telling participants, for example, that these tour guides are unfriendly for whatever reason – the theory served more to give participants an outlook, or an explanatory system within which they could then interpret 'reality'. Importantly though, these theories do not operate independent of reality. While we may be 'primed' to see the world a certain way, we will not do so unless the world *is* that way in some sense. This is where fit comes into the picture: 'Fit ties perception firmly to reality; however perceptually 'ready' we may be to see a given object or event in terms of category accessibility, we do not do so until something with at least requisite characteristics enters the perceptual field' (Oakes, et al., 1994, p. 116).

Theories as ingroup beliefs

Our analysis of stereotype content and of the role of theories in determining that content thus far has focused primarily on the individual cognitive determinants of content. That is, stereotype content is an outcome of the categorization process reflecting an interaction between the data that the perceiver has encountered and the perceiver's background theories and knowledge. However, an important part of many definitions of stereotypes is that they are shared within social groups (Tajfel, 1981b; see McGarty, Yzerbyt & Spears, this volume). Recent research by Haslam and colleagues (Haslam, 1997; Haslam, Oakes, Turner, McGarty, Reynolds & Eggins, 1996; Haslam, Turner, Oakes, McGarty & Reynolds, 1998) has demonstrated how stereotype content is shaped by shared ingroup norms. In a similar vein, we argue that stereotype content is shaped by ingroup theories, knowledge and ideologies.

Haslam (1997; Haslam et al., 1998, following from Turner, 1991) argues that one of the consequences of self-categorization in terms of a social category is that one expects to agree with others one categorizes as similar to one's self. Through a process of 'referent informational influence' our beliefs become shared (Turner, 1991). Similarly, McGarty and Turner (1992) argue that categorizing is a 'social normative' activity that is anchored in our reference groups. Thus the way we categorize others, in terms of both process and content, is influenced by our self-categorizations. Because in categorizing others we always also implicitly categorize ourselves, all our stereotypes of others will be from the perspective of our ingroup, and will be influenced by the norms of our ingroup. Presumably they are also influenced by knowledge, theories and ideologies shared within our ingroup.

In the experiment discussed in the previous section theories were made accessible to participants in an individualized fashion. That is, we were concerned with making theories accessible to each participant personally, and did not consider the extent to which these theories may be shared within (or originate within) an individual's social group. Other research considering the influence of different theories on social judgements has also taken an individual-based approach (e.g., Chiu et al., 1997; Dweck et al., 1993; Levy et al., 1998; Wittenbrink et al., 1997). In the experiment discussed below (Brown & Turner, 2001a) we attempted to link theories to an individual's ingroup.

We also aimed to demonstrate that the *meaning* of a social category could vary with different background theories by showing that the perceived prototypicality of a given person with a given social category and the content of that category would vary with different theories. In this experiment, rather than considering a specific content dimension relevant to differences between groups, we considered content that was related to a specific social category and that should vary with different background theories. Thus we were investigating changes in the *type* of content associated with a category rather than in the *degree* of a specific content dimension associated with a category (as in the previous experiment).

An experiment was designed so as to manipulate the broad theories and background knowledge accessible to participants and then to measure their stereotyping of a category whose meaning should change in line with these theories. Rather than giving participants theories, they were presented with an extreme statement which it was felt they would disagree with, and they were then encouraged to generate their own theories by focusing on why they disagreed with this statement and articulating an alternative position. We attempted to make an ingroup identity salient by getting participants to compare themselves and other ingroup members who (like them) would disagree with the statement with outgroup members who would agree with the statement. Two extreme statements were constructed to act as stimulus statements, both of which outlined a 'theory' about the determinants of success in our society. Statement A argued that success was entirely due to individual factors, whereas Statement B argued that success was entirely due to factors external to the individual.

The category chosen for participants to make judgements about was the long-term unemployed. This category was chosen because of its link with the stimulus statements. That is, the reasons for long-term unemployment are related to the reasons for success or otherwise in our society. Participants, who were introductory psychology students at the Australian National University, were initially randomly presented with one or the other of the extreme statements (Statement A or Statement B) and asked to indicate their level of agreement or disagreement with the statement. As expected, the majority of participants disagreed with the statements. Only those participants initially disagreeing with the statement were invited back to take part in the second part of the study.[3] They were informed that they had been recalled to this stage of the study because they disagreed with the statement and that we were interested to compare their opinions with other students who had agreed with the statement (making self-categorization salient). Participants were then presented with the initial statement again and asked to write a short paragraph indicating why they disagreed with it and to express their own alternative view of the reasons for success in society (to generate theories). A high degree of consistency was found in the types of theories generated within each condition. Participants then listened to one of two audio-taped interviews with the stimulus person, who was either consistent (typical) or inconsistent (atypical) with the category long-term unemployed.[4] Participants then completed a number of measures including ratings of the perceived prototypicality of the target person with the category and a Katz-Braly type checklist of traits they felt applied to the

Table 4.1. *Percentage of participants choosing adjectives characterizing long-term unemployed across interview type and statement type*

Interview:	Consistent		Inconsistent	
Statement:	A	B	A	B
N:	13	12	14	11
unlucky	38	50	93	91
unmotivated	62	92	43	55
underprivileged	62	25	71	45
dependent	54	50	43	45
whingeing	23	32	14	–
ignorant	31	25	7	9

Notes: Only traits marked by at least 30% of participants in at least one condition included, – = < 30%
Statement A produced collectivistic theories, Statement B produced individualistic theories.

category long-term unemployed. It was predicted that both judgements of prototypicality and stereotype content should differ across theory type.

Results showed some differences in judgements of prototypicality. Specifically, the 'consistent' target person was judged as more prototypical of the category long-term unemployed when participants were exposed to Statement B (which generated more individualistic theories) versus Statement A (more collectivist theories). Thus, the *same* stimulus person (who had previously been judged to be highly prototypical of the category long-term unemployed) was judged to be *differentially* prototypical of the *same* social category, depending on the type of background theory which was made accessible. Previous research (e.g., Haslam et al., 1995) has shown that judgements of prototypicality are context-dependent. The current research suggests that they are also theory-dependent.

In terms of stereotype content, again differences were apparent across theory type (see Table 4.1). For example, those participants exposed to Statement B were more likely to characterize the unemployed as 'unmotivated', whereas those exposed to Statement A were more likely to characterize them as 'underprivileged'. A more systematic analysis of the traits chosen was carried out based upon the method employed by Haslam et al. (1992). It was expected that participants would stereotype the long-term unemployed in terms of content consistent with their theories. Independent raters chose traits from the checklist that they believed were consistent with a person unemployed for reasons to do with them personally (internal traits, e.g., unmotivated, dependent) and traits consistent with a person unemployed for reasons beyond their control (external traits, e.g., unlucky, underprivileged). For each participant, a score was calculated in terms of the internal and external traits they had chosen to characterize the unemployed. For internal content, differences were apparent across theory-type, with participants given Statement B choosing more internal traits (consistent with their theory) compared to those given Statement A. For external content, differences were more apparent across interview type, with more external traits chosen by those exposed to the inconsistent versus consistent interview. Importantly, the meaning of the category 'long-term unemployed' did not stay constant but varied across both interview and theory type. Participants tended to characterize the long-term unemployed in terms of content that was consistent with their theory. It appears that theories can influence not just the *degree* to which a specific content is applied to a category (as per previous experiment) but also the *type* of content applied to a category. Participants in the current study also tended to characterize the long-term unemployed in terms of content consistent with the stimulus person they had been exposed to. This finding is interesting in light of research on stereotype change, which suggests that stereotypes tend to be quite resistant to change especially in the face of a single disconfirming exemplar (e.g., Johnston & Hewstone, 1992; Johnston et al., 1994). The results of the current study suggest that stereotype content is not fixed or rigid but is sensitive to both theories and reality (as represented by the stimulus information).

Conclusions

In this chapter we have argued that stereotype content forms to reflect an interaction between theory and data, and that fit plays a crucial role in providing the link between these two factors. We propose that fit does not represent a fixed 'match' between stimuli and some stored representation of a category. Instead, we have argued that fit is not fixed and that the fit between category and content is interpreted within a broader context of relevant background theories and knowledge.

The research reviewed in this chapter suggests that the interpretation of fit is both context- and theory-dependent. This implies that stereotype content is also context- and theory-dependent. We believe that stereotype content is not fixed and does not exist in any ongoing fashion, but reflects the application of background knowledge and theories to the representation and interpretation of stimulus reality within a specific context or frame of reference (for a discussion of related points, leading to a somewhat different conclusion, see McGarty, 1999, and McGarty this volume).

We conceptualize theories as higher-order knowledge structures that are much broader than categories or schemas. We believe that theoretical knowledge may be quite complex and multi-faceted, and that the knowledge brought to bear upon any given judgement may represent only a sub-set of our total knowledge store. This implies that the theories used on any given occasion may be quite variable. The parts of theoretical knowledge, which are applied to a judgement, will depend upon which parts of that knowledge are made accessible and are relevant. We believe that the theories people employ are often tied to group memberships and that theories, unlike schemas, tend to be collectively produced and shared within groups. The way in which theories are generated collectively remains an under-explored topic, ripe for further research (see Turner & Reynolds, in press).

The analysis of stereotype content presented in this chapter suggests that content can reflect a perceiver's broad ideologies and ways of understanding the world. This is consistent with the overall theme of this volume; that stereotypes are meaningful beliefs about groups and can be considered explanations. Stereotype content reflects the way we *explain* and '*make sense of*' the stimuli we encounter. Given that there is generally more than one way to explain any stimulus situation, likewise there is generally more than one set of content that can meaningfully represent a group. The content produced on any given occasion will be the content that best allows us to explain and make sense of the differences we perceive between groups in light of relevant theories and knowledge.

Stereotype content has tended to be either ignored in the stereotyping literature or treated as something that can be measured and hopefully changed. However, given the flexibility of content, attempts to define and measure the fixed or specific content associated with any given social group may ultimately prove to be a fruitless exercise. This does not mean, however, that we should abandon attempts to study and attempt to change content. Our analysis of content implies that it is meaningfully produced and reflects an interaction between stimulus reality, motives, and background theories and knowledge. The production of content is inseparable from the categorization process itself, which can be seen as the application, or working out, of higher-order content in interaction with stimulus data. The categorization process allows us to make sense of the world and is not content free. Understanding the *process* which produces content should in turn allow us to predict the content produced on any given occasion. Likewise to change the content of stereotypes we also need to look to the process, the context and theories which have produced that content.

Acknowledgement

The authors would like to thank Craig McGarty, Vincent Yzerbyt and Russell Spears for their helpful comments on a previous draft of this chapter.

NOTES

1. The majority of participants in the study indicated that they agreed with the theory they were presented with.
2. A pre-test indicated that in general tour guides were perceived to be relatively more friendly than chess players.
3. A potential weakness in this study concerns the self-selection of participants; that is, only those who disagreed with the initial statement were eligible to participate further in the study. However, it should be noted that statements were randomly allocated to the initial sample and that the majority of the initial sample disagreed with both statements (in addition, the mean level of disagreement was significantly different from the neutral position for both statements). Nevertheless, this potential problem with participant allocation should be addressed in future studies.
4. A pre-test indicated that one stimulus person was significantly more typical of the category 'long-term unemployed' than the other stimulus person.

5 Illusory correlation and stereotype formation: making sense of group differences and cognitive biases

Mariëtte Berndsen, Russell Spears, Joop van der Pligt and Craig McGarty

Women are more romantic than men. Scientists are duller than artists. We often make such judgements about groups. Some of these judgements are based on folklore, others are based on observation or experience. When we do rely on observed data how good are we at detecting relationships between group membership and behaviour? Do we find it easy to detect differences between groups? Are our judgements biased? This chapter deals with these issues and focuses on the paradigm that has dominated research on the *formation* of stereotypic differences between groups over the last three decades: *the illusory correlation paradigm*. In this paradigm respondents are exposed to a series of behavioural instances each linked to an individual belonging to a specific group. The term *illusory correlation* refers to perceived associations between attributes and instances other than those contained in the data. In the present case it generally refers to the perception of a stereotypic association of certain features with a given group, typically when the available data is presumed to give little evidence for this (hence 'illusory').

Detecting relationships between events in the environment, between group membership and behaviour, is an essential ingredient of adaptive behaviour. The information derived from these relationships or covariations allow us to make sense of the world by explaining the past, controlling the present and predicting the future (Alloy & Tabachnik, 1984; Crocker, 1981). In these terms, detecting contingency is clearly important for our well-being and even our survival. Although it is well-known that people are able to detect relations between stimuli, they are certainly not perfect in this regard (e.g., Jennings, Amabile & Ross, 1990). For example, it is known that people find it difficult to detect non-contingency (Peterson, 1980) and see relationships where these do not exist. Part of our argument below is that they also see them where *researchers* think that they do not exist, but we are jumping ahead of ourselves. The central theme in this chapter concerns the perception of socially relevant stimuli, as in the examples above. In this chapter we describe a research program focusing on the processes and conditions that influence the perceived covariation of social stimuli.

Research on illusory correlation

As described above, the term *illusory correlation* refers to the perception of covariation between two classes of stimuli that are uncorrelated, or less strongly correlated than perceived. Chapman (1967) originally introduced the term to describe the over-association of semantically related word-pairs or word-pairs of unusual length. Hamilton and Gifford (1976) applied the concept of illusory correlation to the perception of social groups. In their first study, they presented participants with desirable and undesirable behavioural instances from two groups, called Group A and Group B. Group A represented the majority and Group B the minority. These two groups exhibited the same ratio of desirable to undesirable behaviours according to the distribution depicted in Table 5.1.

In other words, there was no correlation between type of behaviour and group membership. Examples of desirable items are: 'a member of Group A offers to work overtime when work piles up', and 'a member of Group B sees the funny side of little things that happen'. Examples of undesirable items are: 'a member of Group A finds co-workers ignorant and unintelligent', and 'a member of Group B comments loudly on people's clothes at a party'.

Hamilton and Gifford demonstrated that the co-occurrence of the infrequent (undesirable) behaviours and the infrequent group (B) was overestimated. An example of a typical response pattern is given in parentheses in Table 5.1. This pattern reflects the characteristic illusory correlation effect, namely the attribution of a relatively high proportion of (infrequent) negative behaviours to Group B as compared to Group A, resulting in a relatively negative impression of this group. Hamilton and Gifford argued that this 'paired-distinctiveness' pattern occurs because the combination of statistically infrequent categories is particularly salient to the perceiver. These categories thus receive more attention, are more efficiently encoded, and, consequently, are more accessible in memory than nondistinctive categories (Tversky & Kahneman, 1973).

A number of studies have identified factors that can weaken or eliminate the distinctiveness-based illusory correlation effect such as the self-relevance of stimulus-attitudes (Spears, van der Pligt & Eiser, 1985) and ingroup bias (Schaller & Maass, 1989). Other research revealed that illusory correlation effects can occur without the statistical infrequency of a particular category (Berndsen, McGarty, van der Pligt & Spears,

Table 5.1. *Distribution of the stimuli in the standard illusory correlation task*

	Desirable behaviours	Undesirable behaviours
Group A	18 (19)	8 (7)
Group B	9 (8)	4 (5)

2001; McGarty, Haslam, Turner & Oakes, 1993; Spears, van der Pligt & Eiser, 1986). However, research findings indicate that the paired distinctiveness effect is a reliable phenomenon (see e.g., McConnell, Sherman & Hamilton, 1994a; Mullen & Johnson, 1990).

The paired-distinctiveness illusory correlation just described is based on *data* and has been used to explain the *formation* of stereotypes about minorities and/or infrequently encountered groups (Hamilton & Gifford, 1976). Illusory correlation that is based on *expectations or theories*, on the other hand may offer an explanation for the *maintenance* of stereotypes (although this effect is less relevant to the focus on stereotype formation in current volume). Stereotypes can be defined as shared beliefs about behaviours and/or personality traits displayed by a group of people (for general reviews see e.g., Leyens, Yzerbyt & Schadron, 1994; Messick & Mackie, 1989; Oakes, Haslam & Turner, 1994). Within social psychology the dominant explanation for the origin and maintenance of stereotypic beliefs is that they result from information processing biases. This view is often based on the assumption that the information in our social environment is too complex for our processing capabilities, and stereotypes allow us to simplify this information (see e.g., Fiske & Taylor, 1984, 1991; Hamilton, 1981a). According to this view, stereotypes are erroneous generalizations based on distorted impressions of individuals in terms of group characteristics. Other researchers have taken the view that stereotypes are not necessarily erroneous but from the stereotyper's perspective may represent valid interpretations of the social properties of group members (Leyens, Yzerbyt & Schadron, 1994; McGarty & de la Haye, 1997; Oakes et al., 1994; Spears & Haslam, 1997). If this is true, illusory correlations might not be completely 'illusory.' Indeed researchers in this tradition have argued that illusory correlations (and stereotypes generally) may represent inferences based on behaviour-reflecting attempts to make sense of the situation (McGarty & de la Haye, 1997; McGarty, this volume). In this chapter we develop the idea that illusory correlations are not merely distortions but also the product of imposing sense on the world (and in the experimental context). Before we do this, we briefly review the prevailing explanations of the illusory correlation effect.

Illusory correlation: a product of data-based distortion or of sense-making processes?

In this section we present several models that explain the occurrence of illusory correlation. We begin by describing those models in which illusory correlation is considered to be a distortion produced by information processing biases. Next, we present the categorization approach, which advocates the view that illusory correlation results from a sense-making process.

Illusory correlation as data-based distortions

Enhanced memory The original explanation of the distinctiveness-based illusory correlation effect formulated by Hamilton and Gifford (1976) involves a bias towards distinctive stimuli because these stimuli attract the observer's attention. More recently, McConnell, Sherman and Hamilton (1994a) extended this explanation by proposing that illusory correlation does not depend on distinctiveness at the time of encoding but on distinctiveness at the time of judgement. Information can become distinctive when old information is reconsidered in the light of new information. Thus information that was not distinctive at the time of encoding (for example because the relative frequency of classes of information is not yet established) can still become distinctive at a later moment, affecting subsequent judgements. Both the original and extended explanation refer to enhanced memory for distinctive stimuli.

Information loss and memory processes In contrast to the distinctiveness explanation Fiedler (1991; see also Fiedler, Russer & Gramm, 1993) considers the illusory correlation phenomenon to be a consequence of 'information loss.' Fiedler has argued that the illusory correlation pattern can be explained by the tendency for each group to be seen more positively than negatively, being diluted by random processes of information loss that disproportionately affects the smaller/less frequent group (B). Because participants perceive more statements about Group A, the perceived positivity of this group is less susceptible to the effects of information loss. However, the positivity of Group B is relatively more difficult to detect given the smaller sample of instances. Another way of stating this is that regression effects (e.g., to a baseline assumption that the group is neither positive nor negative) are stronger in small samples (Group B) than in large samples (Group A). This differential information loss could account for the typical illusory correlation pattern. Fiedler et al. (1993) used signal-detection analysis to show a lower sensitivity (i.e., impaired memory) for infrequent behaviours than for frequent behaviours.

This explanation is closely related to that of Smith (1991). He demonstrated by means of computer simulations that the repeated observations of positive and negative behaviours in two groups of different frequency should result in different memory traces that can explain the illusory correlation effect. Specifically, memory traces associated with the positivity of the majority Group A are more established (being more numerous in absolute terms) and thus more easily activated by a prompt than those of the minority Group B (see also Rothbart, 1981). Thus, differential accessibility, like differential loss of the information in memory, can account for the illusory correlation effect.

Despite these different explanations for the illusory correlation effect, the approaches of Hamilton, McConnell, Fiedler and Smith all have in common the fact that they consider the illusory correlation effect to be a consequence of stimulus- or data-based distortions. Although these accounts differ about whether infrequent information is processed better or worse than other classes of information, they all support the view that illusory correlation is based on skewed distributions and reflects the differential processing of infrequent information. In sum, infrequent stimuli are assumed to lead to biased memory processes involving either selective attention (Hamilton, McConnell) and selective access to information (Smith), or selective loss (Fiedler) of information in memory. We present an alternative theoretical view next. Meanwhile it is worth noting that doubts about the viability of these memory-based accounts have emerged in recent evidence using a source monitoring analysis to separate component processes. This shows that the effects reflect processes involved in 'response bias' rather than memory processes (Klauer & Meiser, 2000; Klauer, Ehrenberg & Cataldegirmen, 2001; see also Spears, this volume). This finding is in line with our preferred approach in which the data-based distortions and memory processes are not necessary to explain the formation of 'illusory correlations.' We now outline this approach.

Illusory correlation as a sense-making process

Research by McGarty et al. (1993) has shown that the perception of infrequent stimuli is not necessary to obtain illusory correlations. They argued that illusory correlation could result from attempts to differentiate meaningfully between groups. Their explanation is grounded in self-categorization theory (Turner, Hogg, Oakes, Reicher & Wetherell, 1987; see also McGarty, 1999, this volume) which in turn is rooted in Tajfel's work on social categorization and accentuation processes (e.g., Tajfel, 1969, 1981b). According to these accounts, categories are formed on the basis of the perception of similarities among, and differences between stimuli, and the categorization process therefore reflects an attempt to determine the basis of similarities/differences and to focus attention on them. Consequently, categorization results in the tendency to enhance the differences between distinct categories on a certain dimension and to minimize the differences within each of the categories. In order to accentuate differences between Group A and B, it is therefore clearly necessary to perceive differences between them.

With this in mind McGarty et al. stressed the importance of certain characteristics of the original task of Hamilton and Gifford (1976, Study 1). The most important characteristic in their view is that there is actually more evidence (in absolute terms) for the hypothesis that Group A is 'good' and Group B is 'bad' (18 + 4 stimuli) than for the opposite hypothesis (9 + 8 stimuli). These differences serve as a basis for further accentuation of group differences. Because of these potentially valid interpretations of the available stimuli, McGarty et al. argue that illusory correlation reflects a sense-making process based on real differences in the task which create expectations of intergroup differences. This approach has been variously referred to as the categorization approach (Berndsen et al., 1998), the evaluative differentiation approach (Klauer & Meiser, 2000) and the differentiated meaning approach (Haslam, McGarty & Brown, 1996; McGarty & de la Haye, 1997). In this book we use the last of these terminologies (see also McGarty, this volume; Spears, this volume; Yzerbyt & Rocher, this volume).

Currently it seems unlikely that any one of the models reviewed above can exclusively explain all aspects of this illusory correlation paradigm, and it seems more likely that they all contribute to the explanation of at least some aspects of this effect. In this chapter, we develop the differentiated meaning approach further, and outline a programme of research designed to evaluate and extend this approach. We show how the illusory correlation phenomenon is both produced and influenced by features of the task that impinge on this category differentiation process. Specifically, we first analyse the effects of the task instruction and the nature of the stimuli on the perception of illusory correlation. Thereafter, we focus on the process underlying the formation of illusory correlation, and show *how* illusory correlations are formed.

Task features inducing the perception of illusory correlation

In this section we discuss two features of the illusory correlation task that, in our view, are likely to elicit group differentiation. The first feature involves participants' interpretation of the task instructions. The second feature concerns the form and content of the stimuli. We examine how these features affect the process of categorical differentiation, resulting in the perception of illusory correlations.

The standard instructions

The instructions used by Hamilton and Gifford (1976) informed participants that they would be shown descriptions of behaviour performed by members of two groups, labelled A and B, and that in the real-world Group B is smaller than Group A. This standard instruction includes two related aspects that encourage categorical differentiation: the term *'group'* and the *labels A and B*. In our view both aspects affect the perception of illusory correlation by influencing the tendency to categorically differentiate between the groups. This is because the term 'group' can induce expectations of similarities within a group, whereas the labels A and B can induce expectations of differences between the groups.

Following ideas developed by Grice (1975), researchers have argued that experiments create a conversational context whereby the experimenter communicates information, sometimes unwittingly, to the participants (Bless, Strack & Schwarz, 1993; Gigerenzer, 1991; Grice, 1975; Hilton, 1995; Yzerbyt, Schadron, Leyens & Rocher, 1994). Participants expect experimenters to follow the conversational rules of being informative, relevant, truthful and unambiguous (Grice, 1975). Although experimenters try to make the information presented in the task informative and meaningful, they often do not provide all information (to do so might reveal the deception necessary to many experiments or introduce demand characteristics). For example, participants are not informed about the purpose of the illusory correlation task. However, if the purpose or meaning of a task is not clear to participants, they need to go 'beyond the information given' in order to make sense of the task.

Yzerbyt, Leyens and Rocher (1997) and Abele and Petzold (1998) also demonstrated that participants try to use all information presented by making sense of both explicit information and subtle cues ('meta-information') in the task. Applying the conversational rules to the illusory correlation task it is possible to argue that this task creates certain expectations, and notably the expectation that there are genuine differences between the two groups. Based on this, and drawing on the concept of *differentiated meaning* (McGarty & Turner, 1992), McGarty et al. (1993) argued that participants in the illusory correlation paradigm try to make sense of the stimulus situation by attempting to allocate the stimuli to meaningful (i.e., clear and separable) categories. In their view the task in the illusory correlation paradigm evokes expectations such as finding out how Group A and B differ from each other. Participants might even reason to themselves 'presumably there must be differences between the two groups, otherwise why should they have been given different names'. We now turn to research investigating this issue.

Labels A and B: expecting intergroup differences

The previous line of reasoning suggests that undermining the expectation to find meaningful differences between the groups should eliminate the illusory correlation effect. This prediction was supported by Haslam, McGarty and Brown (1996) and Berndsen, Spears, van der Pligt and McGarty (1999). Haslam et al. (1996) showed that the illusory correlation effect disappears when the stimulus groups are labelled as right- and left-handed persons rather than as Group A and B, suggesting that it is less meaningful to categorize right- and left-handed people in evaluatively different groups, or at least to distinguish these in terms of good or bad people (at least not since the middle ages).

However, it is possible that the study of Haslam et al. (1996) did not deal with 'raw' stereotype *formation* as is the case in the standard illusory correlation task, because of the general shared knowledge that there are no evaluative differences between left- and right-handed people. Thus the attenuated illusory correlation effects might be due to the knowledge or pre-existing stereotype about well-known groups (even perhaps an expectation-based illusory correlation based on the knowledge of no difference). Therefore, we (Berndsen et al., 1999, see also Yzerbyt & Rocher, this volume, who describe related research by Yzerbyt, Rocher, McGarty & Haslam, 1999) used other stimulus groups, namely students from previous study years (1993, 1994) as the basis for the group categorization. We argued that participants *expect* that these student groups will probably not differ from each other rather than already knowing this. Therefore these stimulus groups may provide a better test of the process of stereotype formation than was the case for Haslam et al. (1996).

As predicted, respondents indicated that they expected fewer differences between student groups than between stimulus groups A and B. Moreover, the illusory correlation effect was obtained for the Group A vs. B condition but disappeared in the condition with student groups.

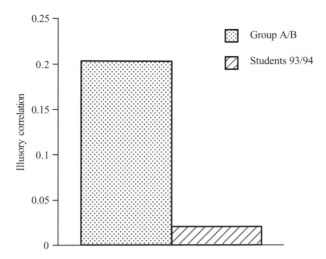

Figure 5.1 Illusory correlation as a function of expectation.
Note: Adapted from Berndsen et al. (1999), p. 208.

These effects are displayed in Figure 5.1. Thus, the labels A and B seem to induce expectations about intergroup differences. Ironically, the labels A and B were originally used to eliminate expectations associated with real groups that might otherwise explain illusory correlations (see e.g., Hamilton & Rose, 1980). However, our research shows that labelling the groups A and B does nothing to undermine the suspicion that the groups should differ from each other, and can actually reinforce this. We now consider the impact of the term 'group' on the perception of illusory correlation.

Groups: expecting intragroup similarities

It seems reasonable to assume that expectations involving differences between the groups also include the expectation that members belonging to a particular group are expected to display similar behaviours, because the term 'group' suggests that individuals who belong to it share behaviours, outlooks, or attitudes, at least to some degree. Following the categorization approach, strengthening the expectation of group coherence should therefore enhance the perception of illusory correlation compared to the case where less coherent groups are expected. This prediction is in contrast with that of Hamilton and Sherman (1996) who argued that perceiving a coherent group evokes on-line processing, which is assumed to eliminate illusory correlations derived from paired distinctiveness. We manipulated the degree of coherence by informing participants either that group members shared the opinions and attitudes belonging to their group, or that group members strongly differed in their opinions and attitudes. The results supported our prediction showing that when participants expected group coherence illusory correlation was higher (Berndsen, Spears, McGarty & van der Pligt, 1998).

We have also attempted to undermine expectations of intragroup similarities by manipulating the standard instructions in another way. Participants were either provided with the standard instructions or were provided with an instruction in which their attention would be drawn to differences in behaviour *within* each group. The idea was that they should thereby be less likely to perceive the groups as homogeneous, attenuating the illusory correlation effect. As expected, focusing on within-group differences eliminated the illusory correlation effect, whereas the effect was obtained with the standard instructions (Berndsen et al., 1999; see also Yzerbyt & Rocher, this volume). Thus the instructions used in the standard task seem to encourage a focus on intergroup differences, and group differentiation, although participants are not explicitly asked to do this.

To summarize, we argue that illusory correlation depends on expectations involving intragroup coherence and intergroup differences. When such expectations are undermined the illusory correlation effect does not emerge. This then suggests that general expectations involving similarities within and differences between groups play an important role in data-based as well as expectation-based illusory correlations. Perceived group coherence can also be influenced by the nature of the stimuli presented to participants. Next, we examine how stimulus features affect the process of categorical differentiation.

The nature of the stimuli

We now discuss two aspects of the stimulus information that can facilitate categorization and thus illusory correlation. Firstly, we discuss whether the content of the stimuli contributes to categorical differentiation. Secondly, we discuss the possibility that the nature of the skewed frequency distributions of the stimuli presented in the illusory correlation task can enhance the tendency to categorically differentiate between the groups.

Stimulus content Earlier we saw that individuals belonging to the same group are expected to display coherent behaviour, which is in line with the differentiated meaning approach. Following this approach, perceived group coherence is considered an important ingredient in illusory correlation. We (Berndsen et al., 1998) tested the effect of group coherence in terms of the stimulus data by manipulating the content of the

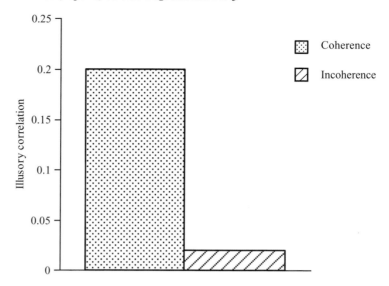

Figure 5.2 Illusory correlation as a function of data-based coherence. *Note:* Adapted from Berndsen et al. (1998), p. 1455.

stimuli. In one condition the stimuli referred to extreme behavioural acts (based on pretesting), that is, behaviours that were either extremely positive or negative. In the other condition the behaviours were moderately positive and negative. The idea was that evaluatively extreme behaviours should undermine the ability to perceive the groups as homogeneous or coherent. This should then attenuate the illusory correlation effect, compared to the condition in which participants were presented with sets of evaluatively moderate behaviours. The results are displayed in Figure 5.2.

These results supported the differentiated meaning prediction that the emergence of illusory correlation depends on group coherence. Specifically the effect should be higher where there is high behavioural similarity within the groups. This pattern is, however, inconsistent with the paired distinctiveness explanation (Hamilton & Gifford, 1976) and also the modified version of this by McConnell et al. (1994a). According to this view the extreme behaviour conditions should if anything render the most distinctive cell even more distinctive and accessible to memory according to the availability heuristic. Thus, the occurrence of the illusory correlation effect seems to be constrained by a certain level of similarity or coherence within the sets of behaviours describing a group. If within-group differences are so extreme that they imply that within-group differences are greater than between-group differences, meaningful categorization is undermined, explaining the elimination of the illusory correlation effect.

Another important aspect of stimulus content involves the behavioural domain. Does illusory correlation occur with domains other than social (un)desirable behaviours? Berndsen, Van der Pligt and Spears (1994) found that the effect did not always emerge for behaviours that varied in terms of risk. Risk behaviours can be distinguished on an evaluative dimension (positive versus negative) and on a descriptive dimension (riskiness). For example, evaluatively opposite but descriptively similar risk-related terms are 'careful' vs. 'overcautious'. Both refer to risk-avoiding behaviour, but careful behaviour is evaluated more positively than overcautious behaviour. Descriptively opposite but evaluatively consistent terms are 'careful' and 'adventurous'. Both terms have a positive connotation, but 'careful' refers to risk-avoiding behaviours while 'adventurous' refers to risk-seeking behaviours. Results of this study revealed illusory correlations when the behaviours were evaluatively different, but not when they were descriptively different.

One interpretation of these results is that illusory correlation is more likely to occur for behaviours that vary on an evaluative dimension. McGarty et al.'s (1993) results showed the importance of the evaluative dimension in distinguishing between the groups and research by Klauer and colleagues also points to the importance of evaluative differentiation in producing the illusory correlation effect (Klauer & Meiser, 2000; Klauer et al., 2001; see also Spears, this volume). Although the evaluative dimension seems to be extremely important for the generation of illusory correlation, the research just described also points to clear restrictions: if the evaluations within the groups are extremely positive and negative, group coherence is undermined.

Another plausible interpretation for the attenuated illusory correlations when the behaviours are descriptively different can also be sought in the concept of coherence. It is possible that for some groups and some dimensions, descriptive inconsistency is more likely to undermine coherent group impressions than evaluative inconsistency. That is, it seems harder to reconcile descriptively opposite behaviours within a group – for example reckless and overcautious gamblers, or careful and adventurous nurses – than evaluatively inconsistent behaviours (e.g., reckless and adventurous gamblers or overcautious and careful nurses). If so, this could also explain the reduced illusory correlation effect for groups comprising descriptively opposite tendencies. Ironically, then, although the evaluative dimension may be very powerful, it may be more open to variation than the descriptive dimension (even serial killers may be nice some of the time).

Skewed frequency distributions We now discuss the impact of the skewness of stimulus distributions on illusory correlation. According to our approach, illusory correlation arises primarily as a product of meaningful categorical differentiation rather than of paired-distinctive stimuli. McGarty et al. (1993) demonstrated that the perception of paired-distinctive stimuli is not necessary to obtain illusory correlations. They constrained the stimulus series without introducing distinctiveness and still found illusory correlation effects. We tested the effects of another way of constraining the stimulus situation on the occurrence of illusory correlation (Berndsen et al., 2001). Specifically, participants were presented with either stimuli describing only one stimulus group (Group A) performing positive (24) and negative (12) behaviours, or with stimuli describing only positive behaviours performed by the two groups (24 Group A and 12 Group B). We predicted and found illusory correlations in both constrained conditions. Thus perceiving statements that are skewed on one dimension (group or behaviour), or providing general information about two groups and a comparative dimension of evaluation (as in the work of McGarty et al., 1993), seem sufficient for the occurrence of illusory correlation without any paired distinctiveness.

This raises the question whether paired distinctiveness is confounded with factors that are likely to facilitate the illusory correlation effect. We (Berndsen et al., 1998) found that not all levels of paired distinctiveness lead to the perception of illusory correlation. Put differently, particular levels of skewness in the distribution enhance the perception of group coherence and hence the perception of illusory correlation. In Study 1 (described above) we demonstrated that perceptions of non-coherent behaviours eliminated the illusory correlation effect as opposed to perceiving moderately coherent sets of behaviours. But what would happen if the groups were perceived as extremely coherent? Following the differentiated meaning explanation, accentuating differences between very coherent groups might be too difficult (if the groups are very similar to each other) or not meaningful (if the groups are very different from each other). Following this reasoning, judgements of extremely coherent groups should reduce the perception of illusory correlation. This implies that the relation between coherence and illusory correlation is curvilinear: illusory correlations would occur when groups are perceived as moderately coherent, but not when they are seen as non-coherent or strongly coherent. We (Berndsen et al., 1998) tested this prediction by varying the within-group behaviour distributions while holding the differential group sizes constant as shown in Table 5.2.

Results supported the prediction that illusory correlations were eliminated for very coherent as well as for non-coherent groups but were

Table 5.2. *Distribution of the presented positive and negative stimuli (Berndsen et al., 1998)*

	Noncoherence		Moderate coherence		Strong coherence	
	positive	negative	positive	negative	positive	negative
Group A	14	12	18	8	22	4
Group B	7	6	9	4	11	2

reliable (and reliably higher) for moderate levels of coherence. The latter condition is similar to the standard distribution of Hamilton and Gifford (1976, Study 1). Thus, level of coherence in the stimulus distribution is related to the illusory correlation effect. Moreover, there was no support for the paired-distinctiveness prediction that illusory correlation should be higher in the strong coherence condition compared to the other conditions, due to the greater distinctiveness of the cell with the negative behaviours performed by Group B. In sum, it seems that it is not distinctiveness per se, but data-based coherence (created by the stimulus content and/or by the stimulus distribution) that facilitates the perception of illusory correlation. This is once again difficult to explain in terms of either the paired distinctiveness explanation (Hamilton & Gifford, 1976) or the modified version of this account (McConnell et al., 1994a). In the next section we discuss how data-based coherence could be reinforced and whether particular task features contribute to this process.

Hypothesis testing and differentiated meaning

Thus far we have considered the effects of inputs (data and expectations) that serve as a basis for the perception of intergroup differences and intragroup similarities that feed differentiated meaning. We now consider how this is further accentuated through judgements of the behaviours attributed to the stimulus groups. We argue that the stimuli are not perceived as fixed data, but are continuously reinterpreted in order to facilitate categorical differentiation (much in the way that McConnell et al., 1994a, argue that stimuli are continuously reinterpreted to assess their distinctiveness). Firstly, we discuss how particular features of the illusory correlation task contribute to these reinterpretative processes. Secondly, we provide detailed analyses of the whole process of categorical differentiation including hypothesis testing and reinterpretations, which can result in the illusory correlation effect.

Accentuation and task features

We examined whether features of the illusory correlation task mentioned above facilitated reinterpretive processes. Asch (1952) has noted that perceived meaning is not fixed but interpreted in context. Previous research (Berndsen, van der Pligt, Spears & McGarty, 1996; Berndsen et al., 2001, Study 1) showed that reinterpretive processes play an important role in the perception of illusory correlation. We used a rating task in which participants were presented with behavioural items ascribed to Group A and B, and were asked to rate these items on a desirability scale. Results show that participants accentuated the evaluations of the behaviours enabling them to distinguish between the groups. For example, supposedly positive behaviours of Group B were interpreted as less positive and negative behaviours of Group A as less negative, after perceiving the stimulus set. We argue that these reinterpretations allow participants to differentiate meaningfully between the stimulus groups such that Group B was associated with negative behaviours and Group A with positive behaviours. In other words, evaluative reinterpretations can help to reinforce perceived intragroup similarity, thereby contributing to the perception of illusory correlation. This result challenges the conventional assumption that illusory correlation is based on the detection or storage of stable stimulus information. On the contrary, perceptions of the differences between groups vary dynamically with the process of categorical differentiation. Next, we discuss whether particular features of the illusory correlation task can elicit reinterpretive processes.

Standard instructions and stimulus content

We (Berndsen et al., 1998) investigated whether the standard instruction of the illusory correlation task can lead to a tendency to reinterpret behaviours by manipulating the scope for reinterpretation. In one condition the scope for reinterpretation was constrained by providing the information that two thirds of the behaviours were positive and one third negative, reflecting the real distribution of the presented stimuli. In the other condition the scope for reinterpretation was not so constrained by omitting this information (as is the case in the standard procedure). Our prediction that the constrained scope would result in less reinterpretation than the standard condition (where there was scope for reinterpretations) was supported. Moreover, the constrained-scope condition resulted in significantly weaker illusory correlations, implying that the standard instruction facilitated illusory correlation by providing the opportunity to reinterpret the behaviours (see Figure 5.3).

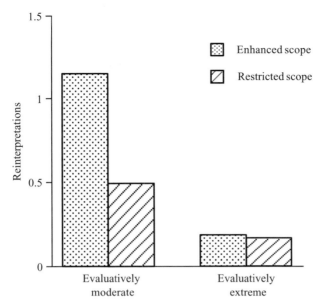

Figure 5.3 Reinterpretations as a function of scope for reinterpretation and evaluative behavioural dimension.
Note: Adapted from Berndsen et al. (1998), p. 1455.

Another feature of the illusory correlation task that affects the degree of reinterpretation is the *content* of the stimuli. We (Berndsen et al., 1998) presented participants with behavioural sets containing either extremely positive and negative behaviours, or moderately positive and negative behaviours for both stimulus groups. The evaluatively moderate behaviours were similar to those used in the standard illusory correlation task. We predicted more reinterpretations for moderately positive and negative behaviours than for extreme behaviours because the extremity of behaviours in itself is expected to limit the range for reinterpretation. Figure 5.3 shows that this prediction was supported, indicating that the standard stimuli allow reinterpretations of behaviours. In sum, both the instruction and the content of the stimuli used in the standard task open the way to reinterpretative processes, offering an additional explanation for the illusory correlation effect.

In previous work (Berndsen & colleagues, 1996, 1998) we demonstrated that these reinterpretations occur in the early stages of perceiving the stimuli. This suggests that respondents seem to develop the idea, or hypothesis, that Group A is more positive than Group B, and are likely to reinterpret the behaviours in line with this developing hypothesis as was revealed by the clear illusory correlation effects in the second half of the rating task. In another study (Berndsen et al., 2001, Study 2), we used a think-aloud task, in order to assess the whole process of meaningful categorical differentiation; we now turn to this research.

A dynamic process

By using the think-aloud technique, we obtained process-tracing data involving the formation of illusory correlation in the standard task (Berndsen et al., 2001, Study 2). We used the standard task because we have shown that it includes a number of factors that affect (and facilitate) the degree of illusory correlation. To recap, these factors are: expectations of intragroup similarities and intergroup differences, the perception of data-based coherence, and reinterpretive processes. Results supported the categorization approach by showing that most participants started to make sense of the task situation by expressing a general search involving either the meaning of the task (e.g., 'What am I supposed to do? I think I've got to remember which behaviour belongs to which group . . . '), or the general relation between groups and behaviours (e.g., 'I'm sure that there is a sort of system in this . . . '). This implies that the formation of illusory correlation started during the perception of statements, and not only when completing the various response measures. After a while most respondents had the impression that Group A was better than Group B, which was subsequently tested against the remaining statements. This reveals that the formation of illusory correlation resembles *hypothesis testing* behaviour, in which a particular hypothesis is tested against data that can confirm or disconfirm the hypothesis. This process is clearly in line with the original arguments developed by McGarty et al. (1993).

Berndsen et al.'s study revealed that illusory correlation depends on a search for differentiation and in particular on the *strategy used to test* the differences between the groups. Participants who reported no illusory correlations, started with the same hypothesis (i.e., the positivity of Group A over Group B) as participants who displayed illusory correlations. The only difference between them was the test strategy; the former group of participants focused on disconfirmations, resulting in attenuated illusory correlations, whereas the latter group searched for confirmations. Thus the absence of illusory correlation seems here not to result from 'accurate' perception, as is generally assumed, but from a different test strategy.

It was also interesting to see that being attentive to disconfirming evidence did more than simply reduce the perception of illusory correlation. We found that many respondents reinterpreted the disconfirming behaviours (the negative Group A or the positive Group B behaviours) in line with their original impression or hypothesis. This behaviour is consistent with the idea of the 'motivated tactician' (Fiske & Taylor, 1991), who selects information-processing strategies on the basis of goals, motives and needs. In line with this view, Kunda (1990) has also suggested that people often use evidence in ways that make their inferences come out in desirable ways for them.

The following example from our research illustrates this behaviour. The (supposedly negative) statement 'A member of Group A often does not finish things he/she just started work on', was interpreted positively by saying 'that must be a very dynamic person, the people belonging to Group A are spontaneous and interested in so many things'. Such reinterpretations serve to reinforce the hypothesis that Group A is better than Group B, and complement a confirmatory hypothesis testing strategy. Thus reinterpretations strengthen the illusory correlation effect which in turn encourages the reinterpretation of subsequent behaviours. Taken together, the data confirm that the formation of illusory correlation reflects a dynamic process in which the perception of illusory correlation and reinterpretations of behaviours are mutually reinforcing.

Conclusions

Following the differentiated meaning approach, we argued that illusory correlation can arise as a product of imposing sense on the stimulus situation. In line with this approach, we have argued and demonstrated that there are two important determinants of illusory correlation: (a) cues that elicit expectations of intragroup similarities and intergroup differences, and (b) the perception of coherent behaviours. In Figure 5.4 we present these factors and their relation to illusory correlation.

In this chapter we described empirical evidence providing support for the various links presented in Figure 5.4. Haslam et al. (1996) and Berndsen et al. (1999) showed that the illusory correlation effect does not emerge in the absence of expectations involving intergroup differences. Similarly, when expectations of group coherence are reduced, the illusory correlation effect is eliminated (Berndsen et al., 1998, 1999; Yzerbyt & Rocher, this volume). On the other hand, if these general expectations are present but the behaviours are perceived as non-coherent due to the stimulus content or the distribution of the stimuli, the effect also disappears (Berndsen et al., 1994, 1998).

We have also shown that these two determinants (expectations and perceiving coherent behaviours) operate in the standard illusory correlation

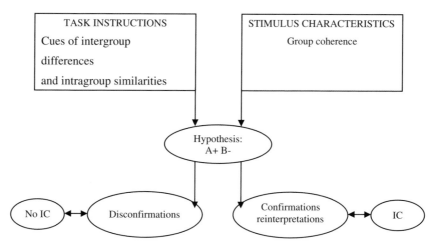

Figure 5.4 Factors affecting illusory correlation. Rectangles refer to antecedent conditions and ovals to dependent variables. The two-sided arrows indicate that (dis)confirmations/reinterpretations and illusory correlation influence each other.

task. More specifically, general expectations are created through the standard instructions, and both the skewed distribution and the content of the stimuli inform perceivers as to the coherence within the groups. Furthermore, the standard illusory correlation task seems to elicit reinterpretive processes because both the instructions and the stimulus content provide scope for reinterpretation. Thus participants make sense of the situation by actively reinterpreting their evaluations of the stimuli so that they become categorically meaningful. This reinterpretive process represents an additional mechanism leading to the occurrence of illusory correlation.

An important contribution of our research programme is that it shows that expectations play an important role in the formation of illusory correlation. This calls into question the viability of making a neat distinction between data-based and expectation-based illusory correlation at all. These two types of illusory correlation are usually treated separately because expectation-based illusory correlations are considered as explanations for maintaining stereotypes about socially meaningful groups (e.g., Hamilton & Rose, 1980) whereas data-based illusory correlations are seen as explanations for the formation of stereotypes (as discussed here). Based on the research in this chapter, we argue that these two types of illusory correlation are not as distinct or diametrically opposed as is often assumed, and have in common that they both deal with expectations of differences and similarities. Indeed these ideas have been used by McGarty (1999, this volume) as part of the platform for the development of the constraint relations formulation treatment of categorization in general and of stereotype formation in particular.

Another contribution of our research is that we are able to answer the three questions raised at the very beginning of this chapter. On what basis do we form relations between social stimuli such as group membership and behaviour? Our research reveals a number of important features involved in the formation of illusory correlation. In line with the differentiated meaning approach, we consider illusory correlation and its development as a sense-making process involving the search for differences between groups, which is reflected by hypothesis testing occurring in the initial phase of the illusory correlation task. Any disconfirmation of the hypothesis that Group A is better than Group B, is reinterpreted in such a way that it confirms the original hypothesis and simultaneously increases the coherence within the groups. This active process of forming coherent impressions of groups reveals that intragroup similarity is a precursor (expectations and stimuli) as well as a product (reinterpretations) of differentiation and illusory correlation. In other words, the formation of categories reflects the mutually reinforcing nature of similarity over time.

This active sense-making process also provides an answer to the question of whether people find it easy to detect relations between groups and their behaviours. Most explanations of illusory correlation suggest that we do not spend much energy on perceiving relations by emphasizing the automatic aspects of information processing due to enhanced or impaired memory. However, our view is exactly the opposite: we have shown that perceivers expend considerable effort to understand the meaning of the task and the nature of the groups and not just when they are subsequently asked to recall the information or form impressions.

The final question we raised in this chapter was whether our perception of group relations is biased. Put differently, how does a sense-making process of differentiation in the illusory correlation paradigm relate to the process of stereotyping social groups? The dominant view of stereotypes is that they are erroneous generalizations based on illusory perceptions that result from cognitive limitations (see e.g., Fiske & Neuberg, 1990; Hamilton, 1981a). This suggests that 'accurate' perception should result in the absence of illusory correlation. However, the research reported in this chapter suggests something quite different, namely that the absence of illusory correlation is a consequence of a different test strategy. Focusing on any disconfirmations of the hypothesis involving the positivity of Group A over Group B, eliminated the illusory correlation effect in contrast to a focus on confirmation. Thus both the perception of illusory correlation and its absence can arise from the same functional sense-making process.

Extending this idea to the area of stereotypes, this implies that stereotypes are not necessarily distortions but rather reflect detection of important features of the perceiver's social world. We should not forget either that even the experts disagree about whether the actual stimuli contained in this paradigm contain evidence justifying the conclusion that these stereotypes are based on genuine group differences (see also McGarty, this volume; van Knippenberg & Spears, in press; Spears, this volume). As is often the case, the participants in our studies may be more rational than previously thought. If there is bias this may be as much a product of the tools and concepts researchers have used to understand our participants behaviour, as of the tools and concepts participants have used to understand our paradigms.

6 Dependence and the formation of stereotyped beliefs about groups: from interpersonal to intergroup perception

Olivier Corneille and Vincent Yzerbyt

Introduction

Since the seminal publications of Allport (1954) and Tajfel (1969, 1978a, 1981b), scholars interested in intergroup relations have made substantial progress in their understanding of the conditions under which categorization influences the perception of individuals and groups (for a recent discussion, see McGarty, 1999). Among the most basic and powerful categorization effects underlying social perception are accentuation effects which consist in the perceiver's tendency to come up with more extreme and more homogeneous impressions of stimuli that are positioned along a perceptual continuum whenever these stimuli are assigned to distinct categories. Depending on the specific perceptual setting, categorization may result from a natural disposition of the perceptual system (see, for instance, Harnad, 1987) or from an explicit association between the stimuli and category labels at the time of judgement (see, for instance, Tajfel & Wilkes, 1963). These distinctions notwithstanding, category assignment or the mere presence of a context category at the judgement stage (which conceptually amounts to the same thing) will result in the accentuation of the perceived difference between and perceived resemblance within the two classes of stimuli (in the social psychology literature) or in a better discrimination across than within the category boundaries (in the cognitive psychology literature).

The accentuation effects can be seen as a natural consequence of the categorization process. As Rosch and colleagues noted twenty-five years ago (Rosch & Mervis, 1975; Rosch, Mervis, Grey, Johnson & Boyes-Braem, 1976), the function of categorization not only is to assemble objects that share a resemblance with each other but, *simultaneously*, to gather objects that share a difference with members of alternative categories. It follows from that definition that the structural properties of a category will change as a function of context. More specifically, categorization will shift so as to produce the best discrimination among the

111

stimuli present in the perceptual setting (think of the 'cluster analogy' used by Rosch). Note that this relationship between accentuation effects and the categorization process is still widely accepted in more recent perspectives on the categorization process, both in cognitive (see, for instance, Corter & Gluck, 1992) and social psychology (see, for instance, the meta-contrast principle proposed by Turner, 1985).

To the extent that stereotyping can be seen as an exaggeration of the differences existing between and of the resemblances existing within social categories ('(all) Males come from Mars and (all) Females from Venus'), accentuation effects are of central concern for social psychologists. With social targets, however, the categorization process is likely to be complicated. *Firstly*, contrary to what happens in judging the length of straight lines (Tajfel & Wilkes, 1963; see also Corneille, Klein, Lambert & Judd, 2001), social targets, whether individuals or groups, can reasonably be categorized along a *multitude of dimensions* (e.g., physical appearance, norms, attitudes, status). So, the question here not only is when but also where (on which dimensions) accentuation effects will occur (see Corneille & Judd, 1999; Ford & Stangor, 1992; Goldstone, 1994, 1996, 1998; Livingston, Andrews & Harnad, 1998; Oakes, 1987; Oakes, Turner & Haslam, 1991; Oakes, Haslam & Turner, 1994; Yzerbyt & Rocher, this volume; Yzerbyt, Rocher & Schadron, 1997; Yzerbyt & Schadron, 1996). A *second* peculiarity of social categorization is that perceivers facing social stimuli generally belong or at least compare themselves to the social categories they are judging. As a consequence, perceivers engaged in a social categorization process will generally be both the actors *and the targets* of accentuation effects. Clearly, social identity theory (Tajfel & Turner, 1979, 1986) and self-categorization theory (Turner, Hogg, Oakes, Reicher & Wetherell, 1987) provided a thorough analysis of the way accentuation effects relate to the construal of the perceiver's self-definition.

The impressive literature associated with the SIT and SCT strand of research helped a great deal to understand the specificity of accentuation effects as these relate to social categorization. Surprisingly, however, only a handful of studies have been concerned with the influence that *group interdependence*, a *third* factor that is distinct from social categorization, may have on these effects. Admittedly, substantial progress has been done regarding the impact of relative group *status* on stereotyping (see for instance Doosje, Ellemers & Spears, 1995; Doosje, Spears & Koomen, 1995; Doosje & Ellemers, 1997; Lorenzi-Cioldi, 1988, 1993; Lee & Ottati, 1995; Simon & Brown, 1987). At the same time, however, only a few experimental studies examined the question of how the respective power (outcome control rather than social prestige) of groups could impact on their mutual perception. Indeed, and as surprising as this may appear, only a few (and recent) experimental studies were concerned with the impact of interdependence on group perception (we mean here group *perception, not* discrimination as in the work by Gaertner & Insko, 2000; Ng, 1981, 1982; Rabbie & Horwitz, 1988; Rabbie, Schot & Visser, 1989).

We think that the issue of the link between interdependence and stereotyping is crucially important for anyone interested in intergroup relations. Although symbolic concerns have been shown to play a major role in stereotyping, the relations that groups experience with each other are far from being purely symbolic. And, even though interdependence might not be *necessary* for discrimination or stereotyping to occur (Bourhis, Turner & Gagnon, 1997; Gagnon & Bourhis, 1996; Sachdev & Bourhis, 1985, 1991; however see Gaertner & Insko, 2000, for a recent reconsideration of this argument), this factor may nevertheless play a substantial role in the regulation of stereotyping and conflict at the intergroup level. The present chapter aims at contributing to better understand this issue by reviewing and discussing the available evidence about the impact of dependence (relative deprivation of outcome control) on stereotyping. Specifically, we will propose that dependence likely increases stereotyping at the group level.

We first note that most experimental studies concerned with dependence have focused on information processing rather than impression formation, and on person rather than group perception. Thus, and as surprising as this may appear, experimental studies conducted in the intergroup relations literature only paid remote attention to the impact of dependence on the way people perceive groups. Fortunately, a few recent studies have begun to tackle this important issue. In line with our above proposal, this literature suggests that more extreme and more homogeneous beliefs are likely to emerge about competing, hostile and powerful outgroups. These findings are discussed in the second section of the present chapter. Our final section deals with the circumstances under which dependence is likely to prevent or facilitate the formation of stereotypical beliefs. We propose that dependence generally reduces stereotyping at the interpersonal level while it generally enhances it in the context of intergroup relations.

Dependence and the individuation of powerful targets

As just noted, experimental studies that linked stereotyping to interdependence generally worked in the context of interpersonal rather than intergroup dependence, and focused on person rather than group perception. This state of affairs is nicely illustrated in the now classic research programme initiated by Susan Fiske and her colleagues on outcome dependence (Fiske, Lin & Neuberg, 1999; Fiske & Neuberg, 1990). In an impressive series of experiments, these authors demonstrated that people attend longer to inconsistent information about social targets who have control over their outcomes. The idea here is that, by attending to the inconsistent information, powerless perceivers may think they are increasing their chances to better know powerful targets and restore some control in the interpersonal setting (Dépret & Fiske, 1999; Erber & Fiske, 1984; Neuberg & Fiske, 1987; Ruscher & Fiske, 1990).

Most studies conducted by Fiske and her colleagues have been concerned with the impact of dependence on stereotyping at the interpersonal level. Exceptions can be found in a series of studies reported by Ruscher, Fiske, Miki and Van Manen (1991) and, more recently, by Dépret and Fiske (1999). Ruscher and colleagues (1991) noted that in most situations of intergroup competition, perceivers are dependent both upon the outgroup (negative dependence) and the ingroup (positive dependence). Under those circumstances, a puzzling issue is whether perceivers choose to devote their attention to the ingroup members or, on the contrary, to the outgroup members. The results obtained by Ruscher and colleagues (1991, Study 2) indicate that people under intergroup competition actually devote similar amounts of attention to both groups, but pay more (less) attention to inconsistent than to consistent information regarding the ingroup (outgroup).

These findings from Ruscher and colleagues suggest that intergroup competition probably interferes with the formation of individuated impressions about outgroup members (to what extent it does so, however, is difficult to estimate in the absence of a no-competition control condition). They, however, remain silent as to whether intergroup dependence impacts on *group perception*. Indeed, the above study was mainly concerned with the attention devoted to, and the number of inferences drawn about, individual group targets under the various experimental conditions, *not* with the impact of dependence on the perception of groups as a whole. A second limitation of Ruscher et al.'s study concerns the structural relation that probably existed between the attentional resources devoted to the ingroup and to the outgroup members. A stronger test of the role played by dependence in the individuation of outgroup targets would require the level of attention devoted to the ingroup members under the different experimental conditions to be kept constant.

In an attempt to address that issue, Dépret and Fiske (1999) conducted a study where individual participants were, or were not, made highly dependent upon three individuals who were believed to form either a coherent entity (same major) or a mere aggregate of individuals (different majors). Higher dependence resulted in more attention paid to the inconsistent information under the aggregate but *not* under the coherent group conditions. Indeed, Dépret and Fiske had predicted that dependence would not lead to the individuation of the coherent outgroup because of the threat embodied by such a group. Under the latter circumstances, the authors noted: 'Because outgroup members are perceived as committed to their own group norms (Leyens & Schadron, 1980), and out-groups are perceived as cohesive entities (Horwitz & Rabbie, 1982) which are expected to discriminate against the ingroup (as in Fiske & Ruscher, 1983), information seeking is not the most appropriate strategy to restore control' (Dépret & Fiske, p. 465). Rather, the authors suggested, the most beneficial way of coping with dependence is to accentuate one's stereotyped beliefs concerning the powerful outgroup: 'If (perceivers) do not expect to be able to influence the target, and if they think negative outcomes are probable, they may attend to and interpret information to sustain beliefs about their worst expectations and stereotypes and shift their focus to the ingroup for protection' (Dépret & Fiske, p. 466).

As it will become evident in the remainder of the present chapter, we have much sympathy with the view that higher dependence does not necessarily result in less stereotyping at the intergroup level. Indeed, and consistent with Dépret and Fiske's (1999) line of reasoning, situations characterized by a high level of dependence of the perceiver upon hostile and powerful outgroups may very well exacerbate the stereotyping process. Unfortunately, Dépret and Fiske's (1999) study did not include measures regarding the impressions formed by participants at the group level. Rather, impression formation measures were computed across judgements made about outgroup individuals. We now turn our attention to studies that involved such measures.

Dependence and the formation of stereotyped beliefs about groups

Attentional processes and stereotyping

The research programme initiated by Fiske and colleagues, although clearly indicative of the role played by dependence in the attention paid to inconsistent information, provided limited evidence to support the claim that powerful targets elicit less stereotypical impressions. In our view, the lack of correspondence between attentional and impression formation measures is a real challenge for these studies (see Nolan, Haslam, Spears & Oakes, 1999; Reynolds & Oakes, 2000; Spears & Haslam, 1997;

Spears, Haslam & Jansen, 1999, for a related argument). This is especially true given what we know from recent literature on stereotyping. As a matter of fact, more attention paid to inconsistent information sometimes results in *more* stereotyping. For instance, Yzerbyt and colleagues (Yzerbyt, Coull & Rocher, 1999; Coull & Yzerbyt, 1999) found that participants exposed to inconsistent information about a group member changed their stereotype of the group as a whole more when they were under high rather than under low cognitive load. When cognitive resources were invested in a concurrent task, participants were unable to reconcile the inconsistent information with their stereotype of the group. As a result, they had to reconsider, if only momentarily, the validity of their stereotype. In sharp contrast, participants who were not distracted during the reception of the inconsistent information managed to retain their stereotypic views of the group.

Although not specifically concerned with the issue of dependence, studies such as these strongly suggest that the attention paid to inconsistent information may boost rather than reduce stereotyping at the group level. In fact, Yzerbyt and colleagues (1999) argued that people often have a vested interest in their stereotypes and would rather stick to their *a priori* views whenever they can make up for the inconsistency. Consistent with that reasoning, Coull, Yzerbyt, Castano, Paladino and Leemans (2001) found that only participants who strongly identified with their group spontaneously withdrew their attention from a secondary task when exposed to inconsistent information about an ingroup member. Presumably, high identifiers allocated extra intellectual resources in order to solve the inconsistency and protect their positive view of the group. Once again, this pattern suggests the intimate link between attentional resources devoted to the inconsistent information and the perpetuation, not to mention the exacerbation, of stereotypic beliefs.

The experience of discrimination

The work discussed in the previous section indicates that people's identification to their group contributes to the maintenance of stereotypical beliefs about the ingroup when inconsistent information is encountered. In a similar vein, Doosje and colleagues (1995) had provided evidence for higher perceived homogeneity of the ingroup among high identifiers exposed to negative information about their group (while the opposite trend was obtained for low identifiers). Recently, Rothgerber (1997) examined the link between identification and group perceptions in conditions of objective rather than symbolic threat. In that study, Texas A&M students were led to believe that they would be asked to write an essay that would be evaluated either by an ingroup (Texas A&M) or by an outgroup (University of Texas -UT) member. Participants were also told that they would themselves have to rate an essay written either by an ingroup or by an outgroup member. Some Texas A&M participants learned that the outgroup (UT) participants had discriminated against Texas A&M students in their evaluations (negative dependence condition). Other participants were not provided with information about the way the outgroup had treated their ingroup (control condition).

Rothgerber predicted that the experience of discrimination would increase participants' perceived similarity to their ingroup ('We all are the victims') and perceived dissimilarity to the outgroup ('They all harm us'). This process was expected to magnify stereotyping. These predictions were clearly supported by the results. Specifically, the experience of discrimination accentuated the perceived similarity of the self to the ingroup and the perceived dissimilarity of the self to the outgroup. Also, discrimination resulted in a higher perceived homogeneity of the outgroup and of the ingroup. Put another way, the experience of negative intergroup dependence boosted participants' ingroup identification (see also Branscombe, Schmitt & Harvey, 1999, and Dépret & Fiske, 1999) and resulted in a clear accentuation effect: an increase in the perceived differences between *and* of the perceived resemblances within the two groups.

The experience of competition

That negative dependence can lead to accentuation effects at the intergroup level is also nicely illustrated in a study reported by Brewer, Weber and Carini (1995, Study 2). In that study, participants received bogus feedback concerning their category identity ('overestimators' or 'underestimators') on the basis of a perceptual test. After they were informed about their category identity, participants were randomly assigned to one of three experimental conditions. In a first condition (Categorization-only), participants were simply asked to wait for a few minutes while the experimenter prepared the next phase of the study. In a second condition (Salience), overestimators and underestimators were separated into different rooms and were asked to take part in a group task. At this point, the two groups were told that they would engage in a different task in order to avoid competitive behaviour. Finally, participants in a third condition (Intergroup) were placed in the same conditions as the Salience participants (different rooms and completion of a group task) but they were led to believe that both groups would engage in a similar task and that their scores would be used to determine which of the two perceptual styles was 'the more creative, socially intelligent, and adept at group problem solving'. The latter instructions clearly aimed at increasing negative dependence between the two groups.

After the experimental manipulation had taken place and participants had completed the group task (or waited for a similar amount of time in the Categorization-only condition), all participants were asked to watch a videotaped group discussion that showed three overestimators and three underestimators who briefly described themselves and talked about their lives as students (the category membership of the discussants was signified by way of their sweatshirts' colour). At the end of the video, participants were provided with twenty-four one-sentence transcriptions of statements heard in the videotape and asked to identify which of the six individuals had made each statement. Consistent with previous who-said-what paradigm studies (Taylor, Fiske, Etcoff & Ruderman, 1978), Brewer and colleagues (1995) compared the number of between- and within-category confusions in the sentence assignments across the three experimental conditions. In line with the authors' predictions (and Rothgerber's findings discussed above), the number of within-category confusions was higher both for the ingroup and the outgroup under conditions of strong interdependence (when the two groups had been in competition with each other). In addition, negative dependence increased the perceived dissimilarity between the two groups as indexed by the reduction in between-category confusions. Thus, negative dependence in these studies also led to a clear accentuation effect: less differentiation within the categories *and* more differentiation between the categories.

The anticipation of negative dependence

The findings reported by Rothgerber (1997) and Brewer and colleagues (1995) strongly support the view that negative dependence elicits accentuation effects at the intergroup level. In particular, competition has the potential to create stereotypes when none or very few exists before. Another question of interest is whether the mere *anticipation* (rather than the actual experience) of dependence leads to similar consequences. Situations where negative dependence is anticipated rather than experienced are common in social life. For instance, whenever some party is gaining relative political power, supporters of other parties may feel that they are likely to become more dependent on the emerging force. We recently conducted a series of studies to look at the impact that such anticipated dependence may have on impressions made about the outgroup. To that end, we relied on a paradigm associated with an intriguing phenomenon, the Group Attribution Error (for a review, see Allison, Mackie & Messick, 1996).

In studies on the Group Attribution Error (GAE; see also Allison & Messick, 1985; Allison, Beggan, Midgley & Wallace, 1995; Worth, Allison & Messick, 1987), participants are generally told that a specific percentage of voters supported a stance on the occasion of a ballot. Depending on the conditions, information about the group decisions rules is manipulated so that the percentage of support is either sufficient or not for the vote to pass. Then, participants have to report what they think is the attitude of a typical member of the group with respect to the vote proposition. The typical result is that participants rely on the decision rule to make the latter estimation. Specifically, the typical group member is rated as more supportive of the vote proposition when the vote passed than when it failed. This pattern emerges despite the fact that the percentage of support is held constant across the two conditions.

In two studies (Corneille, Yzerbyt, Rogier & Buidin, 2001) we provided participants with a scenario where supporters of an extreme-right political party (the French Front National in Alisseau, a bogus French town) had gathered to vote on a specific issue (hiring veterans to set up night security patrols in Alisseau). In line with prior studies on the GAE, we manipulated the vote outcome: all participants were informed that 57 per cent of the Front National (FN) members had supported the policy but, depending on the condition, the group decision rules were allegedly such that either 50 per cent or 66 per cent of support was necessary for the vote to pass. Thus, participants were led to believe that the vote respectively passed and failed under the former and latter conditions. In addition to the vote outcome factor (passed versus failed), we manipulated the threat from the group that participants would experience. In the low threat condition, we told participants that the FN had very little support in the Alisseau population (4% of the votes on the last election) so that the vote outcome would probably not impact on the future of the community. In the high threat condition, we told participants that the FN was quite popular in Alisseau (40% of the votes on the last election) and that the vote outcome would therefore most likely affect the future of the community. We reasoned that, given the set of values associated with the FN in general and with the vote issue in particular, our student population would deem the Alisseau FN as much more threatening under the latter (much political power) than under the former (negligible political power) condition. Consistent with that reasoning, participants rated the FN as a more threatening political force and reported being more reluctant to live in that city under the high than under the low threat conditions. Note that the threat factor was here clearly associated with a loss of control of the ingroup relative to the outgroup.

In these two studies, we predicted higher extremity and similarity ratings of the FN supporters toward the vote issue under the high than the low threat conditions. In Study 1, we asked participants to read carefully the instructions and to estimate the attitude of a typical Alisseau FN supporter toward the vote proposal using a Likert-type scale going from 1 (= not at all in favour of the policy) to 9 (= totally in favour of the policy). We also included a similarity measure: participants had to indicate to what extent they thought that Alisseau FN supporters held a common position on the vote proposal. Consistent with our predictions, (a) the Alisseau FN members were seen as holding a more common political stance in the high than in the low threat conditions, and (b) the GAE appeared to be higher in the high than in the low threat condition.

In a second study, we reasoned that participants in the high threat condition may experience a state of cognitive dissonance when facing the failure information. Indeed, whereas the presence of threat should lead participants to expect a high level of homogeneity within the group, the failure information (57% of support under the 66% decision rule) should render salient the diversity of opinions shared among the group members. We predicted that participants would manage this conflict by inferring that the voters actually favoured an alternative proposition. In Study 1 and 2, we indeed told participants (before we provided the outcome information) that the FN supporters would have the opportunity to vote on a second proposition (to organize political propaganda around secondary schools) should the first one (setting up security patrols) fail. It was thus most instructive to look at participants' estimates of the FN supporters attitudes regarding each one of the vote proposals. In order to collect this information, Study 2 used a bipolar attitude scale: participants estimated the attitude of the typical group member on a scale ranging from 1 (= totally in favour of proposition 2) to 9 (= totally in favour of proposition 1).

Several results emerged from Study 2. Firstly, replicating Study 1's findings, the presence of threat increased the perceived homogeneity *and* the perceived extremity of the voters' attitudes. Thus, participants under the high threat conditions thought more strongly that the voters shared a common attitude. Also, these participants considered that the voters were less favourable to the vote proposal in the 'failed' condition and more favourable to the vote proposal in the 'passed' condition than participants in the low threat condition. Moreover, and in line with our predictions, participants in the high threat and failure condition estimated that the voters actually favoured proposition 2 over proposition 1 (see Figure 6.1). Thus, despite the information that a fair amount of voters (57%) had supported proposition 1 and despite the total lack of information regarding

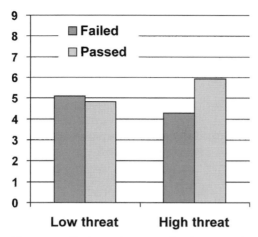

Figure 6.1 Estimated support for the propositions as a function of vote outcome and level of threat (after Corneille, Yzerbyt, Rogier & Buidin, 2001).
Note: The scale ranges from 1 (= favourable to the propaganda proposition) to 9 (= favourable to the security patrols proposition).

the voters' support to proposition 2, these participants inferred that the latter proposition was more strongly supported among the FN supporters than the former proposition. This inference, we think, helped these participants exposed to a vote failure information to protect their beliefs about the homogeneity of the group.

One should note here that, although information about absolute group size was never mentioned to the participants, the relative size of the group was explicitly communicated (4% versus 40% of support in the last election). The fact that participants came up with more homogeneous impressions about the relatively larger group (see also McGarty et al., 1995) suggests that a similar process may also emerge when *absolute* group size is manipulated. Indeed, according to the present analysis, larger groups may be perceived as less variable when their size relates to their power. Needless to say, such tendency would likely be biased for one should generally expect more variability among large than small groups. That social perceivers may be tempted to see less variability in groups that actually become more variable certainly deserves further empirical attention.

Finally, the above two experiments suggest that the experience of threat tends to lead to more inaccurate judgements about the outgroup. Such bases for evaluating the accuracy of participants' judgements are generally lacking in the research on interdependence and stereotyping (for a recent exception, see Guinote, Judd & Brauer, in press). As a result, it is often difficult to conclude from the existing literature whether interdependence results in more biased or, on the contrary, in more accurate impressions about the outgroup. The studies discussed in the present section suggest that negative dependence likely increases biased perceptions about the outgroup.

When and why would interdependence lead to accentuation in group perception?

The two studies discussed in the previous section are among the very few experiments that addressed the impact of dependence on stereotyping at the intergroup level (once again, our low and high threat conditions amounted to situations where the ingroup was respectively totally independent or highly dependent upon an hostile outgroup's decisions). Along with the studies conducted by Rothgerber (1997) and Brewer and colleagues (1995) discussed above, these studies strongly suggest that, at the group level, stereotyping is enhanced under conditions of negative dependence. Note also that these studies were concerned with a situation where dependence was merely anticipated rather than truly experienced by the participants. In fact, dependence was quite indirect: participants did not even anticipate being personally dependent upon the outgroup. Rather, they imagined similar others to be so.

Situations where negative dependence is merely anticipated (or anticipated for similar others) are pretty common in social life and they may lead to noticeable accentuation effects. In Europe, for instance, the recent constitution of an Austrian government that comprised extreme-right leaders provoked strong reactions in the rest of the European Union. In many media, what had previously been referred to as a quiet conservative country ('Mozart's country') was apparently on its way to reinstate the Third-Reich ('Hitler's country'). And, in the streets surrounding the Brussels' European Parliament, a German representative had a very hard time getting a cab. Apparently, taxi drivers had assimilated the whole German-speaking population to what they considered to be a modern instantiation of a Nazi regime.

In our view, negative dependence is likely to increase stereotyping at the group level to the extent this process helps to justify general actions (or retaliations) toward the outgroup as a whole. This is typically the case in war situations where economical embargoes and air strike actions penalize populations that are definitely not concerned with the heart of the conflict (see Brewer et al., 1995; Rothgerber, 1997; Vanbeselaere, 1991; Wilder, 1978, 1986; see also Rothbart & Hallmark, 1988). A related process may be that, in conflictual settings, misses (having Austria really reinstating a Third-Reich programme) appear more costly than false alarms (refusing to give a ride to a German representative).

These processes and their associated functional explanation notwithstanding, negative dependence at the group level may also elicit perceptual accentuation because active groups generally *do* behave in more stereotyped ways. Indeed, we know from classic studies in intergroup relations that common fate is a powerful factor in the creation of group strategies channelling the behaviours of the individual group members (see Sherif, 1966b, Sherif, Harvey, White, Hood & Sherif, 1961; see also Campbell, 1958). The idea here is that people engaged in intergroup relations may actively participate in the construction of the reality of their groups. They tend to behave according to the norms of the group rather than as a bunch of individuals. This process may certainly lead to a reinforcement of the stereotype, the group being perceived in more stereotyped ways because it really does become more normative in its thinking and behaviours (Oakes et al., 1994). As McGarty, Haslam, Hutchinson and Grace (1995, p. 241) put it, '... unlike other (i.e., non-social) targets of perception, we know that groups of people act in ways which maximize similarities and differences. Conformity involves changing behaviour to match ingroup norms which are in part defined in contrast to other groups. In other words, social influence also involves the accentuation of similarities within groups and differences between groups as individual members regulate their behaviour on the basis of these norms.' We think that the active role that group members can have in the construction (rather than the mere perception) of intergroup differences and intragroup similarities has been largely under-addressed in the current intergroup literature and would certainly deserve further empirical attention (Abrams & Hogg, 1990; Hogg & Turner, 1987b; Turner, 1991; see also Abelson, Dasgupta, Park & Banaji, 1998).

To be sure, the present analysis does not suggest that higher dependence will always result in more stereotyping at the intergroup level. It is, however, likely to do so whenever perceivers have no opportunity to or have nothing to gain from forming individuated impressions about the outgroup. *A contrario* evidence to this comes from a couple of studies recently conducted by Guinote and Fiske (2000) in which participants were or were not made dependent upon a group whose size was limited enough (six members) to elicit a sense of control among participants. Under these circumstances, higher dependence resulted in a higher perceived *heterogeneity* of the outgroup (Study 1). Interestingly, Guinote and Fiske (Study 2) conducted a second study in which participants were made highly dependent either upon a small outgroup or upon a small ingroup (four participants). In the ingroup dependence condition, the classic outgroup homogeneity effect was obtained (higher perceived homogeneity of the outgroup). In the outgroup dependence conditions, however, the authors obtained an ingroup homogeneity effect (higher perceived homogeneity of the ingroup).

The originality of Guinote and Fiske's Study 2 is to suggest that dependence rather than (or independently from) group membership influences group stereotypicality (at least, its homogeneity component). The fact that people made dependent upon the outgroup perceived the ingroup as more homogeneous than the outgroup is a strong finding that clearly supports the authors' line of reasoning. One has, however, to stress the fact that these groups were quite limited in size. In these studies, participants could reasonably hope to be able to restore control by individuating the six (Study 1) or four (Study 2) powerful targets. Most intergroup situations may, however, be characterized by a much lower sense of control. A good understanding of how dependence relates to stereotyping may thus require to distinguish between interpersonal, small group and intergroup settings. Gaining information about a game partner can certainly make perceivers think this will help restore their control in the situation. Gaining information about a few teammates, though feasible, is probably less likely to give rise to the same sense of control. Gaining information about a large social category or even an entire nation will certainly do so even less. Thus, whereas people dependent upon one or a few specific individuals may very well tend to individuate these targets, people who are dependent upon an outgroup will likely accentuate the perceived homogeneity among members of that group.

This reversal in the impact of interdependence on stereotyping, going from interpersonal to intergroup settings, may occur for at least three reasons. The first one is cognitive: as one goes from interpersonal to intergroup settings informational constraints definitely increase (but see also McGarty, 1999): there is obviously less information to process in one Chinese person than in the entire population of China. The second reason is pragmatic: as one goes from interpersonal to intergroup situations the opportunity to restore control decreases. Tennis players may think they are restoring control when gaining individuated information about their opponents, but soldiers will probably not gain much control in individuating a competing army for their opportunity to control this army will be negligible anyway – both in terms of the behavioural freedom of the perceiver and in terms of the number of the targets that have to be controlled (see also Fiske, 2000). The third reason, both cognitive and motivational in tone, relates to the perceivers' identity: as we know from the SIT and SCT literature, perceivers who find themselves in a setting that makes their group membership salient have been found to switch from an individual identity to a group identity (Verkuyten & Hagendoorn, 1998). And, importantly, people may assign quite different meanings to a same situation depending on whether they define themselves on an individual or on a collective basis. To use the example of Oakes (1994) and Spears and Haslam (1997), for protesters to treat baton-charging police officers as individuals may be a difficult thing to do not only because it requires cognitive resources but because it makes no sense for capturing the reality which confronts those perceivers (note that similar arguments in quite different terms can be derived from social judgeability theory; see Leyens et al., 1994).

In sum, the present line of reasoning by no means contradicts Fiske and colleagues' demonstration that high-dependent perceivers individuate more individual targets in interpersonal settings than low-dependent perceivers do. Importantly, however, this demonstration should not be taken as evidence for less stereotyping by people belonging to powerless groups. Consistent with the last conclusion, Judd, Park, Brauer, Ryan and Kraus (1995) reported the presence of outgroup homogeneity and ethnocentrism among African Americans toward White Americans but not among White Americans toward African Americans, a finding that is clearly at odds with the view that stereotyping is to be found among powerful groups (see also Guinote, Judd & Brauer, in press).

Conclusions

Although group interdependence should in all likelihood be among the main preoccupations of scholars interested in intergroup relations, the last thirty years of research witnessed almost no empirical work examining the potential impact of dependence on group perception. The discovery that ingroup favouritism emerged even in minimal group situations led researchers to devote the best of their efforts to understand the way identity concerns influence intergroup relations and perceptions. Somewhat paradoxically though, this journey into the intricacies of the relations between social identity and self-esteem took people's attention away from those factors that may play a substantial role in the way group members perceive each other in non-minimal situations. Admittedly, one group of researchers explored the link between group interdependence and group perception. In doing so, however, they mainly focused on the impact of group perception on anticipated interdependence. Illustrative of this line of research are the numerous studies conducted by Insko, Schopler and their colleagues on the individual-group discontinuity effect, which revealed that groups elicit more distrust than individuals and that people anticipate more competition from homogeneous than heterogeneous groups (see Insko & Schopler, 1998, and Wildschut, Insko & Pinter, in press; see also Dasgupta, Banaji & Abelson, 1999, and Yzerbyt et al., 2000).

Needless to say, the study of the links between group interdependence and group perception did not stand very high either on the research agenda of those scholars working in the social cognition tradition. To the best of our knowledge, Fiske and colleagues were among the few who examined this issue in somewhat more detail. As we noted, however, these authors were mainly interested in interpersonal settings and provided only limited information on the way dependence affects group perception. Interestingly, Fiske and colleagues suggested at some points that interdependence may magnify the stereotyping process. Hence, Fiske and Ruscher concluded that 'People attend more to individuating information when they are interdependent, and thus interdependence opens the door to nonstereotyped reactions. But interdependence allows interruptions and negative effects. Hence, ironically, interdependence is potentially both a cause and a cure for prejudice' (Fiske & Ruscher, 1993, p. 264; see also Dépret & Fiske, 1999). The present analysis suggests that dependence may very well be a cure for stereotyping in the context of interpersonal encounters but one of its major causes in the context of intergroup relations. One should finally note that the various situations we discussed here were all characterized by the presence of *negative* dependence. Thus, the question remains as to whether dependence in general or, instead, negative dependence only leads to accentuation effects. This is a question that, we hope, future research will address.

7 Four degrees of stereotype formation: differentiation by any means necessary

Russell Spears

Introduction

Stereotype formation is a strangely neglected topic within social psychology. Research in the social cognition tradition tends to treat stereotypes as givens: cognitive heuristics, which are part of our mental repertoire (or cognitive toolbox), that are activated and then applied (e.g., Gilbert & Hixon, 1991). This two-step process already presumes the fact of formation. So, although this general approach has proved to be of considerable heuristic value, it is not clear that this tells us too much about how stereotypes are formed in the first place. This approach kicks in after the stereotypes are in place so to speak. There has also been some debate in recent years about whether stereotypes are constructs we can always take 'off the peg' in this pre-packaged way (see e.g., Spears & Haslam, 1997). In this chapter we have our cake and eat it: we accept that stereotypes sometimes represent well learned knowledge structures about social groups that are simply activated, but at other times they have to be constructed in context from the resources available. However, if we are to consider stereotype *formation* it is surely self-evident that we cannot rely exclusively on prior knowledge or fixed structures.

Arguably if we want to look at how stereotypes are formed, we have to consider more dynamic and social processes that govern the relations between groups: how meaning is extracted, constructed and developed over time. This does not mean to say that this always refers to the beginning of group life; stereotypes can develop and change with the comparative context. This side of stereotyping has not been neglected. Social identity and self-categorization theories, with their common theoretical tradition, have had much to say about how we extract and develop the meaning that forms the basis for group identity and social stereotyping. One strength of these approaches is that they are dynamic. They involve intergroup comparison and therefore vary with context, with the result that they do not take stereotypic content as fixed. Below we contrast this view of stereotyping and stereotype formation with the activation/application approach current within social cognition, but also aim to integrate these two visions. The difference between the two and the relation between them should become clearer as we proceed. Firstly, we develop the theoretical principles derived from these two traditions and outline how they combine to produce (at least) four degrees of stereotype formation.

Theoretical principles and resources

In the present chapter we draw heavily on social identity and self-categorization principles. Specifically we assume that stereotype formation will generally reflect the process of social categorization into two or more groups, often implicating the self through ingroup membership. Stereotype formation is therefore likely to involve efforts to differentiate groups (in line with accentuation theory), and where social reality allows us to positively distinguish ingroup from outgroup (in line with social identity and self-categorization theories). We can break this theoretical framework down into a number of closely related principles which, although analytically separable, often go together in practice. The *meaning principle* holds that we often use differentiation between categories as a way to make sense of the situation (see McGarty & Turner, 1992; McGarty, this volume; Tajfel, 1981b), using available knowledge to help us where possible. Where the collective self is salient this will involve the closely related *distinctiveness principle*, the attempt to gain an identity for the ingroup that is distinct from relevant comparison groups (Tajfel & Turner, 1986; see Spears, Jetten & Scheepers, 2002). This process in turn is closely related to the *enhancement principle*: where possible we prefer positive social identities to negative ones (Tajfel & Turner, 1986; Turner, Hogg, Oakes, Reicher & Wetherell, 1987). All the principles are both fed and constrained by the *reality principle*: the social world provides the raw materials with which to construct stereotypic differentiation according to the other principles (Oakes, Haslam & Turner, 1994). Although the terminology varies this analysis shares many processes and principles outlined in the social judgeability approach of Leyens, Yzerbyt and colleagues (Leyens, Yzerbyt & Schadron, 1992, 1994; see also Yzerbyt & Rocher, this volume). These principles and processes have sometimes been distinguished by the degree to which they are controlled by motivational forces or are more or less automatic responses of the perceptual/cognitive system. These debates will not detain us here (important though they are), except to say that all of these principles are likely to contain elements of both, with motivation becoming more important to the extent that the self is implicated.

In line with self-categorization theorists, we do not have to see this differentiation process (or processes) as biased, but as often emphasizing real and relevant differences, be these contained in current data or past experience (Oakes, Haslam & Turner, 1994; Spears & Haslam, 1997; see also McCauley, Stitt and Segal, 1980). Differences between groups may put social constraints on who we differentiate, and the dimensions on which stereotypes are formed (for an elaborated discussion of these constraints see McGarty, 1999, this volume). The principles of comparative fit and meta-contrast are important here (Oakes, 1987; Turner, 1985). Elsewhere we have described reality-based differentiation as 'reflective' distinctiveness, because it reflects the reality of perceived group differences in available data (Spears, Jetten & Scheepers, 2002). However we will also argue below that the size or even the presence of the difference does not necessarily limit the possibility (or degree) of differentiation. The question arises of what happens when we have 'nothing to go on' – a question particularly pertinent to the issue of stereotype formation. Assuming we are committed to the idea of a group we have to create differences. When all else fails we have the distinctiveness and enhancement principles, and we can sometimes create differentiation from these motivations in the absence of clear differences. We have termed this process 'creative distinctiveness' to distinguish it from reflective distinctiveness (and also from 'reactive distinctiveness', a similar differentiation motive arising when distinctiveness is threatened by a similar outgroup; Spears et al., 2002). A recurring theme in the following concerns the trade-off between the descriptive and evaluative dimensions of stereotypic differentiation, that relate closely to reflective and creative distinctiveness respectively. Although both dimensions are important, when the descriptive differentiation fails, we argue that evaluative differentiation becomes available to fill the gap (or 'form' the gap).

People not only discover the differences between groups and the contents of stereotypes inductively and at first hand, we also learn about such differences at second hand and from a range of social sources (Haslam, 1997). Normative fit refers to the expectations associated with the contents of group stereotypes. We bring expectations and knowledge to these contexts, and not always in a form that reflects preformed stereotypes. Stereotypic knowledge does not have to be tagged directly with a group but can be constructed in context from more general knowledge about the groups and the relations between them. We may also have more meta-cognitive beliefs about the nature of group differences, including expectations that our group will be better (e.g., Howard & Rothbart, 1980). Moreover expectations about one group, even when these are relatively fixed or preformed knowledge structures (e.g. skinheads are aggressive; librarians are introverted) can be used as a comparison standard from which to construct content about another group where the stereotypes are as yet ill-defined (including stereotypes of one's own group).

These issues bring us to the battleground of two contrasting visions of stereotypes and stereotyping, reflecting key meta-theoretical differences in our discipline. Are stereotypes fixed pictures in our heads as Lippmann (1922) once proposed, and as much as social cognition research assumes? Or are they flexible and dynamic constructions instantiated on line and in context? We admit to preferring the latter vision. However, this does not mean that stereotypes can never reflect well worn or routinized knowledge structures associated with groups. In this sense we think both visions have validity and we will accommodate this distinction in our approach. Specifically, we propose that there are two realms to social stereotyping. One, associated more with social cognition research, refers basically to knowledge activation and application processes. In this case perceivers have a degree of certainty and closure about relevant stereotypic knowledge/content. This content (and its activation) is not generally sensitive to the self, or the position of the perceiver, and the relation to the social stimulus. In this sense it does not implicate a distinctively 'social' process (one that implicates perceivers' consciousness of themselves as social entities). In practical terms this approach tends to study our stereotypes about other groups and is less concerned with self-stereotyping and indeed less concerned with the self per se. The second realm involves the perceiver *in relation to* the stimulus and implicates social comparison between groups. This approach is more associated with social identity and self-categorization theories (for a related perspective, see Leyens, Yzerbyt & Schadron, 1994; Yzerbyt, Castano, Leyens & Paladino, 2000).

As we have already suggested a central theme of this chapter is that this second realm is more appropriate to the study of stereotype formation, although we shall argue below that stereotypes as knowledge schemas can also feed into stereotype formation in a comparative sense. Armed with these theoretical resources we now try to identify different forms of stereotype formation, distinguished by the amount of prior knowledge or information in context that is available about the target groups.

Four degrees of stereotype formation

We structure the present chapter by moving from cases where there is some clear basis for stereotypic differentiation, to ones where there is progressively less information ('out there' or in the head) that can feed stereotype formation. We focus here on the resources offered by the context and the person, that allow for stereotypic definition, usually concerning one group in relation to another. We address first groups and contexts that lend themselves to clear stereotypic differentiation between two relevant comparison groups (often but not always ingroup and outgroup), through to conditions that provide the most meagre and minimal basis for inter-group differentiation. We distinguish between the sources of formation grounded in the available data in the social stimuli versus (prior) knowledge and expectation, as well as neither of these. At the 'information rich' end we consider conditions where people generate stereotypes from the data ('bottom up'), the case most commonly associated with stereotype formation (Case 1 below). At an intermediate level we can distinguish stereotype formation based on very limited data from one or both of the groups allowing one to infer stereotypic differences (Case 2). Stereotypes can also be generated form some form of knowledge or expectations ('top down'), albeit from sometimes very limited information such as background knowledge or category labels (Case 3). Finally at the 'information poor' end of the spectrum we consider how stereotypes might form in the absence of either 'bottom up' or 'top down' information (Case 4):

1. 'Bottom up': Where differences between groups are evident in situ providing the basis for stereotype formation.
2. A bit of 'bottom up': Where stereotypic data for one or both groups is limited but can be inferred from available data.
3. A bit of 'top down': Where there is sufficient knowledge to construct or infer stereotypes in the comparative context.
4. Neither up nor down: Where there are no clear or obvious differences between the groups as a basis for differentiation.

In line with the theoretical section we propose the main process driving stereotype formation will be one of category differentiation, as opposed to information processing or memory biases as often proposed in the social cognition tradition. In this sense we argue for a relatively unitary ('single process') approach to stereotype formation. However, we propose that different (re)sources will form the basis of differentiation as we move through the degrees, with the evaluative dimension (the enhancement principle, 'creative distinctiveness') becoming progressively more important, as descriptive and reality-based differences ('reflective distinctiveness') become less possible.

1.   'Bottom up' stereotype formation: a case of clear
      and present differences

This section is concerned with stereotype formation based on available evidence of group properties and intergroup differences, without making or using any assumptions about group differences. This is probably the most straightforward case of stereotype formation, and what is perhaps most commonly understood to represent this process (and one that unites the 'information processing' approach of the social cognition tradition with the analysis of self-categorization theorists). There are many examples of this and the research is already well documented. Research by self-categorization theorists in which comparative fit, or meta-contrast is manipulated provide direct evidence of stereotyping based on the accentuation of intergroup difference and within groups similarities (Haslam et al., this volume; Oakes, Haslam & Turner, 1994). In this section we consider representative examples of stereotyping of groups to which the perceiver is not related, and then to groups in which they are implicated (ingroups and outgroups).

A clear example of the former is provided in a study by Ford and Stangor (1992) in which participants were presented with information about two groups that varied in friendliness and intelligence, although differences were varied so that they were greater on either the former or the latter dimension. Participants tended to form stereotypes on those dimensions corresponding to greater differences between groups presented in the data. When groups differed more clearly in terms of friendliness than intelligence, this dimension formed the basis of stereotyping. However, when groups differed in terms of intelligence and not friendliness this dimension formed the basis of stereotype formation. Reducing the variability on the stereotypic dimension within groups also increased stereotyping. These findings can be interpreted in terms of the meta-contrast principle: the dimensions that lead to greatest differentiation are the most diagnostic and form the basis for stereotypic differentiation (e.g., Turner, 1985; see also Rosch, 1978).

But what happens when people themselves are members of the groups involved? Self-enhancement principles and the evaluative dimension then become more important. The social identity principle that other things being equal, groups will prefer to see their own groups as positively distinct will come into play. Some studies conducted by Doosje, Spears and Koomen (1995) examined this possibility. These studies involved experimental groups created in the laboratory (labeled inductive and deductive thinkers) so that there were no prior expectations about what the groups were actually like. In these studies we provided perceivers with sample information about their own group and another group: behaviours performed by members of both groups. Specifically, we provided information that the groups differed from each other on the focal dimension of prosocial behaviour, with the ingroup more prosocial than the outgroup, or the outgroup more prosocial than the ingroup. Our prediction was that group members would form stereotypes that generally reflected these group differences, as reflected by their perceptions of the sample information, and also their generalizations to the sample population.

However, as well as respecting social reality, in line with predictions from social identity theory we expected group members to characterize their own group as positive where possible. Obviously this was more difficult in the conditions where the group was characterized in negative terms, because such stereotypes conflict with social reality (see also Spears, Jetten & Doosje, 2001). However, we also manipulated the reliability of the sample information in order to see whether perceivers were inclined to resist the information of negative ingroup stereotypes when the sample information was less constraining. In one study we altered the variability of the sample information, the idea being that homogeneous samples would provide clearer evidence of group differences than heterogeneous and overlapping samples. In another study we varied sample size, larger samples being more reliable than smaller samples. In both studies, there was evidence that participants correctly perceived the differences between the samples. Participants also tended to generalize the sample differences to the category populations when these were favourable to their own groups (ingroup being more prosocial than the outgroup) irrespective of the reliability of sample information. When the intergroup comparisons were unfavourable, however, although group differences were respected when these were reliable, for the less reliable feedback (heterogeneous or small samples), group members downplayed group differences, thereby avoiding a negative social identity (Doosje, Spears & Koomen, 1995; see also Spears, Jetten & Doosje, 2001).

In the studies addressed so far we have considered how aspects of the comparative fit in the data can facilitate stereotype formation and also provide a reality constraint on the enhancement principle. In developing the ideas of Bruner (1957a), Oakes (1987) argued that category salience would be a product of fit and category accessibility, or perceptual readiness to perceive the social stimulus in terms of the accessible categories and their associated stereotypes. Accessibility is somewhat less relevant than fit to the current concerns because it suggests prior stereotypic knowledge and thus stereotypes that are already formed. Various features of both person and context may increase the tendency to categorize independent of prior knowledge. These include aspects of the perceiver such as group identification, and also features of the context other than fit that make categories salient and meaningful. We have used the category confusion paradigm (Taylor et al., 1978) to show how both contextual and person-based factors can increase the impact of comparative fit, reinforcing the categorization processes that accentuate group stereotypes (Spears, Doosje & Ellemers, 1997, 1999). For example, in line with the meaning principle we found degree of categorization to increase when people were asked to form impression of the groups, rather than simply to remember the information (see Hamilton, Katz & Leirer, 1980), and also when category salience was intensified by requiring participants to distribute rewards to the two groups beforehand (see Leyens, Yzerbyt & Schadron, 1994). As predicted, these effects were further moderated by group identification, being generally stronger for high identifiers (Spears & Doosje, 1996; Spears et al., 1999).

To summarize, the evidence from studies in which people are presented with sample information is that this information is used as the basis of stereotypic differentiation between groups, especially when favourable to the ingroup. This is consistent with the related principles of comparative fit and meta-contrast elaborated in self-categorization theory. In general the greater and more clear-cut the group differences the more likely these will be used as a basis for stereotype formation, consistent with the view that they provide a meaningful basis to interpret social reality. This point is important because this theoretical legacy of Bruner's work on categorization processes has not always incorporated this aspect of differentiation. In particular his work has been developed by social cognition researchers in terms of knowledge accessibility and applicability (Higgins, 1996, see also McGarty, 1999), which relate closely to the stereotype activation and application processes discussed earlier. Although the accessibility component seems similar to the self-categorization interpretation of Bruner's ideas, there are important differences between the notion of applicability and fit. Specifically, stereotype applicability lacks the comparative differentiation of comparative fit, and simply refers to the overlap between stored features (stereotypic knowledge) and the attended stimulus features (Higgins, 1996). Recent research by Wegener and Klauer (2000) has attempted to contrast these two interpretations of Bruner's work by assessing whether fit or applicability better predicted memory for category membership in the category confusion paradigm. It turned out that fit was the better predictor of category salience and use, supporting the view that contrastive comparisons between categories are important for category-based effects such as stereotyping. Once again this suggests the importance of a category differentiation process as a basis of stereotype formation.

There is an important theoretical caveat to add to this story, however. Although it is true that the greater the distance or difference between groups the greater the average meta-contrast, an interesting phenomenon occurs when groups become progressively similar (and get closer) on a given comparison dimension. The closer two groups become, the more that extreme positions far away from the comparison outgroup become (relatively) prototypical (see Spears, Jetten & Scheepers, 2002, for a more detailed exposition of this analysis). In other words although the absolute level of meta-contrast reduces as groups become more similar, the tendency to differentiate does not recede, but even intensifies, as indicated by the relative shift in prototypicality. This theoretical point helps to resolve an apparent contradiction between social identity theory and self-categorization theory. Whereas SIT has emphasized the fact that group similarity can increase differentiation (because of threats to group distinctiveness), SCT has typically been taken to emphasize group difference as a basis for category salience and stereotyping (Oakes, 1987). On the basis of the present analysis SCT is also able to accommodate differentiation pressure based on group similarity, however. This point also suggests that groups may not need to differ very much before differences can provide a basis for intergroup differentiation and stereotype formation. Thus a lack of clear difference may actually intensify differentiation for perceptual (SCT) as well as motivational (SIT) reasons (see Spears, Jetten & Scheepers, 2002). We now consider the case for stereotype formation on the basis of more subtle or inferred differences.

2.   A bit of 'bottom up': a little data can go a long way

In this section we consider cases where some basis for the derivation of group stereotypes may be found in the data, but this is subtle, or has to be inferred in the comparative context. Once again we begin by considering a case where the perceiver is not actually implicated in the groups (the illusory correlation paradigm) followed by an example involving ingroups and outgroups.

The illusory correlation paradigm offers an ideal paradigm to consider the formation of stereotype beliefs in the absence of obvious prior group differences (see also Berndsen et al., this volume for a more detailed treatment). Indeed this paradigm is traditionally considered as one where there are *no* differences presented between the groups, although as we shall see, there is some controversy about this claim which is why we consider this research in the present section and not the previous one. In order to explain this we need to outline the basic paradigm as developed by Hamilton and Gifford (1976). In the typical experiment participants are presented with a series of behaviours performed by people from two groups (A and B), in which a higher proportion of behaviours derive from one group (usually A, the majority group). Moreover, the distribution of behaviours is also skewed such that a majority of behaviours are usually positive. Importantly, the proportion of positive to negative behaviours is identical in both groups (usually about 2:1), although the absolute number of behaviours differs due to the greater prevalence of Group A. On the basis of proportions, then, it is possible to argue that there is no difference between these groups in terms of the evaluative proportion of positive to negative behaviours.

Despite the absence of apparent group differences, a consistent and robust finding of this paradigm is that the less prevalent group tends to be perceived in more negative terms. The original explanation for this effect proposed by Hamilton and Gifford (1976), was in terms of the greater distinctiveness of the most infrequent combination (negative behaviours in Group B), which are consequently most accessible in memory, and subsequently influence groups judgements in line with the availability heuristic (see also McConnell, Sherman & Hamilton, 1994a, for a modified distinctiveness account). Other approaches have also provided explanations that are also based on biased memory processes, but argue that the distribution frequencies provide more reliable evidence that *information about Group A* is better encoded in memory and thus that A is more positive (Fiedler, 1991; Smith, 1991). For example, Fiedler, Russer and Gramm (1993) showed that memory for infrequent events is actually poorer than memory for frequent events, contra the paired distinctiveness account. This line of explanation has received further support with evidence that stereotypic expectations are more likely to take root in larger more prevalent groups (in line with 'the law of large numbers'), compared to smaller more distinctive groups as, might be predicted by paired distinctiveness processes (Van Knippenberg & Spears, 2001).

Another class of explanation proposed by self-categorization theorists (McGarty, Haslam, Turner & Oakes, 1993) fits closely with the categorical differentiation theme that runs through the present chapter (see also Berndsen et al., this volume). This explanation has important features in common with the alternative memory explanations, in so far as it also proposes that the information presented in the skewed frequency distinctions provides a firmer basis to draw the conclusion that A is a more positive group than B. However, this line of explanation does not rely on memory processes. Rather it proposes a judgement process based on meaningful categorical differentiation on the evaluative dimension, reflecting actual differences that are present in the stimuli. This relies on the fact that people take into account the absolute quantity of evidence for the contrasting hypotheses that Group A is more positive (and B more negative) or vice versa. For example, in the classic distribution used by Hamilton and Gifford (1976: $A+ = 18, A- = 8; B+ = 9, B- = 4$), there is actually more evidence supporting the hypothesis that A is the positive group and B the more negative one ($18 + 4 = 22$) than for the alternative hypothesis that B is positive and A negative ($9 + 8 = 17$; McGarty et al., 1993). An important feature of this account is that it focuses on the importance of evaluation and meaning in differentiating between the groups, whereas the cognitive information processing accounts make few assumptions about the status of information involved in terms of meaning or valence.

There is now increasing evidence to support this evaluative category differentiation explanation of the illusory correlation effect (Berndsen, Spears, McGarty & Van der Pligt, 1998; Haslam, McGarty & Brown, 1996; McGarty & De la Haye, 1997; McGarty, Haslam, Turner & Oakes, 1993; Van Knippenberg & Spears, 2001; Yzerybt & Rocher, this volume). A study by Berndsen, Van der Pligt and Spears (1994) provided some evidence that illusory correlation only occurs when the attribute dimension is based on evaluative and not descriptive distinctions, in line with the differentiated meaning view that perceivers seek to distinguish the groups according to evaluative criteria (see Berndsen et al., this volume). Recent work by Klauer and Meiser, (2000) has given this explanation a further boost. These researchers employed a source monitoring technique in which they supplemented the items used in the illusory correlation task with distracter items at the recall phase in order to distinguish between memory biases and response bias. They showed that the illusory correlation effect was not attributable to differential memory for items or group membership, but resulted from a response bias. A further study (Study 4) caused even more fundamental problems for the memory-based accounts. In this study Klauer and Meiser substituted gender (male vs. female) for the evaluative dimension: instead of presenting positive and negative behaviours, behaviours were performed by either males or females emanating from Group A and B. In this study, there was no evidence of illusory correlation, whereas illusory correlation was replicated when valence rather than gender was used as in the standard paradigm. This study suggests that evaluative differentiation, and not just a cognitive process associated with infrequency, is crucial to the illusory correlation effect. This is in keeping with the differentiated meaning analysis.

One potential problem remains for the differentiated meaning explanation of the illusory correlation effect, however. A critical finding of the illusory correlation literature is that evaluative illusory correlation seems to occur for group targets, but not when the two targets are individual persons (i.e., people read behaviours performed by two individuals). The standard explanation for this is that whereas groups tend to evoke memory biased processing it is argued that perceivers tend to form impressions of individuals 'on-line' building up an impression piece-by-piece (Sanbonmatsu, Sherman & Hamilton, 1987). The rationale is that, assuming that groups are more heterogeneous than individuals, there is a lower expectation of coherence for groups, so that impressions are deferred until all the information is in. Given that people tend to have superior recall for information under impression than memory set conditions (Hamilton et al., 1980), this should give a memory advantage to person compared to group targets, attenuating or eliminating the memory bias (McConnell, Sherman & Hamilton, 1994b; Pryor, 1986; Sanbonmatsu et al., 1987).

How then do we make sense of the difference for personal and group targets? One alternative explanation for the person/group target effect that fits with the differentiated meaning account, is that whereas it may be relatively natural to seek evaluative differentiation between groups, it may be less natural to differentiate evaluatively between individuals. A central theme of this chapter is that the evaluative dimension is central to intergroup differentiation. This tendency may also be true of situations where the self is not directly implicated (although the possibility that the perceiver could be a member of one of the categories is rarely explicitly ruled out in most illusory correlation studies). Research on the person-group discontinuity confirms that the evaluative and affective dimension may be stronger or more relevant for groups than individuals (e.g., Schopler & Insko, 1992).

Although we know of no direct test of this analysis in the illusory correlation paradigm, some of the published research that compares group versus person targets can be interpreted in this light. For example, the study conducted by Fiedler, Russer and Gramm (1993) provided an encoding manipulation that required participants to keep a running tally of whether or not the behaviours contributed to a positive or negative impression of the person/group, contrasted with the standard memory instruction (control). This instruction was intended as a memory load manipulation, designed to undermine on-line impression formation, increase reliance on memory, and therefore produce illusory correlation in the person target condition (illusory correlation was already expected for group targets). As predicted, illusory correlation was lowest for person targets under standard conditions, but increased to levels similar to what was found for group targets with valence monitoring. This effect was interpreted as evidence that the extra load had interfered with on-line processing enhancing reliance on memory. However, the forced focus on the evaluative dimension may also have made this dimension particularly important, leading participants to differentiate evaluatively between the person targets on this dimension. This interpretation seems more plausible than the argument that on-line impression formation was disrupted, because the very task demanded on-line impression formation about the two targets, on the central dimension (evaluation). This interpretation in terms of evaluative contrast also fits better with the evidence that evaluative differentiation seems to be crucial to the illusory correlation effect

(Berndsen et al., 1994; Klauer & Meiser, 2000; McGarty & De la Haye, 1997).

To summarize, there is growing evidence that real evaluative differences available in the stimuli may help to explain the illusory correlation effect, and thus be a source of group differentiation and stereotype formation in the face of disputable group differences. The subtlety of the differences certainly seems to be no barrier to the emergence of perceived group differences. It is important to note that the evaluative dimension seems to be crucial here. Although illusory correlation has been found for other dimensions such as attitudes rather than evaluative behaviours (e.g., Spears, Van der Pligt & Eiser, 1985; 1986) the evaluative dimension was clearly relevant in these contexts too (especially to those with strong attitudes) and attitude intensity played a role in the resulting differentiation. Moreover, although the self is not typically implicated in the illusory correlation paradigm, when it is the evaluative dimension becomes even more critical in so far as ingroup bias then overrides the effect (see Schaller & Maass, 1989).

We now turn to a paradigm where the self is implicated (through ingroup membership) but the database for stereotypic differentiation is equally subtle and even more indirect. Sometimes we only become aware of the stereotype of a group with reference to 'what it is not', by comparing it to a comparison standard or a relevant comparison group. In this section we illustrate this point by drawing on our research on so called 'automatic behaviour' which involves activating a knowledge associated with a particular target group. In this case we are concerned with how activated knowledge 'stereotypic' of the outgroup might affect the perception and behaviour of one's own group (the process of self- and ingroup stereotyping). We use the term 'stereotypic' advisedly here because for many cases of the research described below the features linked to the outgroup had no prior stereotypic basis, avoiding effects of prior expectations (see section 3 below) for either outgroup or ingroup.

This line of research conveniently illustrates the difference between the two realms represented by the social cognition and social identity traditions, and their contrasting implications for the stereotyping process. A good example of the effects of stereotypes producing pure knowledge activation without implicating the social self is provided in a classic study on automatic behaviour by Bargh, Chen and Burrows (1996). In one of these studies, Bargh et al. activated the stereotype of the elderly by means of a task in which participants had to make grammatical sentences out of scrambled ones, and in which words associated with the elderly were embedded (grey, traditional, forgetful, etc). Crucially, none of the words related to the more sedentary activity levels associated with the elderly stereotype. After completing this test, participants thought the experiment was over and left the room. However, an experimenter surreptitiously measured the time it took them to walk a length of corridor. Those who had been primed with the elderly stereotype (as opposed to a neutral prime) actually walked away more slowly. Bargh and colleagues viewed this as evidence that behaviour can be automatically triggered by activated knowledge structures, in this case a stereotype: 'We see and we do.'

We can see this effect as akin to an assimilation effect: we soak up information in the environment and act in line with that information (Bargh and others have also called this a 'chameleon' effect). The students appear to adopt the stereotype of the elderly and, at least momentarily, make it their own. Indeed, readers may legitimately question whether this behaviour actually reflects the operation of a (self) stereotype in a fuller sense of the word used throughout this book (e.g., as conscious and consensual characterizations of group level properties that reflect justification, explanation, essence and so forth). We share this scepticism and acknowledge that we are using this term here in its most minimal sense of simply reflecting an (albeit unconscious) representation of a group, which in this case influences behaviour. In this case we might more accurately talk of a 'stereotypical depiction' (see McGarty, Chapter 2) – and an ephemeral and atypical one at that – in the sense that this behavioural tendency is unlikely to be internalized or become a conscious feature of the groups' self-stereotype.

Indeed one reason to question the status of this automatic behaviour as reflecting the operation of a (self) stereotype in a stronger sense is that it would seem to contradict everything we know about stereotypes of the young as (for the most part) lively and active. From the perspective of more intergroup approaches to stereotyping this effect is somewhat bizarre. Research in the social identity and self-categorization tradition, shows that groups tend to differentiate themselves from outgroups. It would be plausible to assume that if the youthful students participating in Bargh et al.'s study were asked, they would not define themselves in terms of the elderly stereotype. However, taking this minimalist approach allows us to pose the question of when group perceptions (or behavioural tendencies) *become* stereotypic and of course, in line with arguments throughout this book, the role of more social processes is central to turning mere depictions into the socially shared images that are stereotypes.

Indeed, we argue that there is one important social process that is missing from such examples of automatic behaviour that arguably prevents them becoming social stereotypes: namely a social comparison process. We would argue that for differentiating contrast to occur in this kind of paradigm, some sort of (intergroup) social comparison process is necessary that either implicitly or explicitly contrasts one's own group from the outgroup and its stereotype. In further research using this paradigm we have shown that activating an individual exemplar associated with the stereotype can stimulate the comparison process that produces contrast (Dijksterhuis, Spears et al., 1998). Priming people with the elderly stereotype, but coupled with the elderly Dutch Queen mother, led them to walk away more quickly than controls (a contrast effect). The idea here is that a concrete exemplar is likely to evoke a spontaneous comparison between the individual and the self (Gilbert, Giesler & Morris, 1995), in this case causing a contrast effect. In contrast, simply activating a general stereotype without an exemplar provides an interpretative framework that colours judgement and produces assimilation (Stapel, Koomen & van der Pligt, 1997).

Whereas simple knowledge of a stereotype does not necessarily evoke a spontaneous comparison process, then, we reasoned that this would be much more likely when this was activated in an intergroup context, or at least where an intergroup comparison is made salient. To examine this we conducted a number of studies where we have primed participants with an outgroup stereotype, in which we either did or did not make the intergroup comparison salient (Spears et al., 2000). In many of these cases (and unlike the elderly-slow, young-fast example) the content of the *ingroup* stereotype cannot be assumed a priori from prior knowledge. Rather this stereotype only makes sense as a means of contrasting one's own group away from the outgroup. For example, in one study we presented participants with a supposed creativity test which involved colouring in pictures. We told participants that, in order to get a reliable measure of creativity, we need to assess their choice of colour combinations twice, separated by a filler task. The filler task actually contained a priming manipulation (a scrambled sentence test). The scrambled sentences were described as being composed by either psychology (ingroup) or economic students (outgroup), in order to assess whether sentences made by one's own group were easier to solve by their own group. After solving the sentences, participants indicated their own study major, and that of the researchers composing the test. In this context we aimed to make the group identity and the intergroup comparison salient. Crucially, we primed the construct 'neatness' in the sentences and coupled this (or synonyms) with the group responsible for the sentences in their sentences.

The dependent measure of automatic behaviour in this study was the degree to which participants slipped over the lines of the second drawing they were required to colour in (providing a measure of neatness). We predicted that, when primed with the 'neat outgroup' (Economics students) respondents would automatically contrast their behaviour, and become more messy in their colouring behaviour. This is what we found.

In this case, making ingroup identity and the intergroup context more salient led to an automatic behavioural contrast effect (one might also expect more neatness in the ingroup stereotype condition – an assimilation effect – although we found no support for this; however the nature of our paradigm provided more scope to become messy in the colouring as opposed to neater than baseline). In order to explain this we have to assume that respondents wanted to differentiate themselves from the outgroup on the dimension made salient in the study. They constructed a 'messy' (or non-neat) ingroup stereotype and conformed to this in their behaviour.

In further studies, we showed that making the intergroup comparison salient, and thereby activating a 'we-they' comparison is crucial. In the absence of this comparison, simple stereotype activation, and even assimilation effects can occur, as the research of Bargh et al. had suggested. For example, in another study we primed Dutch students with a stereotype of Germans as being brusque, or as being polite. These were manipulated in a scenario describing German students visiting Amsterdam. The dependent measure here was how long it took participants to request their credit slip from an experimenter who was deep in conversation with another experimenter. In this case assimilation occurred: those primed with the rude stereotype interrupted more quickly than those primed with the polite stereotype. This can be explained as a straightforward knowledge activation effect impacting on behaviour. Although one might expect the Dutch students to differentiate themselves from the Germans (which they probably would have done if the behaviour was conscious) because the intergroup comparison was not made salient in this study no intergroup comparison occurred and no contrast resulted.

In a further study we demonstrated evidence of assimilation turning to contrast within the same participants. We primed participants with the stereotype of 'business people' in which the busy lives of a group of business people were described in the priming text. Participants in a control condition received a different text, neutral with respect to this stereotype. We then measured the time it took for respondents to fill out some general questions after reading this text. In line with the knowledge activation prediction, respondents were marginally quicker in completing these questions than controls (an assimilation effect). At this point in the study the experimenter entered the room, collected the completed questionnaire, and handed out a final questionnaire. This contained items measuring identification with study major (Psychology students). The experimenter then stated that he would return shortly to collect this questionnaire, and administer the course credit for participation, adding that they could be found in a designated room if this took too long. The dependent measure was the time it took before participants went looking for the experimenter (who never returned). Here we predicted a contrast effect, namely that those in the 'business stereotype' condition would actually wait longer after completing the psychology student identification measure. The idea here was that making group identity salient would trigger an intergroup comparison ('we psychology students are unlike business types'). As predicted, the very same respondents who had filled in the earlier measure more quickly, now waited reliably longer before setting off to find the experimenter.

These studies tell us something about the possibility of automatic behaviour. However, they also tell us something about spontaneous stereotype formation. What is the stereotype of a psychology student? Are they generally messy, impolite and slow? Although some of us may be tempted to say yes, these traits were not selected a priori as being prototypical of this group. Rather we would argue that these properties only make sense in the local contexts devised in our studies, where the comparison outgroups were defined in contrasting terms. Indeed, in one study psychology students demonstrated themselves to be either polite or impolite, assimilating their behaviour to the manipulated stereotype of Germans. In another they were both faster *and* slower depending on whether or not they assimilated themselves to or contrasted their group from the busy business people. In short, rather than tapping into some pre-existing knowledge of the ingroup, these self-stereotypes seem to have been constructed on-line, as a result of a social comparison. Psychology students are not messy, slow or quick by nature, but they can become so in the appropriate context. In this sense we have demonstrated some evidence for spontaneous self-stereotype formation, rather than mere knowledge activation.

A sceptic might reasonably ponder whether the contrast effects reflect stereotyping (or indeed stereotype formation), as opposed to simply the momentary products of priming. But what makes a stereotype? We are not claiming here that these self-perceptions and their accompanying behaviours reflect longstanding or even very meaningful stereotypes, but then again it is not necessary to see stereotypes as longstanding and stable images (Oakes, Haslam & Turner, 1994; Spears, Oakes, Ellemers & Haslam, 1997). Although, as we have claimed, it is certainly true that these would qualify more as stereotypes when they become conscious and shared (e.g., Haslam, 1997; see Haslam et al., this volume), if group difference is the essence of the stereotype (as we argue) then we have identified one possible mechanism of stereotype formation. Indeed if we top up automatic behavioural contrast with self-perception processes (Bem, 1967) and the potential to internalize one's behaviour, then under certain conditions such behaviour may well lead to more fully fledged self-stereotypes.

We suspect that other features of the group context, some much more conscious, will serve to feed and build the stereotyping process based on comparative differentiation. Automatic assimilation to an outgroup on the other hand may quickly become overridden and contradicted, especially when these conflict with other aspects of ingroup (or outgroup) knowledge. However, the deeper theoretical question remains of whether it is even possible to consider assimilation effects based on knowledge activation as examples of (spontaneous) 'self-stereotyping' in quite the same way as the contrast effects (which implicate a social comparison process). We would argue that there is a qualitative difference here, in the sense that comparison-based contrast is intrinsically related to the intergroup context, whereas assimilation based on mere knowledge activation is not. Therefore we are tempted to say that comparative contrast in these studies reflects a more social self-stereotyping process, whereas the assimilation effects reflect a less social priming process. This point speaks to the difference between the two realms of social *cognition* (knowledge activation/application) and *social* cognition implicating self and social comparison.

The research from the two paradigms studied in this section demonstrates that a little data can often go a long way, and enable us to go beyond the data in our stereotypic inferences. In the illusory correlation paradigm, the group differences in the data are sufficiently subtle that it is only recently that researchers have recognized these differences at all. However, the evidence seems to be that people do use the real evaluative differences between the groups as a basis for evaluative differentiation, and the evaluative dimension of differentiation seems to be critical. The evaluative dimension is also crucial to contexts that implicate perceivers as group members, in the sense that they try to distance themselves from outgroup attributes. The research on automatic behaviour shows the ingroup stereotypes (or at least depictions of the ingroup) can be generated on the basis of knowledge of outgroup stereotypes or attributes. Stereotypes of unknown outgroups may often be generated in much the same way in contrast to knowledge of the *ingroup*. Once again the content of these stereotypes is likely to be informed by what we know about our own group, and will likely be (evaluatively) differentiated away from group attributes on relevant comparison dimensions. We now consider the case where we have some familiarity with both of the groups being compared and perhaps some limited knowledge of them, but as yet no specific stereotype relating the two.

3.   A bit of 'top down': a little knowledge goes just as far

Clearly when perceivers already have knowledge of the target groups concerned it makes little sense to talk of stereotype formation. However, in this section we consider the case where people have *some* knowledge of the groups, which allows stereotypes to be constructed in context. Even when people have minimal knowledge this may often allow them to 'go beyond the information given' (Bruner, 1957b) and form coherent stereotypes of the groups in question. This knowledge can come from different sources, from outside of the groups (background knowledge) or from mere category labels that allow and even encourage further inferences to be made. We consider an example of both of these possibilities from our own research, referring to naturally occurring and more minimal group settings respectively.

Although some groups may have well established stereotypes associated with them, for many other groups stereotypes have to be worked out in relation to specific intergroup comparisons. For example, what is the stereotype of a psychology student, our most familiar participant population? The answer to this seems to depend on a number of factors, including the comparative context. We can often rely on prior knowledge to inform these judgements, but this knowledge is not always declarative knowledge of the content of group stereotypes. It may involve meta-knowledge of what is an appropriate dimension to distinguish between the groups (in line with social identity arguments this can implicate social creativity strategies; see Tajfel & Turner, 1986). This may involve 'background knowledge' or theories about the nature of the categories (Brown & Turner, this volume, McGarty, this volume; Yzerbyt & Rocher, this volume; see also McGarty, 1999). It may involve knowledge of comparative and normative fit which varies according to the two groups involved (ingroup and outgroup).

So, to return to our example of psychology students, we may generate certain features of psychology students, but almost any stereotypic attribute could be reversed depending on the context. For example are they studious and hard-working, or sociable and party-loving (Doosje, Ellemers & Spears, 1999; Reicher, Spears & Postmes, 1995)? Identities and stereotypes may often be 'contradictory' in this regard: they may be both. Note that this is not just a matter of the group consisting of different 'subtypes'; the *same* psychology students may define themselves as studious *and/or* party-loving depending on the context. One defining attribute could be said to be that they study psychology. However, even this information may not be very diagnostic, especially when one group of psychology students (e.g., from one university) is compared with another.

In such cases we have to seek other dimensions of differentiation that have much less to do with psychology (Jetten, Spears & Manstead, 1998; Spears, Doosje & Ellemers, 1999; Van Rijswijk & Ellemers, 2000).

To illustrate some of these issues consider a study by Spears and Manstead (1989; Study 1). In this study we investigated the stereotypes of students at two universities in the UK about each other: Manchester and Exeter. Now although people may have stereotypes of students, these would presumably be of little use in distinguishing these groups. Secondly, we thought it quite unlikely that these students had preestablished stereotypes about the stereotypes of students at these universities, at least *in relation to each other*. Although they may have developed ingroup stereotypes based on their familiarity and experience with the ingroup, they were unlikely to have thought in any depth about the specific stereotype of the outgroup, or how the two groups might differ (this would imply that they had given *prior* consideration to the stereotypes of the 150+ universities in the UK). Moreover, many of the students involved had probably not even been to the other city, still less met students from the other university. However, we expected that people would be able to generate stereotypes of the groups in relation to each other on the basis of background knowledge and theories associated with the universities, and the places in which they are located.

As expected, clear stereotypes emerged that many people familiar with the UK and its academic scene could probably generate. Here we are assuming that participants are drawing as much on their general knowledge about North and South, and the cities in which these universities are located, to generate the more specific stereotypes of the university students at these locations, rather than relying on preformed stereotypes of these groups. In a 'complete design' students from both Exeter and Manchester rated students from Exeter as more articulate, self-assured and high achievers, whereas Manchester students were rated as being more politically aware, aware of music and fashion, practically minded and easygoing. In short there seemed to be some stereotypic consensus about the two groups. It seems likely that these stereotypes were generated from knowledge of these different cities or university milieus, with richer and more academically oriented students going to Exeter, and with Manchester representing a more socially lively and politically progressive environment in the more industrial North.

Of course we cannot rule out that students went around with an idea in their head about what the ingroup or the outgroup was. However, in a related study we showed that the ingroup stereotype was not fixed and stable but varied considerably depending on the outgroup(s) in the frame of reference (e.g., Oxford University, Manchester Polytechnic). In the presence of comparisons with Manchester Polytechnic, Manchester University students now rated themselves as high achievers and the Polytechnic students as more politically aware and practically minded. The point is that this stereotypic knowledge is highly contextually variable, but can be quite easily generated with a degree of consensus, depending on knowledge of the groups and their context (see also Diab, 1963; Haslam et al., 1992). The lesson of this research is that stereotypes are not fixed properties of groups (even though they may often be experienced as such; see Hegarty & Pratto, 2001; Yzerbyt & Rocher, this volume), but relational constructs that allow us to differentiate different groups. This is not to deny that we often have some basic stereotypic knowledge of groups or that we may come to see whatever stereotypic knowledge is being generated in context as linked to essential differences between groups (for a presentation of a subjective essentialistic view of stereotypes: see Yzerbyt & Rocher, this volume; Yzerbyt, Rocher & Schadron, 1997). Our point is simply that the groups in question determine what knowledge and which dimensions will be brought to bear in situ. In this sense it is appropriate to talk about the construction, or even formation of stereotypes on-line.

We now address another more experimentally controlled example to demonstrate how minimal prior knowledge of groups can be used to generate stereotypic group differences. One key paradigm normally used to eliminate knowledge or expectations associated with groups is the 'minimal group paradigm.' Normally within this paradigm people are given no information at all about the groups. However, some information about group differences often sneaks in through the back door. We argue that participants often cling onto these subtle differences in an attempt to make sense of the situation and to differentiate between the groups (Bless, Strack & Schwarz, 1993). We address the case of completely minimal groups, where there is no information to go on, in the next section. In the meantime we consider here what might be termed quasi-minimal groups in which ostensibly trivial details can be used and magnified to feed categorical differentiation.

In the minimal group paradigm, participants are categorized on the basis of a fairly trivial or even arbitrary criterion, such as preference for a painter (Tajfel et al., 1971), or in terms of whether people tend to overestimate or underestimate dots or shapes (e.g., Gerard & Hoyt, 1974; Jetten, Spears & Manstead, 1996). Participants are allocated at random to the two groups, so this actual choice or estimation is irrelevant. Quite often, however, in an attempt to make the task more meaningful to participants, the cover story describes the groups in terms of some ostensibly more significant distinction, albeit one that is actually bogus. Examples of these 'experimental' categories are 'synthetic' versus 'analytic' perceivers

(Ellemers, Doosje, Van Knippenberg & Wilke, 1992), 'deductive' versus 'inductive' thinkers (Doosje, Spears & Koomen, 1995) and 'global' versus 'detailed' perceivers (Jetten, Spears & Manstead, 1996; Spears & Oyen, 1992). These categories are often contentless in the sense that the scope for filling them in is deliberately restricted to what the experimenter tells the participants in the cover story. However, this does not necessarily stop the participants from trying to imbue them with differentiated meaning, and going beyond the information given. Such meaning can also provide participants with a rationale or justification for differentiation (Leyens, Yzerbyt & Schadron, 1992).

A number of chapters in this volume have considered the theories and expectations, and background knowledge people use to make sense of group differences (see e.g., Brown & Turner, this volume; McGarty, this volume). These theories and the knowledge and expectations that people bring to bear are particularly important in those sparse intergroup contexts involving quasi-minimal groups. In a study by Spears and Oyen (1992) we obtained clear evidence that people were able to engage in meaningful stereotypic differentiation in such groups. In this study people were categorized as underestimators and overestimators, ostensibly on the basis of frequency estimates. In addition, underestimators were described in the cover story as being 'detailed perceivers' and overestimators as 'global perceivers.' No more information was given about the meaning of these terms. We had pretested a number of terms for associations with these categories and we constructed bipolar scales with poles representing a more 'detailed' and a more 'global' association (balanced for valence; examples of bipolar labels that correspond to the detailed/global distinction on the basis of pretesting are respectively: introverted/extroverted, shortsighted/visionary, accurate/sloppy, cautious/decisive, organized/chaotic, etc). After completing the Tajfel reward allocation matrices participants then completed the stereotypic ratings of the two groups on these series of bipolar scales.

This study also contained additional manipulations (designed to depersonalize perception and create group norms relating to allocation behaviour) but which are peripheral to the present focus. Although we found evidence for ingroup bias on the reward allocations, the interesting finding with regard to stereotype formation concerns the clear effects on the stereotyping measure where there was a strong and consistent effect of target group. Members of both groups tended to characterize the two groups in terms stereotypically associated with the category (averaged deviations from the midpoint of the 100mm scale were around ten points for both groups on the stereotypic side). In other words people do seem able and inclined to differentiate on the basis of ostensibly trivial categorical differences. Recall that we never told people that the stereotypic labels were associated with detailed or global perceivers. Apparently participants used their naïve (or perhaps more sophisticated) theories to infer these differences, and to imbue the groups with meaning and a distinctive identity. A critic might argue that this simply reflects the demand characteristics of the situation, but this is also partly our point. When there is little basis to go on, people latch onto what little there is in order to differentiate the groups, especially when this can be construed as justifying differentiation (Leyens et al., 1992).

In the examples provided above we focused on the descriptive differences between groups that were focused on. These were dimensions that generally maximize differentiation (fit, meta-contrast, group distinctiveness). However, stereotyping often involves evaluative differentiation too. Social identity principles suggest that particularly when people are able to differentiate in multiple ways on multiple dimensions, other things being equal they will tend to choose those that cast their own groups in a positive light (the enhancement principle). Returning to the well worn example of psychology students: if we take physics students as our comparison group it is possible to differentiate them on dimensions of analytic intelligence, and creativity (Spears, Doosje & Ellemers, 1997, Study 2). Other things being equal we would expect psychology students to emphasize the dimensions of creativity as part of their ingroup stereotype rather than intelligence, as the former not only differentiates but also casts them in more positive terms. Conversely, when the comparison group is art school students the position is reversed, with psychology students likely to emphasize the dimension of intelligence that now positively differentiates. A number of social identity studies provide evidence for this social creativity strategy, as reflected in the importance ascribed to positively differentiating characteristics (e.g., Doosje, Ellemers & Spears, 1995; Mussweiler, Gabriel & Bodenhausen, 2000). Self-enhancement or positive differentiation is not everything, and can sometimes be overridden by the need to differentiate one's group even at the cost of a positive ingroup image (the distinctiveness principle: Spears, Jetten & Scheepers, 2002). For those who value the group, distinctiveness can sometimes be as important, if not more so, than enhancement.

To summarize, the two empirical examples in this section, like the previous one, show how adept people can be in generating stereotypes from minimal information. This ability also belies the notion that stereotypes reflect stored knowledge that is directly tagged to groups in a fixed way. Indeed, such representations would often be inefficient for many groups whose comparative context can vary so much. To return to our question of whether the stereotype of psychology students is that they are intelligent or creative, studious or party-loving; this seems to depend on the context of comparison. We can generate stereotypic differentiation from the bits and pieces of knowledge we have of the groups (where they come from, their history, etc) and this knowledge helps us to construct differences between groups even when we do not have direct data about these differences. We seem able to generate these from theories and expectations (normative fit), and more general background knowledge. This knowledge provides a grounding in social reality that, if not directly 'on stage' and in the data, is 'waiting in the wings' so to speak. People also seemed quite capable of forming relatively rich stereotypes on the basis of a mere group label. We now go one step further and consider the case where there is not even a minimal basis for divining stereotypic differences; the truly minimal group paradigm.

4.   *Neither up nor down: differentiation by any means necessary*

Until now we have been considering situations where there is some substantive basis (albeit sometimes meagre), on which to differentiate between groups, whether in theory, on the basis of expectations, or grounded in the actual data. What happens when we have groups where there is no apparent basis on which to differentiate the groups either in terms of prior stereotypic expectations or in the data? One obvious response to this situation that is consistent with self-categorization principles is that it simply does not provide a basis for category differentiation (either in terms of comparative or normative fit), undermining the very salience of the group distinction. A lack of group difference may promote self and social categorization at more interpersonal or more intergroup levels (Gaertner et al., 1993; Turner et al., 1987). Does this mean that groups with no apparent differences will not be differentiated? Not necessarily. In fact the similarity between groups can *stimulate* the need to differentiate between them for reasons of both enhancement and distinctiveness (Jetten, Spears & Manstead, 1999; Spears, Jetten & Doosje, 2002; Tajfel, 1982). However, within social identity theory threats to distinctiveness usually refer to groups where there is an already established group identity and ingroup stereotype. Here we refer to the case where group identities are not yet formed and where an ingroup identity that is distinctive from the comparison group has to be created. We refer to the tendency to create group distinctiveness by whatever means necessary where it does not yet exist as 'creative distinctiveness' (Spears, Jetten & Doosje, 2002). What determines whether people reject the group level of self-categorization for more fitting alternatives, or decide to persevere with group differentiation? Degree of group identification is likely to be a critical factor that moderates between these two courses of action (Jetten, Spears & Manstead, 1999).

The problem with seeking to differentiate when there are no differences is obvious: stereotypic differentiation has no basis or seed. In these circumstances groups are forced to resort to the evaluative differentiation. We have already seen a hint of this in the minimal group study discussed in the last section (Spears & Oyen, 1992). In this study participants actually showed clearest ingroup bias in the depersonalized condition where there was no normative feedback about reward allocations of other group members – in other words where group salience was high but there was least meaning to group identity. It is part of our argument that in situations of minimal group differences such as the minimal group paradigm people will try to differentiate precisely in order to gain a meaningful and distinctive identity. However, as we argued above, the group in this study was actually 'quasi-minimal' in that participants did have some differences to go on relating to the group label. They were apparently able to translate the global and detailed perceivers into meaningful group differences when given the opportunity to express this on the stereotypic scales.

We now present a series of experiments where these avenues to 'creative distinctiveness' are even more limited. We predict that when the chance to differentiate meaningfully between groups is restricted, that people will try to do this by evaluative differentiation on reward allocation measures or in terms of direct evaluations of the groups or their products. In the first two studies (Scheepers, Spears, Doosje & Manstead, 2000) we set this creative distinctiveness motive in contrast to more instrumental motives for group differentiation where ingroup bias might function to help the group to achieve group goals. In these studies we categorized people ostensibly on the basis of preference for painters (but actually at random) and defined the resulting groups as analytic versus synthetic perceivers. We considered this distinction to be somewhat less meaningful (or at least less interpretable) than the detailed/global criterion used previously. In the first study we simply required group members to rate products (abstract paintings) made by previous groups distinguished in terms of the same category membership. After creating their own group product in the experiment we required them to rate ingroup and outgroup products once more. However, half the participants were told that groups were involved in a competition in which that with the best product would compete for a prize. This introduced an instrumental element: preferring their own group would be consistent with the goal of gaining the group prize.

In line with predictions we found that participants in both conditions differentiated in favour of their groups at the first phase. However, only the condition that was given a subsequent competitive group goal reliably preferred ingroup products when these were rated at the later phase: the group without a goal actually no longer showed ingroup bias. This effect for the competitive goal condition makes sense in terms of more instrumental explanations of ingroup bias (realistic conflict theory, interdependence explanations). What is interesting for us here is that both groups differentiated before a material goal was introduced, and that the differentiation disappeared when this goal was not present, when a renewed opportunity for differentiation arose. We interpreted this as evidence that ingroup bias was serving a differentiation function ('creative distinctiveness'), and that once this motive had been satisfied further differentiation was not necessary (see Spears, Jetten & Scheepers, 2002, for further evidence of the motivated nature of intergroup differentiation when distinctiveness is threatened).

A further study in which we manipulated the prior opportunity to differentiate by means of ingroup bias (and thus gain group distinctiveness) provided further evidence for this interpretation. In this design, as well as manipulating prior differentiation opportunity (present vs. absent) we again manipulated the presence of a group goal. In line with the instrumental motives for differentiation we found that the opportunity for differentiation followed by a competitive group goal led to high levels of intergroup differentiation on group product ratings and evaluative group ratings. However, differentiation was also high in the most minimal cell of the design – the no differentiation opportunity/no competitive goal condition – resulting in a crossover interaction (see Scheepers et al., 2000). We interpreted presence of ingroup bias under such utterly most minimal conditions as evidence of creative distinctiveness: differentiation designed to provide the group with a distinctive and meaningful identity.

We obtained even more direct evidence for the motive to differentiate in order to provide meaning to group identity in another study in which we manipulated the degree of meaning of the minimal groups more directly (Spears, Jetten, Arend, Van Norren & Postmes, in prep.). In one study we used the same basic minimal group procedure as in the above studies, and categorized people on the basis of their preference for a painter. However, in one condition we said that this preference was related to personality, with those showing a preference for Painter A tending to be more extroverted, and those preferring Painter B more introverted (or vice versa). In this study the minimal condition was not accompanied by a label elaborating the painter preference and was thus even more meaningless than the previous study. In this study we predicted and found greater evidence for group differentiation on the matrices and also evaluative ratings in the most minimal conditions, and reliably less bias in the meaningful condition. Once again we argue that the evaluative differentiation occurs here in order to provide a meaningful and distinctive group identity. A follow up study ruled out some alternative explanations of this effect (Spears et al., in prep; see also Spears, Jetten & Scheepers, 2002).

We are not claiming that lack of stereotypic group differences always results in more evaluative differentiation or ingroup bias on reward allocations. However, what these studies clearly illustrate is that intergroup differentiation is not ruled out by the absence of clear group differences. Indeed the absence of group differences may bring more motivational distinctiveness and enhancement principles to the fore, assuming of course group commitment is sufficient to rule out shifting to another identity. Indeed, in keeping with the principles of social identity theory, it may be that precisely where there is no consensus about the social reality (or status relations) that social reality is 'up for grabs' and open to contest in group favouring ways (Tajfel & Tuner, 1986; see also Spears, Jetten & Doosje, 2001). Although we have characterized this as a case where there is no 'top down' information processing, in the absence of concrete differences, there is a sense in which groups may revert to the 'ultimate' intergroup expectation, namely that their group is superior or more deserving than the other one (Tajfel & Turner, 1986; Howard & Rothbart, 1980), in order to derive the group distinctiveness that is their raison d'être as a group.

This process of evaluative differentiation might not seem like stereotype formation in a descriptive sense. However, evaluation is an important dimension of stereotypic differentiation and indeed one that provides the link to prejudice and ethnocentrism. Evaluative differentiation can also form the basis for subsequent differentiation in more descriptive terms, as interaction and experience provide the data, expectations and theories that will feed more descriptive dimensions of differentiation demonstrated in the previous sections. What is interesting from the present section is that the very absence of stereotypic differences, as well as undermining group differences, can provide the conditions for the strongest and perhaps most naked forms of differentiation: ingroup bias.

Conclusions

In this chapter we have examined stereotype formation under a range of different conditions. We identified four degrees of stereotype formation depending on the resources available in terms of data concerning group attributes and differences that are observable in context, and prior knowledge and expectations about the groups and their relations. Although this ordering is meant to be neither exhaustive nor to preclude finer gradations it does cover the classes of information that may be available (or absent), and grist for the mill of stereotype formation.

What the delineation of these degrees does make clear is that stereotype formation is a process that is rich and varied in so far as it occurs in contexts where there is already considerable knowledge about groups (where one might suppose that stereotypes are already formed) and it can occur in extremely minimal and information-poor contexts (where one might suppose that stereotype formation is not even possible). The first key conclusion then is that stereotype formation is not just something that occurs once, at the beginning of group life, or at the start of a perceiver's knowledge of groups. Rather this is a provisional and ongoing process that is therefore probably quite pervasive if the different degrees outlined above are representative. It is important to note that we are not (necessarily) talking of stereotype change rather than formation here (i.e., the adjustment or revision of already formed stereotypes). Often, although we already know the groups involved (and often this will include our own), it is just not yet clear what the appropriate social stereotype is, independent of the particular social context. As examples above should make clear, even under conditions of group familiarity, social stereotypes may often be manufactured on line, and at the interface of particular intergroup relations.

However, the variety of contexts and inputs should not detract from the uniformity of the process of stereotype formation. Although we are not claiming that this is the only route to stereotype formation, most if not all of the stereotyping phenomena described in this chapter can be accounted for by a basic categorization process in which perceivers try to differentiate one group from another in perception and judgement. Sense making, distinctiveness and enhancement principles can further drive and guide the direction of this differentiation process, and this process may also be fed by expectations or meta-cognitive knowledge (see also Leyens, Yzerbyt & Schadron, 1994). Diverse information processing heuristics and biases have been brought to bear to explain stereotype formation, such as in the illusory correlation paradigm. However, category differentiation has also been shown to be an important determinant of this phenomenon. The category differentiation account even extended to the heartland of research on social cognition: automatic behaviour. Although the differentiation process may be less applicable when there is only a single group in the frame (producing assimilation effects) when outgroups are viewed in an intergroup context implicating the ingroup, differentiation once again results. Despite the variety of the contexts and resources at our disposal, there seems to be considerable unity in the principles and processes used to explain the outcomes. Moreover the activation and application approach to stereotyping characteristic of social cognition research (e.g., Fiske & Neuberg, 1990; Gilbert & Hixon, 1991) is of limited help to us here because this approach not only assumes the existence of stereotypes, but tends to treat them as relatively fixed knowledge structures. Although such knowledge structures can influence the formation of new stereotypes, the central question here is how such knowledge is generated in the first place.

Another general message of this chapter is that we can detect a clear trend running through the differing degrees of prior knowledge and available information. As we have noted, the absence of descriptive content within and differences between, groups does not necessarily seem to deter stereotypic differentiation. Indeed, it is possible to make the case that as the search for meaningful differences gets more difficult, the motivation to find meaningful differences gets stronger (McGarty et al. 1993; Spears et al., 2002). Stereotypic differentiation does not therefore disappear when groups differences are less apparent. Rather, what we tend to see is that, as the descriptive dimension fails to deliver, so the evaluative dimension becomes increasingly important. The findings of the illusory correlation paradigm make clear the importance of the evaluative dimension in intergroup differentiation, and this dimension becomes even more critical when the social self is implicated in context through group membership. In the minimal group paradigm, where descriptive differences between groups are even fewer and further between, evaluative differentiation, and ingroup bias through reward allocations, remain the only meaningful way to (positively) differentiate between the groups (Spears, 1995).

This might seem to be a pessimistic conclusion. It would seem that if groups are not stereotyped on the one hand, then they will be hit with discrimination and ingroup bias on the other. A double whammy indeed. However this conclusion is only problematic if stereotyping is defined a priori as bad. In line with other self-categorization theorists, we do not have to see social stereotyping as bad, or even the best of a bad deal (Leyens, Yzerbyt & Schadron, 1994; Oakes, Haslam & Turner, 1994; Spears, Oakes, Ellemers & Haslam, 1997). Indeed this inverse relation seems to confirm the *distinctness* of stereotypic differences from evaluative prejudices. If we question the equation of stereotyping with prejudice, the inverse relation can be framed in much more optimistic terms. This 'compensation hypothesis' would seem to suggest that stereotypic differentiation in descriptive terms if not an *antidote* to discrimination, may inoculate us to some degree against more prejudicial forms of differentiation. Most real-life intergroup contexts, where at least subtle differences are available, should allow for stereotypic differentiation in less evaluative terms (Spears & Manstead, 1989). One potentially interesting implication of this argument is that ideological contexts that allow the flourishing of differences in group identity (e.g. multiculturalism) may actually be more successful ways of avoiding intergroup conflict and prejudice than attempts to deny group differences (Hornsey & Hogg, 2000).

As we have seen, stereotype formation would seem to be rather difficult to hold back in any case. Stereotype formation should therefore satisfy distinctiveness and enhancement motives (Spears et al., 2002), at least to the extent that groups can value attributes more characteristic of their own group (Doosje, Ellemers & Spears, 1995; Mummendey & Schreiber, 1983, 1984). Although we would be reluctant to raise this hypothesis to the status of a general principle we think it is consistent with much research on distinctiveness and enhancement principles and how these may be addressed by social creativity strategies in line with social identity theory (Tajfel & Turner, 1986; see also Wicklund & Gollwitzer, 1982). From this perspective we should probably not try to suppress the formation of social stereotypes any more than we should suppress their activation or use (cf. Macrae, Milne, Bodenhausen & Jetten, 1994). Social stereotypes may not just be an inevitable feature of social level perception, more positively they may actually counteract more pernicious forms of differentiation. Indeed in common with Haslam et al. (this volume) we think that the best means to fight the fire of negative stereotypes is the fire of other stereotypes designed to challenge these views with images and actions at the group level.

Acknowledgement

I am indebted to the collaboration of the following for some of the research reported in this chapter: Ap Dijksterhuis, Bertjan Doosje, Ernestine Gordijn, Naomi Ellemers, Alex Haslam, Jolanda Jetten, Tony Manstead, Daan Scheepers. Because of the collaborative nature of the work reported here I use the collective pronoun. I would also like to acknowledge the patience and feedback of the other editors and also the insightful comments of Alex Haslam.

8   From personal pictures in the head to collective tools in the world: how shared stereotypes allow groups to represent and change social reality

S. Alexander Haslam, John C. Turner, Penelope J. Oakes, Katherine J. Reynolds and Bertjan Doosje

Stereotyping and stereotype formation: two metatheories

When it was initiated some seventy or so years ago, research into stereotype formation was primarily oriented to the question of why it is that certain attributes come to be associated with particular social groups in the minds of members of the same or other groups. Confronted with findings from the very first empirical studies of stereotype content in which Princeton students were asked to select five traits from a list of eighty-four to describe various national and ethnic groups, Katz and Braly (1933) asked why the students believed that Americans were industrious, Germans scientifically minded, Jews shrewd and Negroes superstitious. As can be seen from Table 8.1, social psychology went on to provide a rich array of answers to such questions. Amongst other things, these pointed to the role of processes that are psychodynamic, socio-cultural and cognitive in origin, and to the mediating role of specific mechanisms such as projection, ethnocentrism, learning, accentuation and illusory correlation.

Varied as these mechanisms are, all this research has the shared features of, on the one hand, explaining stereotype content as a product of psychological shortcomings. It suggests, amongst other things, that people hold their stereotypes because of their aberrant personalities, their biased learning and cognition, or their limited information processing capacity. On the other hand, the research also sees that content as itself inappropriate. It suggests that stereotype content is biased, distorted and erroneous (see Oakes, Haslam & Turner, 1994, for a review). In this way, with notable exceptions (e.g., Sherif, 1966a), mainstream metatheory has defined research into stereotyping and stereotype formation as an exercise

Table 8.1. *The history of research into stereotype formation: approaches and key principles implicated in the process (seminal papers in brackets)*

Decade	Approach			
	Psychodynamic	Socio-cultural	Individual cognitive	Social identity and intergroup relations
1940s	projection (Bettelheim, 1947) intolerance of ambiguity (Adorno et al., 1950)	ethnocentrism (Vinacke, 1949)		
1950s		kernel of truth (Fishman, 1956)	accentuation (Allport, 1954)	
1960s			category differentiation (Tajfel & Wilkes, 1963)	intergroup relations (Sherif et al., 1961)
1970s			illusory correlation (Hamilton & Gifford, 1976) distinctiveness (Taylor et al., 1978)	ingroup favouritism (Doise et al., 1972)
1980s		role learning (Eagly & Steffen, 1984) biological essentialism (Hoffmann & Hurst, 1990)		intergroup differentiation and social explanation (Tajfel, 1981b)
1990s				self-categorization and salience (Oakes et al., 1991) differentiated meaning (McGarty et al., 1993)

in bringing to light the mental frailties and failings that give rise to faulty understandings of the world and of the people in it. It invites researchers to voyage to the dark side of the individual mind in an attempt to fathom the depressing deficiencies of human nature.

This, though, is not the only perspective on the social psychology of stereotyping and stereotype formation. As Table 8.1 indicates and as other chapters in this book testify, work in the social identity tradition has also made a major contribution to developments in this area. In the first instance, pioneering work by Tajfel (1969, 1972; Tajfel & Wilkes, 1963) suggested that stereotype content served to accentuate and sharpen group differences on value-laden dimensions that were perceived to be correlated with social categories. Thus if Dimension X (with the potential to vary from X++ to X−−) is perceived by members of a particular social group (Group A say) to be correlated with distinct group memberships (e.g., so that Group A tended to be X+ and Group B X−) and that dimension is important to the group's own value system, then stereotypes might develop whose content both enhances the differences between the groups (the interclass effect; e.g., suggesting A is X++ and B X−−) and the similarities within them (the intraclass effect; e.g., that Group A members are homogeneously X++ and Group B members are homogeneously X−−).

Consistent with this analysis, evidence from minimal group studies (after Tajfel, Flament, Billig & Bundy, 1971) also suggested that, other things being equal and in the absence of groups having any prior meaning or history, individuals tended to assign favourable content to their ingroup and less favourable content to outgroups (Doise, Csepeli, Dann, Gouge & Larsen, 1972). These findings were easily reconciled with *social identity theory*'s subsequent assertion that group members are motivated to enhance or maintain collective self-esteem and that they often achieve this through a process of relative ingroup favouritism (Tajfel & Turner, 1979).

Later still, this body of work contributed to, and provided impetus for, the development of *self-categorization theory* (Turner, 1985; Turner, Hogg, Oakes, Reicher & Wetherell, 1987). In particular, this theory's principles of normative and comparative fit suggested that, in part, social categories are formed and become salient as a function of *expectation-consistent meta-contrast* (Oakes, 1987; Oakes et al., 1994; Turner, Oakes, Haslam & McGarty, 1994). This analysis suggested that stereotype content is sensitive to social comparative context (i.e., the specific array of groups and other social stimuli that comprise the perceiver's frame of reference) with content forming (and, where necessary, *re*forming) so as to positively and clearly differentiate self- and non-self categories. Some early empirical support for these arguments was provided by Ford and Stangor (1992; see also Brown & Turner, this volume) and these ideas were crystallized in arguments that stereotype content forms in a manner that maximizes *differentiated meaning* (McGarty, Haslam, Turner & Oakes 1993; McGarty & Turner, 1992; see also chapters in this volume by Berndsen et al.; McGarty; and Yzerbyt & Rocher). In this vein, self-categorization theorists have concluded:

The formation of stereotypes reflects a process of resolving individual stimuli into meaningfully different social categories where that resolution is rendered appropriate by comparative and normative features of judgemental context. [Stereotypes are] manifestations of the quest for, and the discovery of, subjectively relevant social meaning. (Haslam, McGarty & Brown, 1996, p. 618; see also Oakes et al., 1994; Oakes & Turner, 1990)

Social identity work notwithstanding, it is nonetheless clear that in mainstream work outside the social identity tradition there has been a dramatic narrowing of focus over time. Where originally researchers had concentrated on the formation and expression of stereotypes in *large groups* (Princeton students, people of different nationality, fascists), sixty years later empirical work was concentrated more-or-less exclusively on the individual stereotyper. Where once the research question had implicitly been 'Why do members of this group *share* these stereotypic beliefs?' now it became simply 'Why does this individual hold and express particular stereotypes?'. Indeed, at their most extreme, researchers have come to argue that the groups in which stereotypes are formed are essentially irrelevant to the stereotyping process (e.g., Devine & Elliot, 1995, p. 1147; Hamilton, Stroessner & Driscoll, 1994, p. 298; Judd & Park, 1993, p. 110; McCauley, Stitt & Segal, 1980, p. 197).

Against this trend, and partly in reaction to it, work informed by social identity and self-categorization theories played an important corrective role because it underlined Sherif's earlier point that stereotypers' own group memberships were absolutely central to stereotype formation (e.g., Schaller & Maass, 1989). Moreover, this approach argued that *consensus* in group beliefs was a key social fact that needed to be attended to and explained in stereotyping research (e.g., Oakes et al., 1994; Tajfel, 1981b). In his own powerful critique of developments in the cognitive mainstream, Tajfel argued that any psychological analysis of stereotype formation would be hopelessly restricted and irrelevant without 'a theory of the contents of stereotypes *as shared by social groups*' (1981b, p. 160, emphasis added).

A broad goal of this chapter is to outline and elaborate a theoretical analysis of the processes through which shared stereotypes form and are deployed – one that goes beyond Tajfel's own 'hazy blueprint' for progress and which rises to the significant challenges he laid down (1981b, p. 167). Briefly, it is argued that social identities do not simply provide group members with a common perspective on social reality and common motives for imbuing stereotypes with differentiated meaning, but that they also provide a platform and a motivation for *coordinating* social perspectives and *using* particular stereotypes in the service of social action. The argument here, then, is that stereotypes form not just so that individuals can represent the social world to themselves but so that they can also act meaningfully and *collectively* within it. In contrast to the view (first articulated by Lippmann, 1922, p. 59) that stereotypes are personal 'pictures in our heads' we propose that stereotypes also need to be understood as *tools that are developed by groups both to represent their members' shared social reality and to achieve particular objectives within it.*

The remainder of the chapter then goes on to consider a variety of ways in which this dual function is achieved and a variety of the social parameters by which it is constrained. The key message that emerges from this work is that stereotype formation is both a cognitive and a sociopolitical process (see also, Oakes et al., 1994; Oakes, Reynolds, Haslam & Turner, 1999). Groups develop stereotypes in order to veridically appreciate the socially structured world they confront (which contains groups of different status, different power, different ideology) and as a platform for creating or maintaining a world with the social structure they desire. Mounting a compelling case for this view is therefore an exercise in freeing the analysis of stereotype formation from its metatheoretical and methodological shackles and in realizing the full significance and potential of the process. It takes us on a journey not to the sinister side of the individual mind but to a fundamentally creative aspect of human sociality.

The social identity approach to stereotyping: three phases of research

1.   Social identity and social categorization

For the purposes of charting its development, stereotyping research that has been informed by social identity and self-categorization principles can be seen to have been conducted in three phases (focused, respectively, on issues of *categorization, salience* and *interaction*). The first phase, most closely associated with Tajfel's (e.g., 1969, 1981b) social categorization research, had the twin goals of (a) identifying stereotyping as a process bound up with the realities of group life, particularly intergroup conflict, and (b) uncovering some of the individual cognitive processes that were implicated in that process.

The process of accentuation, alluded to above, was central to this analysis and Tajfel saw it as playing a key role by serving to order and organize social perception. As well as this, though, he saw stereotypes and stereotyping as serving three key *social* functions. Specifically, he argued that they (a) help to *explain* large-scale social events (such as war and peace, persecution and tolerance, disadvantage and privilege), (b) serve to *justify* the activities of groups as they relate to those events (e.g., attacking an enemy, funding an aid programme, collecting and distributing taxes), and (c) contribute to a process of positive intergroup *differentiation* whereby stereotypers strive to represent their ingroup as different from, and better than, outgroups.

Somewhat ironically though, for all its insights, Tajfel's work was actually at least as influential in lending impetus to research that focused on the individual cognitive functions of stereotypes as it was in stimulating research into their collective social functions (e.g., see Hamilton, 1981a). Nonetheless, important early studies succeeded in demonstrating that stereotyping was a process centred on the collective self ('us') and was partly underpinned by motivations to represent that collective self positively (e.g., Doise et al., 1972; Schaller & Maass, 1989; Spears & Manstead, 1989).

2.   *Self-categorization and social identity salience*

Having emphasized the role that group membership and intergroup relations played in the stereotyping process, substantial advances in the social identity tradition were now dependent on a thoroughgoing examination of social identity salience (something that was not provided by social identity theory). What leads a collection of individuals to see themselves as a group and to ascribe common properties (e.g., norms, goals, values and other social attributes) both to it and to the groups with which it interacts? Such questions provided a focus for a second phase of stereotyping research in the social identity tradition – a phase that defined a central project in the development of self-categorization theory and which was most closely associated with the work of Oakes and Turner (1990; Oakes, 1987; Oakes, Turner & Haslam, 1991; Turner, 1985).

This phase of research was founded upon an analysis of the self-concept and of the processes that allow for contextual redefinition of the self across different social contexts (e.g., Turner, 1982, 1985; Turner et al., 1987). A key insight that emerged from this line of enquiry was that stereotypes – both of ingroups and outgroups – are not fixed rigid structures that group members learn and then inevitably cling to like drowning sailors to a liferaft. On the contrary, whether or not individuals see themselves as a group and *how* they see themselves (and others) was understood to depend on features of the social world they confront in interaction with the experiences and perspective that they bring to any situation (e.g., in the form of history, culture and ideology). Building on the work of Bruner (e.g., 1957a), these arguments were formalized in the view that social categories become salient through the interaction of *fit* and *perceiver readiness* (Oakes, 1987; Oakes et al., 1994).

Fit principles clarify the role that context plays in social perception. Specifically, the comparative principle of meta-contrast suggests that a collection of individuals is more likely to be seen as an entity (by themselves and others) where the differences between those individuals are perceived to be smaller than the differences between them and the other individuals that are salient in a given setting. In this way a New Yorker and a Californian are more likely to see themselves (and be seen) as Americans at the Olympic Games (an intergroup context) than at the Superbowl (an intragroup context). However, normative fit – which relates to the perceiver's content-related expectations – is also important here. To be defined as categorically interchangeable, stimuli must be seen to be less different from each other than from comparison with others, but the nature of those differences must also correspond to the perceiver's category expectations. To be seen as Americans at the Olympic Games our New Yorker and Californian should support Americans when they compete with Russian athletes. Yet even here we can see that contextual forces will be at play and that these are bound up with the perceived applicability of content to categories. This means, for example, that support for America should have a more central role in defining the category American when Americans are in conflict with Russians rather than trying to broker peace.

Most of the work that tested and developed ideas of this form was conducted during the 1980s and early 1990s. Two key strands of research focused on the role that context plays both in structuring the perception of groups as entities and in shaping stereotype content. In particular, a plethora of studies showed that ingroups are more likely to be seen as homogeneous and that their members are more likely to engage in self-stereotyping in situations that are intergroup rather than intragroup in nature (i.e., in situations that involve 'us and them' rather than just 'us': e.g., Castano & Yzerbyt, 1998; Haslam, Oakes, Turner & McGarty, 1996; Hogg & Turner, 1987a; Hopkins & Cable, in press; Lee & Ottati, 1995; Reynolds & Oakes, 2000; Spears, Doosje & Ellemers, 1997). Similarly, numerous studies have shown that stereotype content varies lawfully through the operation of fit principles (e.g., Brown & Turner, this volume; Doosje, Haslam, Spears, Oakes & Koomen, 1998; Ford & Stangor, 1992; Haslam & Turner, 1992).

3.   *Self-categorization, influence and consensus*

One indicator of the success of research that addressed the contextual determinants of social categorization and social identity salience is that while twenty years ago researchers were wedded to the view that stereotypes are fixed cognitive structures, demonstrations of context-dependence in stereotyping and stereotype content are now considered unremarkable and old hat. However, for self-categorization theorists, the analysis of social identity salience has provided a platform for a third phase of stereotyping research. Broadly speaking, this has sought to reconnect the analysis of individual cognition with examination of *collective action* in the social world *by which* and *for which* that cognition is structured.

One particular goal of this research has been to develop a theoretical analysis of the processes that lead group members to embrace consensual stereotypes of themselves and others. A central plank of this work has been provided by the fusion of insights from salience research with self-categorization theory's analysis of social influence. Following Turner (1987a, 1991; see also Haslam, 1997; Oakes et al., 1994, Chapter 8), a key point here is that when contextual factors lead individuals to define themselves in terms of a particular group membership, that self-categorization does not only provide them with a similar perspective on the world, but it also serves as a basis for organizing and coordinating that perspective. Individuals expect to agree with other people who are members of the same salient self-category and, so long as that shared self-categorization is sustained (and sustainable), they work actively to ensure that agreement is reached. Stereotypes thus form not only so that each individual can represent, understand and explain the social world but so that those representations, understandings and explanations can have collective meaning and purpose for the groups that hold them.

A particular issue here concerns the management of disagreement. If two Americans at the Olympic Games have different views about Russians and about the way that they should be treated (e.g., disagreeing about whether they should be supported, ignored, rebuked or vilified) what do they do? Turner (1987a) outlines three possible reactions. Firstly, through negotiation, they can attribute their disagreement to relevant differences 'out there' in the stimulus domain. Perhaps one American was thinking about Russian gymnasts and the other about Russian boxers, and, having established this fact they can agree that there are important differences between these two groups that warrant a different response. Secondly, through a similar process, the Americans can explain their disagreement in terms of relevant category-based differences between themselves. Perhaps the two will discover that really they should not be relating to each other in terms of a shared national self-categorization because one is a Democratic 'dove' and the other a Republican 'hawk' and it is these divergent political identities that are most relevant in this setting. Finally, if neither of these alternatives is plausible or fitting, they can engage in a process of mutual influence so that through the exchange of information, discussion, argument and persuasion they work to arrive at a common understanding and a shared stereotypic response – a process Haslam, Turner, Oakes, McGarty and Reynolds (1998) refer to as *group consensualization*.

It is upon this consensualization process – and its grounding in social category salience – that much of our more recent empirical work has concentrated. Early studies in this programme showed that feedback from others only impacted upon stereotype content and consensus when it was provided by ingroup rather than outgroup members and was normatively fitting (Haslam, Oakes, McGarty, et al., 1996; see also Stangor & Sechrist, 2000; Stangor, Sechrist & Jost, 2000, Sechrist & Stangor, 2001). Australian students were thus more willing to embrace positive stereotypes of Australians and negative stereotypes of Americans when they received stereotype-consistent feedback from fellow students rather than inconsistent feedback or feedback from a prejudiced outgroup.

A later series of three studies also showed that Australian students' stereotypes of their national ingroup were more consensual to the extent that a shared national identity was made salient by features of comparative context (e.g., because the experimental setting was intergroup rather than intragroup in nature; Haslam, Turner, Oakes, Reynolds et al., 1998; see also Haslam, Oakes, Reynolds & Turner, 1999). Moreover, consensus was further enhanced by interaction with other ingroup members – especially in intergroup contexts. This meant that students selected quite varied traits to describe Australians when they performed a Katz-Braly checklist task alone and without reference to other nations, but that their choices were much more uniform when they had been made after a group discussion in which Australians were compared with Americans.

Although our presentation of research into stereotype consensus generally focuses on the support it provides for our theoretical analysis of the consensualization process, two additional points flow from the arguments that underpin this work. First, it is apparent that all three of the responses to disagreement outlined above are dynamic and interactive such that none can take place solely in the mind of the individual perceiver. Without a forum for these processes to be played out, consensual stereotypes could never form. This forum is provided in a social world that contains, amongst other things, collective gatherings, shared causes, opinion leaders, academics, books, television interviews and newspaper articles. Moreover this is a *political*[1] realm that all humans necessarily inhabit by virtue of the fact that they belong to groups with divergent (and often conflicting) cultures, histories, interests and goals. By the same token, it is because this political realm is a fundamental (indeed, a defining) feature of human activity that people will always hold – and strive to hold – stereotypes.

Secondly, though, as much as this first point is true, it is also the case that the extent and the contours of stereotype consensus are always in flux. As the three scenarios described above make clear, the fact that group members strive to reach agreement in order to validate their individual perceptions and coordinate social action, does not mean that consensus is guaranteed. Indeed, in many situations disagreement (itself a product of the fact that individuals never have identical cognitions and perspectives) will lead to schism – a redefinition of social categorical boundaries that creates pressure for dissensus (or divergent lower-level consensuses; Sani & Reicher, 1998, 1999). In the Olympic example, the Republican and Democrat will experience less pressure to agree – and may well be motivated to disagree – once they come to define the situation along party political rather than national lines. Similarly, as empirical work by Sani and Reicher (1998, 1999) illustrates, members of a political party or a religious movement will tend (and be motivated) to develop divergent policies and plans once they disagree about the defining features of their shared identity.

It is on dynamic processes such as this that we will focus in the remainder of this chapter. This draws on some of our more recent stereotyping research in an attempt to underscore four lessons that we see as critical to the social identity approach and which clarify its distinctive contribution to the stereotyping field. These are not the only lessons of the approach and all are interdependent extensions of fundamental points that we have already touched upon. All four are also reasonably controversial in light of prevailing metatheory and research practice. Nonetheless, we believe that each has the potential to lead to theoretical progress in our understanding of the stereotyping process and of the social phenomena in which it is implicated.

Self-categorization and the politics of stereotype formation: four lessons

1.   Stereotypes are collective achievements

In many ways the strongest support for our argument that meaningful stereotypes are generally arrived at through an interactive process of negotiation is provided by the results of those experimental studies discussed above in which stereotype consensus was shown to be contingent upon perceivers sharing a common social identity and then interacting in terms of it (e.g., Haslam et al., 1999). There is a danger though, that some of the social processes which contributed to the effects in those studies are hidden by the practice of translating human behaviour into descriptive and inferential statistics. This is not an argument against that practice, but nonetheless (in the spirit of influential research by Reicher and his colleagues) we believe that there are benefits to be gleaned from detailed examination of the substantive features of interaction in such studies. In particular, scrutiny of this form should (a) afford a better understanding of how consensus is achieved, and (b) reinforce the point that consensus is indeed an achievement.

To this end, we conducted a small replication study in which Australian students completed the Katz-Braly checklist individually and then in groups of four people. Two groups were asked to assign traits to Australians and two groups were asked to assign traits to Americans and in each case their discussions was tape-recorded and transcribed.

In the first instance we were able to establish that the pattern of responses in this experiment were broadly representative of those observed in previous studies (e.g., Haslam, Turner, Oakes, Reynolds et al., 1998, Experiment 1; Haslam et al., 1999). Interaction thus had a consensualizing effect on both stereotypes, but, as expected, this was much more pronounced in the intergroup context where participants discussed Americans than in the intragroup context where they discussed Australians (because the former context was expected to make the social identity more salient; see Haslam et al., 1999). In discussing Americans, stereotype consensus (as measured by the consensus coefficient, P_a) increased from .24 to .47 after interaction, but in discussing Australians it increased only from .14 to .19.

Examination of the discussion which led to these effects also served to emphasize a number of the points articulated in the previous section. Firstly, and most significantly, it is clear that the discussions themselves were vigorous and animated and that participants were keen to instigate and participate in a process that might lead to mutual agreement – especially when discussing the American stereotype. This is apparent in the following extracts and indeed, in the second it is notable that the group resorted to humour as an informal mechanism for ensuring consensus:

[Group 1: describing *Americans*]
A: I have, I have a few things down here, (inaudible) things like talkative
B: Nationalistic
C: Arrogant (laughs loudly)
D: Ambitious
A: Ambitious?
D: Loud
A: Yeah I had loud
C: The same
A: Yeah. OK. Great

[Group 4: describing *Australians*]
C: Well do we want to quickly put in ones we've definitely got and then work out a strategy?
D: Umm
C: And then go to the other ones that we'll discuss
D: Umm. Alright
A: And we'll ostracise the person who doesn't agree [laughs]. Like make them feel really uncomfortable.
D: Alright. So we've got straightforward
B: And that means we should tick conservationalist
A: Persuasive [laughs]

As a corollary of this process it is also apparent that individual group members were keen to coordinate their own and others' responses and ensure that none of their contributions were perceived as deviant. As we would expect, this was particularly marked in discussion of the American stereotype, where after making seemingly-idiosyncratic responses individuals moved swiftly into 'damage-repair mode' to make it clear that, after all, they really were aligned with other group members. So, for example, when a group member indicated that he himself had not actually underlined a consensual trait, he indicated that he 'sort of' did, and when one participant's suggestion of a trait to include in the final five was met with silence, he proceeded quickly to offer up another more acceptable one:

[Group 1: describing *Americans*]
B: I had tradition-loving and nationalistic
C: Yeah I did . . . too
D: So yeah . . . we'll have those ones?
C: Yeah
A: I had tradition-loving. Nationalistic. I didn't put it down as the most . . . in the top five . . . but yeah I did put it down . . . sort of, marked it

[Group 2: describing *Americans*]
A: Yeah. Alright agr... extremely nationalistic. Yeah
C: ... and tradition-loving
A: Yeah
C: ... and ostentatious
D: Yeah that was another one
B: [agreeing] another one
A: Yeah. And... talkative. [short silence, then definitively] No. Arrogant

Other points of divergence in the process of stereotyping Americans and Australians consistent with our theoretical analysis can also be identified in the respective discussions of these groups. In particular, there is evidence that when discussing Australians (in the intragroup context), although there was pressure for agreement, disagreement was less problematic for participants partly because they were able to make sense of this disagreement by differentiating within the object of judgement and referring to meaningful lower-level categorizations (cf. Park, Ryan & Judd, 1992; Turner, 1987b). This is exemplified by the following exchanges:

[Group 3: describing *Australians*]
B: Arrogant?
C: No
D: It depends on which part I guess [laughs]
A: Oh, Ok, is it.....
C: Some people... like prime ministers are
B: Yeah
A: Yeah
B: I had arrogant as well on mine
A: Did you? Oh alright
D: It depends on where you live I guess
B: Yeah
D: Like if you live in Sydney they judge, you know, on whether you come from South or North you know

[Group 3: describing *Australians*]
C: And how about persistent?
B: Persistent?
A: It doesn't strike me as one of our ... er things about being Australian ...
C: It depends on how you think about it ... er ... if you look at the good old, good old Australian, you know like the Australian image that other people have of us, say of farmers and stuff in the outback
A: Yeah but
D: It's not like the whole population
B: Yeah. Farmers but not...

Yet when discussing Americans, on the one occasion where a participant ventured to suggest that stereotyping at a generalized level of abstraction might be inappropriate, this suggestion was actively resisted by other group members in the course of again trying to identify a consensual response:

[Group 1: describing *Americans*]
B: I have rude
D: [as if interested] Uhhum?
A: Yeah so did I.. I'm sure . . . A bit . . . A bit of a generalization.
     [D laughs quite loudly]
     From the half-dozen people I've met to a whole nation is a bit of a . . .
     [C laughs quietly]
C: [interrupting] I went there and met people like that.
     [general laughter]
     I guess they just wanted to get where they were going.. but you know
D: [to C] Did you have rude or not?
C: Oh I would have put rude down

One further point to note is that the differences in the emergent consensus between American and Australian stereotypes can be attributed not only (a) to lower-level self- and other-categorizations being more accessible and meaningful and (b) to disagreement being more acceptable in the intragroup context, but also (c) to the fact that the precise meaning of the traits was more a topic for negotiation and debate in the intragroup context. Consistent with the observations of Reicher, Hopkins and Condor (1997) it is thus clear that when participants discussed their own national identity, the precise meaning of terms like 'sportsmanlike' and 'arrogant' was sometimes quite hard for them to agree on, as the following excerpt shows:

[Group 4: describing *Australians*]
C: Sportsmanlike?
B: Not everyone's interested . . .
D: I know but they still talk about it. Like um I know a lot of people um who read books and are very sort of . . .
A: Yeah but isn't there a difference between sitting down and watching say cricket on TV and actually participating. I mean, like when it said sportsmanlike I assumed it was to be er
B: Active
A: Active . . . .
B: Umm
D: Well I sort of picture sportsmanlike means er talking about sports I mean and knowing about it as much as anything. I was sort of thinking about er for example
B: Sort of
D: You know State-of-Origin, they sort of get people who don't play sports at all watching that
B: I don't know what it really means to be sportsmanlike

A: Umm
   (pause)
D: Well a question of attitudes
C: I think there's more sportsmanlike than talkative
B: I don't agree. I think there are more talkative people than there are
   sportsmanlike. 'Cause if you didn't have people talking about sport all the
   time . . .
   (general laughter)

Significantly though, there was little evidence of similar confusion when discussing the meaning of these and other terms in relation to Americans. Along the lines of arguments presented earlier (see also Haslam et al., 1998), we would suggest that this is because the intergroup comparative context served to disambiguate the traits by providing participants with a shared perspective on their meaning-in-context. So, for example, while the meaning of the term 'sportsmanlike' might be relatively unclear when Australians are considered alone, we would expect that it would become more clear if Australians were compared with the Chinese (a comparison that might engender a common reaction by making salient issues related to the consumption of performance-enhancing drugs). In contrast, then, to the assumption that ambiguity is a *stable* feature of any trait, we would argue that it, like other aspects of stereotypes, varies lawfully with changes in social context.

The broader point that emerges from this study, however, is that stereotypes are here shown to be anything but fixed structures, off-the-peg cognitions that group members invoke routinely or carelessly to describe themselves and others. Instead they are creative and intricately tailored constructions that demand collaborative work (see also Condor, 1999). The fact that this proves to be the case where stereotypes are elicited using the Katz-Braly paradigm is all the more remarkable as this procedure is often criticized for being a relatively blunt and uninformative research instrument (for methodological critiques along these lines, see Augoustinos & Walker, 1995; Ehrlich & Rinehart, 1965; Eysenck & Crown, 1948; Reicher & Hopkins, in press).

2.   *Stereotypes are works in progress*

We noted above that one of the first points to emerge from the infusion of self-categorization principles into stereotyping research was an assertion that stereotypes are context-sensitive and fluid rather than fixed and inviolate. In fact a considerable amount of evidence that supported this conclusion had already been assembled by researchers who had used the Katz-Braly paradigm to monitor change in stereotype content over time and context (e.g., Diab, 1962; Meenes, 1943; Karlins, Coffman & Walters, 1969; Seago, 1947; for a review see Oakes et al., 1994, Chapter 2). Nonetheless, this message had been rebuffed until it was resurrected through experimental studies that provided evidence of variation both in the content of stereotypes (e.g., Haslam et al., 1992) and in the generalizability of that content within particular groups (e.g., Haslam et al., 1996).

Important as the latter work was in setting the historical record straight, in many ways its primary focus can be seen to have been on the *representational* rather than the *strategic* aspects of stereotyping (Reicher et al., 1997; Reicher & Hopkins, 2001). Nonetheless, our research programme as a whole has always been clearly guided by the view that categorization is not only about *depiction* but also about *action* (Oakes et al., 1994, after Bruner, 1957a; for related views in the realm of perception, see Gibson, 1982). We stereotype not simply to see people for what they are (to us), but also to clarify what we can (and should) *do* with them (Tajfel, 1972).

This point is made clearly in research by Reicher and Hopkins (1996a, 1996b, 2001) which explores the role that political leadership plays in defining national identity and then making particular policies (e.g., Scottish devolution from England) appear to be natural expressions of that identity. For example, if Scottish identity is defined as being incompatible with being British (e.g., because the Scottish and English are seen to have fundamentally different values and aspirations) then Scots should support devolution – and political leaders use such a definition precisely for the purpose of justifying this policy. Moreover, as a subtle elaboration of this point, Reicher and Hopkins show that the very same attributes can be used to define different relational identities and hence different policies. 'Warmth' for example, can be used to distinguish Scots from the 'cold' English (suggesting devolution) or it can be used to imply that the Scots should be neighbourly towards the English (suggesting alliance).

Similar arguments are also supported by much of our own research. As an example, we can look closely at the results of an experiment reported by Doosje et al. (1998). Participants in the study were asked to judge psychology students (a group to which they belonged) under conditions in which this group was compared with one or two other groups: physics and/or drama students. They did this with respect to two attributes that were each typical of one of these groups – 'scientific' and 'artistic', respectively. They were also asked to indicate how favourable they considered these attributes to be.

Illustrating the sensitivity of ingroup definition to comparative context – and consistent with the meta-contrast principle – psychology students were seen as more scientific when they were compared only with drama students ($M = 5.33$) than when they were compared with physics students (alone or together with drama students; $Ms = 4.81, 4.95$, respectively). They were also seen as more artistic when they were compared only with physics students ($M = 4.37$) than when they were compared with drama students (alone or together with physics students; $Ms = 4.00, 3.90$, respectively).

However, there was more to these judgements than simply description. This much is evident from ratings of attribute favourableness which provided an index of how desirable a particular characteristic was thought to be. Here, in effect, the participants had to answer the question of whether group members thought it was appropriate to be, or to seek to be, scientific or artistic. Significantly, the answer depended on the group with which psychologists were being compared. In a world comprised only of physicists and psychologists, psychologists were not only seen as less scientific, but being scientific was seen as less desirable ($M = 5.19$) than it was in a world comprised only of drama students ($M = 5.33$). On the other hand, in a world comprised only of drama students and psychologists, psychologists were not only seen as less artistic, but being artistic was seen as less desirable ($M = 5.18$) than it was in a world comprised only of physics students ($M = 5.94$).

Of course, in one way it would be possible to see these responses simply as a severe case of sour grapes: group members don't like making judgements that make them look bad, and having had to make them they belittle the exercise and the source of their discomfort. At the same time though, bound up in this reaction is a communicative act concerning 'the way things ought to be' and the actions that can bring it about. To indicate, in the context of a comparison with drama students, that it is good for psychology students to be scientific is to invite fellow psychologists to participate in activities that reinforce their scientific qualities. In the same way, stating in the same context, that it is bad to be artistic tells others what they should *not* be doing.

Again though, we can see that such injunctions, and the stereotypic judgements on which they are predicated, vary with context. What group members think they should be doing, and the shared beliefs they articulate in order to represent themselves and promote group-relevant activity, are not invariant: they change over time and as a function of the particular circumstances they collectively confront. Nonetheless, it is also true that such variability is typically constrained by the emergent ideology (i.e., the higher-order theory of group values and goals) that unites a group's actions across contexts. Moreover, that ideology provides groups with a capacity for sense-making and direction that transcends context and which allows stereotypic variation to be understood as rational and purposive rather than perplexing and chaotic.

3.   *Stereotypes are embedded in a system of dynamic*
       intergroup relations

Arguments that stereotypes change with context and are oriented towards shared goals can be elaborated by considering how those stereotypes (and the behaviour with which they are associated) change as a
function of currents within the broader system of intergroup relations.
An early demonstration of this point was provided by our 'Iraq study'.
This showed how Australians' stereotypes of Americans changed over the
course of the 1991–92 war in the Persian Gulf depending on the nations
Americans were compared with (Haslam, Turner, Oakes, McGarty &
Hayes, 1992). Amongst other things, this meant that at the start of the
war Americans were perceived most negatively when they were compared
with Iraqis, but by its end this comparison led to them being seen most
positively. This change was explained in terms of the increasing involve-
ment of Australia in the conflict: at the beginning of the war Australians
reacted negatively to Americans' perceived bellicosity, but at the end
(by which time Australia had joined the United States in an anti-Iraq
military coalition) they perceived Iraq as a common enemy. Moreover,
such stereotypes clearly played an important role in justifying Australia's
allegiances and motivating its own contribution to the war effort.

Powerful (and very topical) support for related arguments is provided
by Stott and colleagues' extensive studies of football crowds (e.g., Stott,
Hutchinson & Drury, in press; Stott & Reicher, 1998; see also Drury &
Reicher, in press; Stott & Drury, 2000). These provide vivid demonstrations of the way in which the contents of self- and other stereotypes
are shaped by social context and lend themselves to different forms of
collective behaviour. For example, upon finding themselves labelled and
treated as 'hooligans' by the police and supporters of other teams, fol-
lowers of the English football team find particular forms of self-definition
(e.g., 'holiday-makers', 'fans') denied, along with certain forms of group
behaviour. As Stott et al. (in press) show, this means that while a Scottish
fan who lifts up his kilt to passing motorists is seen to be 'having a laugh'
and, together with his friends, can happily enjoy a night of drunken cama-
raderie, an English supporter who drops his trousers is seen as a menace
and is likely to have his night of collaborative carousing transformed into
one of conflict with the authorities.

We can see similar processes to this played out in some recent experimental research that has investigated the dynamics of reciprocity in intergroup settings (Doosje & Haslam, 2000). In an initial study (designed
as an analogue to field research which analysed voting patterns in the
Eurovision Song Contest), Australian participants were asked to assign

points 'for good international citizenship' to people from four countries: the Netherlands, England, the USA and France. They did this either in a control condition (where no background information was provided) or in one of four experimental conditions in which they were provided with (bogus) information about Dutch people's stereotypes of Americans and Australians. This information served either to confirm or contradict the participants' own positive national self-stereotype of Australians (as 'happy-go-lucky', 'straightforward' and 'sportsmanlike' rather than 'ignorant', 'rude' and 'unsophisticated') and either to confirm or contradict their negative stereotype of Americans (as 'extremely nationalistic' 'materialistic' and 'arrogant' rather than 'creative', 'friendly' and 'ambitious'). Significantly, the study was also conducted at a time when Australia was engaged in dispute with the United States over trade tariffs being placed on Australian exports and there was an even more heated quarrel with France over its decision to conduct nuclear testing in the South Pacific.

Our basic hypothesis was that Australians' views about the validity of Dutch-held stereotypes would vary as a function of the feedback provided and, most importantly, that this would impact upon the points awarded both to them and to other groups. As the results presented in Figure 8.1 indicate, this was what we found. Thus Dutch stereotypes were seen to be most valid and the Dutch were awarded most points for international citizenship when they confirmed Australians' positive self-stereotype and their negative beliefs about Americans ($M = 3.65$). On the other hand, when the Dutch articulated the opposite views a very different pattern of point allocation emerged. Here Australian affections, as revealed by the allocation of points, were transferred from the Dutch ($M = 2.15$) to the English ($M = 3.35$). So when Dutch people's stereotypes signalled that they were aligned with Australia's trade enemy (the USA), Australians strategically realigned themselves with the country with which they were least clearly in conflict, at that time (England). Significantly too, stereotypes can help to initiate realignment of this form (as they did in this study) and they are one of the means by which it can be communicated and achieved.

Interestingly too, the study's two other conditions provided evidence of slightly more nuanced responses. In particular, when the Dutch were said to have positive stereotypes of both Australians and Americans, Australians reduced the number of points they awarded to Americans to its lowest level ($M = 2.30$): potentially in an attempt to distance themselves from the American component of the Dutch judgement. On the other hand, when the Dutch were said to have negative stereotypes of both Australians and Americans, Australians increased the number of

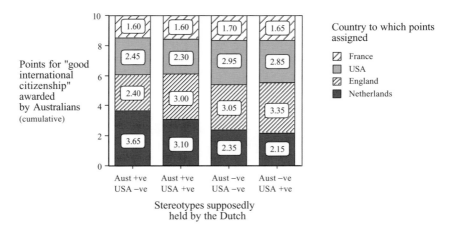

Points for "good international citizenship" awarded by Australians (cumulative)

Country to which points assigned

☑ France
☐ USA
☑ England
■ Netherlands

Stereotypes supposedly held by the Dutch

Figure 8.1 Variation in intergroup behaviour as a function of the stereotypes held by an outgroup.

Note: Aust +ve traits: happy-go-lucky, straightforward, sportsmanlike
Aust −ve traits: ignorant, rude, unsophisticated
USA +ve traits: creative, friendly, ambitious
USA −ve traits: extremely nationalistic, materialistic, arrogant

points they awarded to Americans to its highest level ($M = 2.95$): possibly because this information led to some alignment with the USA as a result of seeing Australians and Americans as 'common victims' of the Netherlands.

The results of this study thus provide compelling evidence for the view that stereotypes – and the behaviour with which they are associated – are highly sensitive to the network of intergroup relations in which groups are located (Bourhis, Turner & Gagnon, 1997; Sherif, Harvey, White, Hood & Sherif, 1961; Sherif, 1966a; Tajfel, 1978b). Changes to one element of this system are thus observed to have ramifications for other non-proximal elements to which they are nonetheless related.

In this study the most intriguing demonstration of this fact comes from the finding that the number of points for good international behaviour awarded by Australians to the English depended partly on the stereotypes that Dutch people were purported to hold of Americans. And in contrast to chaos theory's metaphor of a butterfly flapping its wings in the South American rainforest leading to a stock market crash on Wall Street, we here have evidence that this distal impact is meaningful and strategic. Stereotypes form to reflect the standing of a group in relation to others, but are also structured by the ideological model of social relations which informs all group judgements (a model which in this instance made the English a more fitting recipient of Australian votes than the French). Combined, these facts allow stereotypes to respond meaningfully to changes in the state of the social system as a whole – responses that include the potential for coalition and alliance as well as devolution and schism.

4. Stereotypes help maintain and contest the social power structure

The previous sections give some indication of the way in which stereotypes respond to the realities that perceivers confront as members of interacting groups in a dynamic social system. The studies we have considered also provide evidence that such responses allow both for the subjectively veridical representation of that reality and for coordinated reactions to it. Let us now turn, though, to consider one of the most important ingredients and outcomes of political behaviour: *power*. In a broad range of social milieux – including international relations, organizational life and sexual politics – the maintenance or accretion of power is a key goal (e.g., Bourhis, 1994; Fiske & Dépret, 1996; Kanter, 1979; Mulder, 1977; see also Oakes et al., 1999, pp. 150–153; Chapter 8 in Haslam, 2001). When groups have been dispossessed or deprived of power they generally seek to regain it and when they have acquired it they typically seek to hold on to it.

These ends can also be achieved in a variety of ways. Indeed it follows from social identity theory (e.g., Tajfel & Turner, 1979) that while group power is generally won only through direct collective action (which will typically involve some form of conflict or competition), it can be maintained by both direct and indirect means (see Table 8.2). The latter may include attempts to encourage members of low-power outgroups (a) to adopt a strategy of individual mobility rather than social change, (b) to act in terms of competing subgroup identifications (the strategy of 'divide and rule'), or (c) to embrace socially creative collective understandings that reinforce the status quo rather than challenge it.

It follows from our discussion thus far that because stereotyping is an activity oriented to the achievement of group goals it should have a role to play in the politics of power maintenance and enhancement. Indeed, just such a role is envisioned by Jost and Banaji (1994) in their *system justification approach* to stereotyping. This argues that the most important and enduring function of stereotypes is to maintain the existing power structure and that:

The notion of system justification is necessary to account for previously unexplained phenomena, most notably the participation by disadvantaged individuals and groups in negative stereotypes of themselves, and the consensual nature of stereotypic beliefs despite differences in social relations. (Jost & Banaji, 1994, p. 1)

Table 8.2. *Predicted variation in the form of stereotypes, their manifest function and the breadth of consensus as a function of the group that holds them and the perceived security of intergroup relations**

Group Power	Perceived security of intergroup relations	Nature of ingroup stereotype	Nature of outgroup stereotype	Stereotype function	Breadth of consensus
high	high	positive on status-defining dimensions	positive on status-irrelevant dimensions	indirect maintenance of power relations (system justification)	across ingroup and outgroup
	low	positive on status-defining dimensions	negative on status-defining dimensions	direct maintenance of power relations (social competition)	within ingroup
low	high	positive on status-irrelevant dimensions	positive on status-defining dimensions	collective self-maintenance (social creativity)	across ingroup and outgroup
	low	positive on status-defining dimensions	negative on status-defining dimensions	direct challenge to power relations (social competition)	within ingroup

Notes: *These predictions relate to a two-group context in which the existence of the two groups is consensually recognized (e.g., as might be the case if the groups were based on nationality rather than social class).

However, important as such processes may be (at least for members of powerful groups in particular contexts), the social identity approach suggests that they represent only one of the ways in which stereotypes can impact upon group behaviour and therefore that a system justification analysis provides an incomplete analysis of stereotype consensus. Indeed, in contexts where members of low-power groups perceive status and power relations to be illegitimate, social identity principles predict (see Table 8.2) that they should embrace shared stereotypes that both (a) challenge the existing power structure and (b) articulate a self-definition around which group members can mobilize.

Reynolds, Oakes, Haslam, Nolan and Dolnik (2000) tested this prediction in a study modelled on previous research by Wright and his colleagues (e.g., Wright, Taylor & Moghaddam, 1990). In this, participants were initially assigned to a low-status 'unsophisticated' group but told that they could gain entry to a more powerful 'sophisticated' group if they performed satisfactorily on an ability test administered by representatives of the powerful group. The study had three independent conditions, with participants being told that they had either (a) narrowly failed to make the grade for admission to the sophisticated group (the *open* condition); (b) made the grade but that the powerful group had imposed a quota so that only 10% of the candidates who passed the test would gain entry to their group (the *quota* condition); or (c) made the grade, but that the powerful group had decided not to allow any of the candidates who passed the test to become members of their group because they did not 'want to be swamped' by new members (the *closed* condition).

Here it was predicted that in the open and quota conditions – where the possibility of personal mobility was present and social relations appeared to be legitimate – stereotypes would reproduce the existing power structure and reveal images of the powerful group as relatively benign and favourable. This is what was found. Indeed, along the lines of a system justification analysis, in the open condition stereotypes of the sophisticated outgroup (e.g., as 'analytical' and 'conscientious') were slightly more favourable than those of the unsophisticated ingroup. However, in the closed condition – where an impermeable boundary removed all possibility of personal progress and the treatment meted out to the ingroup appeared to be extremely illegitimate – it was predicted that stereotypes of the powerful group would be far less favourable and would pave the way for strategies of social change. This is what happened. Now members of the low-power group qualified their description of the sophisticated group as 'analytical' with the additional traits 'mean', 'cold' and 'rude'. As well as this there was also evidence of accompanying change in the *ingroup* stereotype. Whereas in the open and quota conditions the un-sophisticated group was described primarily as 'friendly', 'pleasant' and 'sociable', in the closed condition it was more likely to be described as 'conscientious': a self-characterization that foreshadows (and facilitates) a shift from acquiescence to antagonism. Consistent with this general shift, statistical analysis also indicated that unfavourable stereotypes of the sophisticated outgroup played a mediating role in participants' decision to collectively confront that group over its treatment of the ingroup.

These findings clearly challenge the view that members of powerless groups are necessarily resigned to their lowly station and are only capable of submitting passively to the disempowering stereotypes of the powerful.[2] On the contrary, when intergroup relations appear to be insecure and structural relations between groups encourage powerless individuals to band together to mount a collective challenge to the powerful, groups enlist and rely upon stereotypes to prosecute that conflict. So although stereotypes can be part of attempts to dumb down and pacify powerless outgroups it is also the case that – psychological and structural factors permitting – those groups themselves can counter-attack with competing stereotypes of their own.

As a means of examining both sides of this coin, we recently conducted a study in which Australian students were asked to assign traits to a na-tional group under conditions where participants knew that the nation was either powerful or powerless but did not know its actual identity (it was referred to as Nation X). As well as this, five traits in the checklist were written in capitals to give an indication of the way in which Nation X had previously been described either by Australians or by its own nation-als. Furthermore, these traits were either favourable or unfavourable and either consistent with being powerful (e.g., industrious, ostentatious) or consistent with being powerless (e.g., faithful, ignorant). Key dependent measures included the favourableness of the traits used by participants to describe Nation X and the level of consensus in trait selection.

Complex as it was, the study's core aim was to reveal the political di-mensions of stereotype formation. Broadly speaking, we anticipated that participants would consensually endorse those stereotypes that appeared to offer the best prospect for appropriate collective management of the prevailing intergroup situation. In some ways this argument is akin to that of social judgeability theorists who suggest that an individual's capacity to stereotype members of a particular group is a product of social real-ity concerns (e.g., whether the stereotype represents objective features of the world) in interaction with normative and other social constraints (e.g., whether the stereotype is endorsed by others or is seen to be prejudicial; see Corneille & Yzerbyt, this volume, Leyens, Yzerbyt & Schadron, 1994; and also Spears, Jetten & Doosje, in press). However, in order for social judgeability theory to have predictive power, these abstract principles clearly need to be spelled out. In this regard, a distinct advantage of social identity and self-categorization theories is that the theoretical principles they contain led us to make some clear predictions in relation both to emergent stereotype content and consensus.

Central to these predictions was an appreciation of the degree to which the provision of feedback appeared to provide an opportunity either (a) to collectively challenge the power of the powerful group or (b) to maintain the powerlessness of the powerless group. Along the lines of previous research by Haslam et al. (1996), we expected that stereotypes of the powerful group would be very sensitive to the feedback provided by other ingroup members, so that Australians would be much more willing to endorse a negative stereotype of that group where that view was shared by other Australians and there thus appeared to be some basis for a collective challenge to the group's power. As the columns on the left of Figure 8.2 reveal, this was generally what we found. In particular, when Nation X was described using powerful traits the favourableness of stereotype content was very sensitive to the views of ingroup members (with positive feedback Mfav $= -0.21$, with negative feedback Mfav $= -3.29$) at the same time that it was largely unaffected by the views of people in the powerful group itself.

However, although consensus within an ingroup is critical to any challenge to the power of a powerful group, in the absence of overt conflict the opportunity to maintain the powerlessness of a low-power group should depend much more upon that group's willingness to accept its lowly position (Jost & Banaji, 1994). Accordingly, we expected that the content and consensus of Australians' stereotypes of this group would be much more sensitive to Nation X members' self-descriptions. Strong support for this proposition is revealed in the right hand columns of Figure 8.2. In particular, Australians uniformly embraced a very positive stereotype of the powerless Nation X (the most positive and most consensual stereotype in the whole study; Mfav $= 2.33$; $P_a = .289$) when that nation's self-stereotype indicated that its citizens were comfortable with their lowly status (seeing themselves as honest, faithful, loyal to family ties, musical and pleasure-loving).

The overall pattern of results in this study thus shows very clearly that the process of forming stereotypes is not only dictated by the need to represent social reality but is also sensitive to the opportunity to advance one's collective interests within it. And in contrast to the view that those opportunities are only available to powerful groups and are contingent

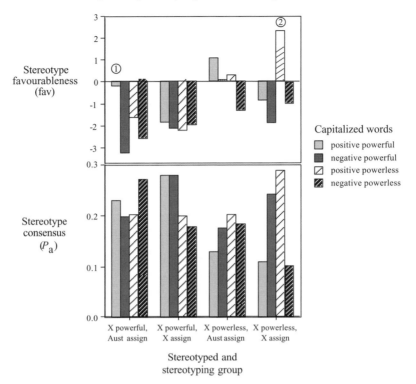

Figure 8.2 Favourableness and consensus of Nation X stereotypes as a function of the stereotypes (positive, negative; powerful, powerless) held by Australians or people from Nation X.

Note: Positive powerful traits = industrious, practical, intelligent, ambitious, progressive

Negative powerful traits = extremely nationalistic, ostentatious, loud, boastful, arrogant

Positive powerless traits = honest, faithful, loyal to family ties, musical, pleasure-loving

Negative powerless traits = lazy, unreliable, superstitious, ignorant, slovenly

1. Stereotypes of the powerful group were most positive when they were described in favourable status-consistent terms by ingroup members
2. Stereotypes of the powerless group were most positive when they were described in favourable status-consistent terms by outgroup members.

only on their behaviour (or whims), it is clear too that the actions and aspirations of powerless groups are every bit as important. Indeed, in this study feedback from the powerless group had *more* impact on the participants' stereotypes than did that from the powerful – a reflection of the fact that powerful groups are generally more motivated to build a workable higher-order consensus with powerless groups than vice versa (Machiavelli, 1513/1984).

Moreover, when the collective consciousness of the powerless is articulated in shared stereotypes, it appears to be palpably real and valid rather than false or enfeebling. On the one hand this is because such stereotypes have the capacity to challenge the status quo where social relations are unstable (as in this case) or illegitimate (Reynolds et al., 2000; Oakes et al., 1999). Indeed, even when this potential is not realized (e.g., because relations are secure and options for conflict are limited) they can play an active role in protecting and maintaining the ingroup's identity (Doosje & Ellemers, 1996; Ellemers, Wilke & van Knippenberg, 1993). Again, then, we are moved to the conclusion that stereotypes are instruments of collective self-actualization rather than mechanisms for passive self-abuse. In a world of intergroup politics they are not lazy traps into which the dispossessed unwittingly and all-too-easily fall but carefully-crafted weapons that are instrumental to their consolidated advancement.

Conclusion: stereotypes are shared tools not just private pictures

Towards the start of this chapter we noted that over time there has been a narrowing of focus in the analysis of stereotyping and stereotype formation, with researchers becoming increasingly preoccupied with the intrapsychic processes that lead isolated individuals to develop particular stereotypes and then to deploy them in different settings. Such issues are important, and indeed, as other chapters in this volume testify, work in the social identity tradition has provided important insights into these processes. Our general view, however, is that focusing on these activities to the exclusion of the social and political realm within which all stereotyping is located can only have a stultifying effect upon social psychological theory and research.

The simple reason for this is that the social world does not provide a backdrop for stereotyping, a context in which various matches between categories and content are treated with equal equanimity and favour. Instead group life is the primary sphere towards which that activity is oriented. Stereotypes form because people belong to groups, and they allow them to act proficiently as group members. And because proficiency in this realm can never be a wholly private act, much of the texture and meaning of stereotypes derives from the way in which they are *collaboratively managed* across a range of social settings.

Contrary to the view that is implicit in much previous research, stereotype formation is not, then, a process in which individuals develop personal (mis)representations of the world that they then resort to habitually and incorrigibly. It is a joint endeavour through which groups develop shared explanations of the world that allow them to represent social relations veridically and manage them appropriately, partly by orienting group members to ideologically-relevant goals. If those goals and relations are enduring stereotypes will be too (and they often are). But if they are not, collaborative work will ensure that stereotypes reform to reflect the group's new exigencies and to provide a platform for the new activities that its members need to undertake together.

For this reason, the very notion of 'stereotype formation' is actually somewhat misleading as it encourages petrification of a process that is, in reality, fluid and ongoing. Like the achievement of consensus, stereotype formation does not signal the endpoint of social and cognitive processes. Instead it represents a milestone that researchers use to mark out a significant phase of a group's life within an evolving system of intergroup relations. Stereotype formation and consensualization come not at the end of a journey but are ongoing processes on the road that takes a group from one significant event to the next.

This is a point that emerges clearly from the experimental work that we have reviewed in the previous four sections as well as from a wealth of research that has examined self-categorization processes in the field (e.g., Reicher & Hopkins, 2001; Sani & Reicher, 1999; Stott et al., in press). It is apparent too that this work paints a picture of the stereotyping process that is far more flattering than that which is offered in the metatheoretical mainstream (see also Oakes & Haslam, 2001; Oakes et al., 1994). For as that process bends itself to the goals and perspective of the stereotyper's group we see veridicality not distortion, meaning not irrationality, flexibility not rigidity, creativity not sameness, vitality not torpor.

Of course to many researchers such assertions will be close to heresy. Pointing to evidence of real human injury, they would argue that for the person who is a victim of a malicious stereotype or of action informed by bigotry, there is little solace in the knowledge that this represents the working of a rational, valid and constructive process (e.g., see Stangor & Jost, 1997). For our part, the goal of the analysis we have presented is certainly not to deny the capacity for stereotypes – and the groups that wield them – to inflict massive damage of this form. They do. However, where this occurs we see this not as a sign of psychological failing but as confirmation of the point that stereotyping is primarily a political process through which groups represent and assert their different (and sometimes conflicting) views, values and ideologies (see Oakes et al., 1994, 1999; Spears, Oakes, Ellemers & Haslam, 1997).

Moreover, we would contend that a key to redressing the problems that this fact can create lies in proper acknowledgement of the political basis and purposes of stereotyping and stereotype formation and in appropriate action of our own. Indeed, to offer the victims of stereotyping and prejudice anything other than a remedy of this form is to send them into a gun fight armed only with a water pistol. And by denying the positive role that self-empowering stereotypes can play in collective resistance to oppression it reinforces the very injustices that we seek to eradicate.

NOTES

1. Throughout this chapter we use the term 'political' to refer to the broad class of activities through which all groups represent and promote their shared interests in relation to others, rather than to the narrow class of activities related to party politics or government.
2. Indeed, even where power relations are perceived to be legitimate and the stereotypes held by low power groups have a latent system-justification function, we would argue that they are not necessarily passive internalizations of the power structure (or a form of 'false consciousness') as system justification theorists argue (see Oakes et al., 1999). Instead, their manifest function is often to allow for collective self-enhancement and group maintenance which is a necessary prelude to subsequent attempts at social change.

9 Conclusion: stereotypes are selective, variable and contested explanations

Craig McGarty, Russell Spears and Vincent Y. Yzerbyt

The chapters in this book make a number of distinct contributions that help us understand the importance of explanation in stereotype formation. Despite the distinctiveness of the various contributions, a number of key themes emerge and recur. Before addressing these in more detail it is useful to remind ourselves of perhaps one key theme that has guided this volume and gives all of its contributions some common ground. Perhaps more implied than explicitly stated, all of the contributions focus on stereotype formation (and more generally 'stereotyping') as a dynamic psychological process embedded in intergroup relations. This point may sound like a truism, but in our view, the partial nature of some previous approaches flows from an emphasis on one or other of these two components. That is, much previous and contemporary research has tended to focus on stereotyping as a psychological process, but to neglect the social and contextual dimensions of this process (e.g., the importance of own group membership, content, the nature of the intergroup relations). Alternatively, where research has recognized the social dimension of stereotyping, it has often neglected the dynamic explanatory psychological processes involved (stereotypes as fixed structures, percepts, pictures in our heads, epiphenomena of intergroup relations or culture). If there is a common theme that brings many of the current contributions together, then, it is the attempt to integrate the cognitive and the social aspects of the stereotyping process by attention to both cognitive and social levels of explanation and analysis. Put another way, the analysis of the psychological processes involved makes most sense when understood in terms of the social relations involved (and vice versa). Indeed the central idea of *stereotypes as explanation* is the bridge that links social perception to the social perspective of the perceiver.

In the following sections we elaborate the particular themes in more detail, which allows us to see in sharper focus the specific ideas that recur in the contributions. These themes also suggest to us a number of profitable directions for future development. However, such continuities should not disguise the potential for divergence and debate (as befits an edited volume with multiple voices) and in the following section we move on to consider some of the potential differences and contradictions that might emerge from the various positions espoused in the book, along with some ideas about how these debates might be resolved or at least motivate further research. First of all, and to introduce an analysis of themes, it may be useful to remind ourselves briefly of the key points put forward in the various contributions.

A brief summary of the chapters

In Chapter 2, McGarty made a number of claims. The most general of these was that stereotype formation can be understood as a process of development of constraints between what we know about categories (background knowledge), perceptions of similarity and difference (perceived equivalence or non-equivalence) and the explicit use of some category labels (category use). In other words, stereotypes can only be said to have formed when there are interrelations between knowledge about social categories and perceptions of those categories. The stereotype should not be considered as either the explanation or the thing to be explained, but as the full set of constraints between knowledge, perceived equivalence and labelling. Nevertheless stereotype formation can be said to be taking place whenever sets of constraints develop in perceiving social stimuli: thus, both perceiving that some set of similarities and differences is associated with a particular category and internalizing those category labels as an explanation of some set of similarities and differences are both aspects of stereotype formation. This central claim was supplemented by three additional ones. Stereotype formation involves explicit processes of justification and implicit processes of explanation. McGarty argued that a key feature of the explicit comparisons was that explicit justification tended to be in symbolic terms that could be communicated to other people. Further, explanations could involve both knowledge of mechanisms and covariations. Finally, he argued that we need to distinguish between groups and categories in terms of how these are stereotyped, a key part of the distinction being that groups are assumed to have collective qualities. This was important because some social categories (such as mental illness categories) seem to be devoid of these qualities.

In Chapter 3 Yzerbyt and Rocher remind us of the extent to which stereotyping often rests on naïve theories. One readily available example of such a naïve theory is the idea that categories have essential qualities in much the same way that natural objects do, and the assumed existence of this underlying essence contributes to the entitativity (coherence) of the categories. Importantly, essentialism should not be restricted to the perception of natural kinds within the social world. In fact, the consequences of subjective essentialism emerge whenever perceivers assume the existence of some meaningful underlying feature accounting for the observable characteristics. The work described by Yzerbyt and Rocher indeed shows an accentuation of similarities and differences when category labels suggest the existence of an underlying essence. These authors also report how the evocation of a meaningful rule for group construction can amplify the illusory correlation effect. Similarly, Yzerbyt and Rocher demonstrate that knowledge about how groups were formed helps people to make decisions about the relevance of dimensions for understanding and indeed stereotyping groups. The process is thus the same in all these situations: the theories that perceivers bring to the perceptions of social categories powerfully constrain the form of those perceptions. Specifically, the way in which groups are thought to come into being can have important consequences for the way they are to be perceived. Finally, Yzerbyt and Rocher suggest that essentialism and entitativity can perpetuate the status quo and the negative treatment of minority groups although they also suggest that this is certainly not an inevitable consequence.

Brown and Turner begin Chapter 4 by arguing that the distinction between stereotype formation and application of stored stereotypes is flawed. Instead they argue that stereotyping involves a single process of categorization based on comparative (data-based) and normative (theory-based) fit, but that fit at the level of data is always interpreted in terms of theories. These ideas were illustrated in two ways. Firstly, the authors showed that perceptions of groups were affected by theories about the malleability of individual group members. Secondly, they suggested how these theories functioned as shared ingroup beliefs. When people were exposed to the rejected theory of an outgroup they perceived the target in stereotypical ways which were more consistent with their own group's theory (a sort of reactance pushed them to come up with a countervailing explanation). Together these observations supplement an earlier point stressed by self-categorization theorists (e.g., Oakes et al., 1994): stereotypes are not only context dependent they are also theory dependent.

In Chapter 5 Berndsen et al. returned the focus to the illusory correlation effect. Illusory correlation has often been understood as a process of data-based distortion, but more recently it has been considered as a process of development of meaningful explanations. Once again the focus here moves us beyond passive perception or information processing to interpretation and sense making. Although one useful earlier distinction in the area of stereotype formation had been made in terms of the difference between expectancy-based and distinctiveness- (or data-) based processes, an up-to-date review of the research reveals that there is no sharp divide between theory- and data-based illusory correlation (although they may refer to different inputs and phases in the sense-making process, suggesting that the analytic distinction may remain useful). This is apparent in a number of ways. First of all the data-based processes that have attracted much of the attention in the field actually involve reinterpretation. The stimuli perceived in the illusory correlation paradigm are not constant over the course of the perception, but change in their meaning depending on the context and expectations brought to the situation. Similarly, coherence is both a property of data and theories that can feed into each other, and enhance the categorical differentiation process. In general, stereotype formation in the illusory correlation paradigm rather than being viewed as an information processing bias, is perhaps best understood as a dynamic hypothesis-testing process. Indeed evidence from think-aloud reports from participants provides intriguing evidence of this.

In Chapter 6 Corneille and Yzerbyt focus on other aspects of social reality that underpin stereotypes and once again demonstrate the interaction between psychological processes and social circumstances. They examine the consequences that actions by social groups have for other social groups and the stereotypes that result, making a strong case that stereotypes can emerge from outcome relationships between perceivers and social actors. For example, knowing that somebody may be able to or wish to harm or control you can lead you to stereotype them, and this may be quite socially functional as well as psychologically appropriate. From this starting point they make two central observations that elaborate on this theme. The first is that dependence generally increases stereotyping at the group level, partly because such stereotypes justify more abstract (group-level) responses to the outgroup. Secondly, they point out that this gap exists because most of the previous research focuses on individuals and on information processing rather than on stereotypes of groups. Their chief contribution then is to fill these empirical and theoretical gaps by examining the role of attentional processes and by studying the impact of anticipated interdependence on stereotyping.

Spears reminds us in Chapter 7 that stereotype formation almost inevitably involves reference to self and context and the neat activation/application distinction that was examined by Brown and Turner is also questioned here – particularly in the realm of stereotype formation. An immediate implication of this point is that the social cognitive approach (or at least its focus on pre-existing knowledge or schemas) will tend to be less relevant than the social identity inspired approach. This is not to deny that there will be important and wide-ranging consequences for the processes that are investigated by the cognitive approach. Social cognitive methods allow us to know when stereotypes have formed even when these are implicit, but much will be lost by not taking into account the role of self-processes. Spears suggests that four closely related principles can be employed to help explain the way perceivers form stereotypes: the reality principle (stereotypes are based on interpretations of real stimuli), the meaning principle (stereotypes form to make sense of the world), the distinctiveness principle (stereotypes form to distinguish between in-groups and outgroups) and the enhancement principle (stereotypes form to distinguish our own group positively). This chapter has several messages for us to consider. One overall theme is that stereotypes reside in the relation between groups and derive from the process of attempting to differentiate between groups. Or put slightly differently, the group essences may reflect at some deeper level the nature of the relation between groups (for the racist the sense of outgroup essence is closely bound up with the sense of otherness). This applies even where there are minimal differences between groups. Stereotyping helps to make sense of minimal group differences and can magnify them where no differences were obvious before. One general conclusion that Spears draws is that most stereotyping phenomena can be understood in terms of a single process of categorization that allows us to make sense of reality by separating groups into meaningful entities. This process draws on many factors (the four principles): the theories and expectations detailed in earlier chapters, but also motivations and interests, especially where expectations and theories, or even social reality ('content', comparative fit), fail to provide the differences that feed stereotype formation.

Finally, in Chapter 8 Haslam et al. strive to relocate the study of stereotype formation in the idea of consensus, and the often neglected realm of social interaction in which this is produced. Stereotypes are interesting and important not so much because they are about groups of people but because they are so frequently shared by groups of people. To put this point in perspective Haslam et al. start with a critique of social cognitive views which have narrowed the focus of stereotypes to be fixed pictures in the individual mind. They reject this view and on the basis of the social identity approach argue that stereotypes are shared or collective tools that are used to understand and to shape reality. Their account reflects four principles. The first is that stereotypes are collective achievements. Groups may not set out with a deliberate plan to stereotype some other group, but the stereotypes that they do develop are nevertheless elaborate attempts to understand complex relationships between groups. The formation of these stereotypes rests on processes of cooperation and influence. Secondly, despite a conventional wisdom to the contrary, stereotypes are constantly changing and are surprisingly responsive to changes in context. Thirdly, stereotypes are embedded in group relations and must be understood in the context of those relations. The fourth principle is that stereotypes are used to both maintain and challenge social orders. Stereotypes exist to understand groups, this is not necessarily for some abstract intellectual enterprise but because developing shared understandings of groups allows group members to act on those beliefs, and these actions can affect the status relations of those groups.

This summary gives just a taste of the individual contributions of the chapters. What we seek to do in the next section is to identify a set of common themes that run through more than one chapter of the book, and then turn to some points of disagreement before attempting to recapitulate the message of this book.

Some unifying themes

1.   Theories and knowledge about social groups have consequences for the dimensions which are selected to distinguish between groups

This idea appears in the chapter by McGarty in that some dimensions are associated with plausible causal mechanisms (e.g., laziness in unemployment). Similarly, Yzerbyt and Rocher suggest that the relevant dimensions chosen for differentiation will tend to be the ones which naïve theories say will cause the difference between the categories. Brown and Turner argue that the selection of dimensions is always driven by theory. Finally, Spears points out that differences on dimensions can either reflect knowledge or create knowledge (and even the absence of knowledge can stimulate the search to discover or create difference).

2.   Theory and data are intimately intertwined in stereotype formation

This point is central to the arguments of Berndsen et al. and Brown and Turner also make it clear that judgements of prototypicality are not just context-dependent they are theory-dependent. Related ideas are discussed in some detail by Yzerbyt and Rocher, McGarty and Spears (and in their discussion of stereotype content Haslam et al. point out that even features such as ambiguity are not stable properties that are perpetually linked to traits).

3.   Meaning and differentiation: beyond cognitive economy?

The first two themes above indicate that we have moved beyond simple perceptualist models of 'bottom up' accentuation. The focus on (differentiated) *meaning* that arises in virtually every chapter reflects this interaction between theory and data. In recent years a focus on meaning has come to signify a challenge to the cognitive-miser-based accounts of stereotyping that have depicted cognitive economy as the driving principle behind categorization and stereotyping. This economy theme has been notable by its absence in the present volume and it is interesting to ask whether this is a deficiency of the current approaches or perhaps reflects the reduced relevance of the economy principle to the question of stereotype formation. Some have resisted the opposition of the principles of meaning vs. economy (does efficiency capture both?) and that debate is ongoing elsewhere. However, such questions do demand some precision. What is meant by 'meaning' that is any different from 'information' (is it more than merely a vacuous comfort term, an attempt at illusory distinctiveness?). In various ways the chapters do make clear that a focus on meaning takes us beyond mere information, and captures the interplay of theory and data, of categories and content, and of the social factors and psychological processes. It also refers to the constructive and temporal process that puts these elements together resulting in interpretations, judgements and even actions. Meaning is also something that is socially shared (in language, by the group) as well as providing personal insight. In short, meaning captures more than information, and is for many of the authors a useful concept in the interactionist attempt to link the psychological and the social domains. Finally, meaning, or at least the meaning which appears so important for stereotype formation, is derived by differentiating between categories.

4.   *Stereotypes are not passive responses to context*

Corneille and Yzerbyt go to some lengths to point out that real or anticipated actions by groups have important consequences for the content of stereotypes, and even for determining which group is stereotyped. Yzerbyt and Rocher are sensitive to this and a related issue occupies a great deal of the chapters by Spears and by Berndsen et al. Contexts are not just taken on board but are interpreted for their relevance to the social actors and their implications for potential courses of action (this is partly what is understood by the more social concept of meaning addressed above). Indeed, one implication of the ideas of Haslam et al. is that beyond the interpretation of context lies the possibility of overturning some context: a group may develop the view that its status is inferior to some other group, but on the basis of the development of perceptions that that status advantage is illegitimate (involving a stereotype of the high status group as being unfairly privileged) the possibility exists for the groups to work to overturn that state of affairs.

5.   The wrong lessons have sometimes been drawn from social cognitive research

In general terms, this is the starting point of the analyses of Spears and of Haslam et al. Similarly, in their general analysis of problems with a distortion-based approach, Berndsen et al. suggest that perceivers' limitation to detect non-contingency may have consequences: stereotyping data may reflect not so much a distortion but a mismatch between perceivers' aptitude and experimental stimuli. This implies previous researchers may have drawn the wrong lesson from evidence of categorization effects because researchers have been locked into the 'bias' framing. This may have prevented them from seeing the more rational and functional sides to these processes and even the outcomes. Once again, and in keeping with our general guiding theme, these processes and outcomes need to be judged against social agendas (e.g., group related goals, or what the experimenter wants), and not just in terms of individual information processing criteria.

6.   Expectancies can produce coherence

Of course this is a key idea in the work of Yzerbyt and Rocher: naïve theories that groups have essential qualities can lead to coherence. Berndsen et al. also discuss in some detail the evidence for the proposition that expecting coherence in groups contributes to the illusory correlation effect. It is worth noting that these are exactly the sort of ideas that the constraints relation formulation discussed by McGarty was designed to describe.

7.   Stereotypes are not necessarily bad

This idea is one of the hallmarks of the self-categorization theory approach and is reiterated here in two chapters in particular. Haslam et al. suggest that stereotypes are weapons that can be used to challenge or maintain the status quo, a position that is also largely compatible with Corneille and Yzerbyt's contribution. The application of those stereotypes can have positive or negative consequences, but that assessment is largely a political judgement. Similarly, Spears tentatively raises a 'compensation hypothesis' in that stereotypic differentiation can be an antidote that serves to inoculate against pernicious forms of discrimination, or at least that it can have this effect. More generally, at least implicitly, most of the contributions take a functional approach to stereotyping, in that they see stereotype formation as relating to individual or social goals, rather than being dysfunctional, distorted or prejudiced (see next theme).

8.   *Stereotypical knowledge is shared*

Although it is a focus of the chapter by Haslam et al. and of the introductory chapter this point can be considered to be a subtext of numerous other contributions to this book (e.g., where McGarty argues that justifications are expressed in explicit symbolic terms to enable people to communicate them). Stereotypes are interesting, and arguably only become important in a social sense where they are shared (if every member of a group had different stereotypes we would pay them little heed). We cannot hope to understand stereotypes fully until we come to understand the process by which consensus is reached.

Some points of difference

In the preceding section we focused on some points where there was actual or implied agreement across several chapters. It is now useful to consider a smaller number of points of disagreement that invite attention, debate (and perhaps even resolution).

> *Debate point 1. 'stereotypes do not exist in any ongoing fashion' vs. 'some aspect of categorical knowledge must have a long-term existence'*

Brown and Turner champion the first position that stereotypes do not have an ongoing existence, and their view is in line with an important tradition of self-categorization theory work (see e.g., Oakes, Haslam & Turner, 1994; Turner, Oakes, Haslam & McGarty, 1994; Turner & Onorato, 1999). The starting point for this view is that little is to be gained from distinguishing between application and activation of categories, and perhaps something to be lost in the realm of formation at least (see also Spears, this volume). The enormous variety of categories that people can deploy and the context-dependent nature of those categorizations means that it is more sensible to focus on the application of categories to particular situations.

The alternative position, espoused by McGarty (1999, and this volume), is that there must be some aspects of stereotypical knowledge that are relatively enduring, and unless this knowledge reflects categories it is relatively useless to learn or communicate. There would be little point learning that the unemployed are lazy (and can be expected to be lazy in the future) if we were not able to store the category *unemployed* in some form. Similarly, there would be little point in communicating such a stereotypical belief and working to build a consensus around it, if the members of groups had no capacity to retain knowledge of categories beyond the time that those categories were salient.

Other authors are either silent on this issue, or in the case of Spears, present a compromise position. He adopts the self-categorization position that stereotypes are context-dependent and relational, but also allows for knowledge structures that have become so routinized that they reflect a certain stability (at least once accessed) and can be triggered along with the relevant category labels. One answer to this question may therefore be that it can be both and this may depend on the nature of the group and one's relation to it.

Is a more general reconciliation possible here? In line with the arguments of Smith and de Coster (1998) and others who have advocated consideration of connectionist principles in social psychology it is reasonable to doubt that categories exist as enduring knowledge structures that are stored in some independent fashion. If we instead consider categories to be instantiated through a set of associations of representations of instances then we can move beyond the limitations of the idea of stored, fixed category and consider mental systems which incorporate both stability and seemingly infinite variety.

Another way out of this impasse is to see the issue of storage and stability as something that operates at the social level rather than the level of cognitive representation. In line with our general theme of uniting social and psychological components, and our view of stereotypes as shared and consensual group products (Haslam, et al.), it is quite consistent to see these as 'stored' in the social structure, the social relations, the culture that they inhabit (until we get the conditions for social change of course). Indeed this has been a traditional response of self-categorization theorists to resolving the apparent contradiction of the rigidity and consistency of stereotypes over time with their notional fluidity and flexibility in the mind. They can be both long-term and ephemeral, but this is not just an individual question but also a broader social one.

Debate point 2: how important is essence?

This point is not so much a debate between opposed positions but a question of emphasis. Yzerbyt and colleagues have stressed the importance of the essential qualities of groups in the perception of groups as coherent entities. In his chapter McGarty does not take issue with the importance of this idea, except to the degree that he argues that these principles need to be supplemented by a consideration of what he terms collective qualities of certain categories (deriving from social organization and adherence to norms).

Of course, both of these ideas are important (and certainly collective qualities are included in the entitativity continuum of Hamilton, Sherman & Lickel, 1998). The question of the relative importance of these two principles is, at this stage, an empirical question, but it may turn out to be important to resolve it. This is because attributing collective qualities to social categories can be interpreted as a process of attributing group formation (and hence self-categorization) to social categories. This has two important consequences. Firstly, where members of social categories are presumed to have engaged in group formation then a whole new class of stereotypical explanations is available. Social perceivers can only plausibly explain stereotypical attributes of social categories in terms of the adherence of the members of the group to social norms where they believe group formation (at some level) has occurred. Secondly, if it is true that perceivers are motivated to have accurate views of social categories then they will only be able to achieve accurate perceptions of social categories to the extent to which they attribute group formation accurately. If collective behaviour is controlled by group processes then in order to accurately explain and predict the behaviour of groups perceivers need to be able to recognize the circumstances when collective behaviour really is collective. Once again, this is not just a matter for cognition alone, but of the interaction between cognition and a social reality in which the degree of essence (at least from a realist perspective) can be assumed to vary.

There is one further way in which the idea of essence may be critically important and this relates to the question of whether stereotypes are relatively fixed or relatively dynamic. In their different ways, all of the contributors to this volume emphasize the potential stereotypes have for variability and change. Despite the relative variability of stereotypes the subjective experience of stereotypes may be that they are relatively enduring and invariant partly because variable surface features are easily attributed to deep essences. Thus, the subjective experience of stereotype flexibility may not be cognitively accessible to perceivers. This suggests one intriguing explanation for the emphasis on stereotype rigidity in the social psychological literature: stereotypes are *experienced* as being more rigid than they really are because people's essentialist stance renders the impact of their background knowledge and the current context mostly transparent and prevents a full consideration of the evolution if not inconsistency of their stereotypic views from one moment to another.

Debate point 3: 'the categorization process tends to (but need not) perpetuate the status quo' vs. 'stereotyping allows both challenges and maintenance of the status quo'

The contributions by Corneille and Yzerbyt and Yzerbyt and Rocher may appear to be more in agreement with the idea that the categorization process tends to perpetuate the status quo whereas that by Haslam et al. suggests a contrary view. This difference can be seen as a recapitulation of an old debate in social psychology about the potential for negative consequences of the way that humans think. Is the cognitive process of categorization inherently conservative? More broadly than this, the question here is whether the processes of categorization and stereotyping are socially conservative, or provide tools for social change.

We think there is a resolution to this point. To the extent that there is a status quo in the relations between two groups it is certainly useful to consider how social psychological processes are involved in maintaining that status quo (alternatives include considering that the status quo is maintained by inertia, or the absence of process, or multiple random processes, which have the effect of cancelling out change in any dominant direction). If a status quo is maintained then it is highly plausible that categorization processes will have played some role because they are ubiquitous cognitive processes. On the other hand, if change does occur (even where this is against the odds) it is essential that this rests on some new interpretation of the relation of the groups as we learned from social identity theory a quarter of a century ago (Tajfel & Turner, 1979). For instance, patterns of domination are easier to maintain where the oppressed 'know their place', but they are also easier to overturn where the oppressors are identified as oppressors rather than as (say) kindly guardians. This example nicely illustrates how the process, (i.e. categorization), and the content, (i.e. stereotypes), may be independent of each other. Again, the members of the dominant group may be keen to stereotype the members of the subordinate group in order to perpetuate their privileges. Conversely, the members of the subordinate group may be tempted to build a derogatory image of the members of the dominant group in order to change the state of affairs. Interestingly, the stereotypes in these two situations serve very clear yet contradictory goals. It thus seems that stereotyping is largely inescapable as a process, be this executed unknowingly or on purpose. In contrast, stereotypes, as content, always end up in the service of those concerns that people have on their agenda. Obviously, social psychological work on isolating the social psychological role of stereotype formation in maintaining or modifying the social structure is in its infancy (albeit long overdue!). However, we think that this question is more likely to be resolved by social factors and forces, rather than by issues of psychological functioning, that swing the balance in favour of false consciousness (for example).

The message of this book

Is it possible then to articulate in just a few words a central message of this book? If it is then our summary would be something like the following (though, of course, we cannot hold the authors to our interpretation of their work).

People form stereotypes to make sense of the world they live in. The things that they tend to make sense of are relations between groups that they encounter, interact with and are dependent on. Perceivers are intent on producing these understandings because they need this knowledge to understand the world and to take and coordinate action.

In forming these stereotypes people bring two key sorts of resources to bear. The first includes naïve (or everyday) theories about the groups, which might take the form of expectations of coherence within, or difference between the groups, or beliefs about the naturalness and essential qualities of the categories that underlie the groups, or beliefs about the collective (group qualities or social organization that underpins the group). The second kind of resource that the perceivers bring involves their perceptions of members of the categories that enable judgements of similarities and differences.

These two resources (theory and data) are utterly intertwined in the process of explaining the relations between groups so that even where others might perceive no difference it is possible for perceivers to interpret the data to show differences in new ways or to choose to focus on new dimensions. The way in which stereotypes emerge from the interaction of theory and data, however, is completely bound by two related features: the dynamic varying nature of the process and its consensual basis. We say that these two are related because it is only through flexibility that consensus is possible (see McGarty, 1999). If we could not change our opinions we would be irreconcilably locked in disagreement and would be unable to reach genuine consensus, regardless of how desirable that consensus may be.

What does all of this achieve? The outcome of the process of stereotype formation is the derivation of knowledge about categories that serves to explain similarities and differences on relevant dimensions at that time in ways which are shared. We can put it no more succinctly than to say: we form stereotypes to explain aspects of and relations between social groups.

We hope readers find this framework useful. Regardless of whether the framework passes the tests both of time and future empirical investigations we hope that the enduring legacy of this work will be that this volume continues the tradition of normalizing the cognitive process of stereotype formation by putting it in its social psychological context, and more strongly, showing its social character. We hope this enterprise is successful because we do not believe that there could be anything more natural or normal than the attempts to form understandings of the social groups that make up such a large part of the world around us.

References

Abele, A. E. and Petzold, P. (1998). Pragmatic use of categorical information in impression formation. *Journal of Personality and Social Psychology*, *75*, 347–58.

Abelson, R. P., Dasgupta, N., Park, J. and Banaji, M. R. (1998). Perceptions of the collective other. *Personality and Social Psychology Review*, *2*, 243–50.

Abrams, D. and Hogg, M. A. (1990). Social identification, self-categorization, and social influence. In W. Stroebe and M. Hewstone (Eds.), *European Review of Social Psychology* (Vol. 1, pp. 195–228). New York: Wiley.

Adorno, T. W., Frenkel-Brunswik, E., Levinson, D. J. and Sanford, R. N. (1950). *The authoritarian personality*. New York: Harper.

Ahn, W-K., Kalish, C. W., Medin, D. L. and Gelman, S. A. (1995). The role of covariation versus mechanism information in causal attribution. *Cognition*, *54*, 299–352.

Allison, S. T., Beggan, J. K, Midgley, E. H. and Wallace, K. A. (1995). Dispositional and behavioral inferences about inherently democratic and unanimous groups. *Social Cognition*, *13*, 105–25.

Allison, S. T., Mackie, D. M. and Messick, D. M. (1996). Outcome biases in social perception: implications for dispositional inference, attitude change, stereotyping, and social behavior. *Advances in Experimental Social Psychology*, *28*, 53–93.

Allison, S. T. and Messick, D. M. (1985). The group attribution error. *Journal of Experimental Social Psychology*, *21*, 563–79.

Alloy, L. B. and Tabachnik, N. (1984). Assessment of covariation by humans and animals: the joint influence of prior expectations and current situational information. *Psychological Review*, *91*, 112–49.

Allport, G. W. (1954). *The nature of prejudice*. Reading, MA: Addison-Wesley.

Andersen, S. M. and Klatzky, R. L. (1987). Traits and social stereotypes: levels of categorisation in person perception. *Journal of Personality and Social Psychology*, *53*, 235–46.

Anderson, C. A. (1995). Implicit theories in broad perspective. *Psychological Inquiry*, *6*, 286–90.

Asch, S. E. (1952). *Social Psychology*. New Jersey: Prentice Hall.

Augoustinos, M. and Walker, I. (1995). *Social Cognition: an integrated introduction*. London: Sage.

Avigdor, R. (1953). Etude expérimentale de la genèse des stéréotypes. *Cahiers Internationaux de Sociologie*, *14*, 154–68.

Bargh, J. A. (1996). Automaticity in social psychology. In E. T. Higgins and A. W. Kruglanski (Eds.), *Social psychology: handbook of basic principles* (pp. 169–83). New York, NY: Guilford Press.

Bargh, J. A., Chen, M. and Burrows, L. (1996). The automaticity of social behavior: direct effects of trait concept and stereotype activation on action. *Journal of Personality and Social Psychology, 71*, 230–44.

Barsalou, L. W. (1985). Ideals, central tendency, and frequency of instantiation as determinants of graded structure in categories. *Journal of Experimental Psychology: Learning, Memory, and Cognition, 11*, 629–54.

Barsalou, L. W. (1991). Deriving categories to achieve goals. In G. H. Bower (Ed.), *The psychology of learning and motivation: advances in theory and research* (Vol. 27). New York, NY: Academic Press.

Bassok, M. and Medin, D. L. (1997). Birds of a feather flock together: similarity judgements with semantically rich stimuli. *Journal of Memory and Language, 36*, 311–36.

Bem, D. J. (1967). Self-perception: an alternative interpretation of cognitive dissonance. *Psychological Review, 74*, 183–200.

Berndsen, M., McGarty, C., van der Pligt, J. and Spears, R. (2001). Meaning-seeking in the illusory correlation paradigm: the active role of participants in the categorization process. *British Journal of Social Psychology, 40*, 209–33.

Berndsen, M. and Spears, R. (1997). Reinterpreting illusory correlation: from biased covariation to meaningful categorisation. *Swiss Journal of Psychology, 57*, 127–38.

Berndsen, M., Spears, R., McGarty, C. and van der Pligt, J. (1998). Dynamics of differentiation: similarity as the precursor and product of stereotype formation. *Journal of Personality and Social Psychology, 74*, 1451–63.

Berndsen, M., Spears, R., Van der Pligt, J. and McGarty, C. (1999). Determinants of intergroup differentiation on the illusory correlation task. *British Journal of Psychology, 90*, 201–20.

Berndsen, M., Van der Pligt, J. and Spears, R. (1994). Voorwaarden voor illusoire correlatie. [Requirements for illusory correlation]. In N. Ellemers et al. (Eds.) *Fundamentele Sociale Psychologie, 8*, (pp. 48–56). Tilburg University Press.

Berndsen, M., van der Pligt, J., Spears, R. and McGarty, C. (1996). Expectation-based and data-based illusory correlation: the effects of confirming versus disconfirming evidence. *European Journal of Social Psychology, 26*, 899–913.

Bettelheim, B. (1947). Dynamism of anti-Semitism in gentile and Jew. *Journal of Abnormal and Social Psychology, 7*, 151–63.

Biernat, M., Vescio, T. K. and Manis, M. (1998). Judging and behaving toward members of stereotyped groups: a shifting standards perspective. In C. R. Sedikides, J. Schopler and C. A. Insko (Eds.), *Intergroup cognition and intergroup behaviour* (pp. 151–75). Mahwah, NJ: Erlbaum.

Bless, H., Strack, F. and Schwarz, N. (1993). The informative functions of research procedures: bias and the logic of conversation. *European Journal of Social Psychology, 23*, 149–65.

Bliuc, A-M. (forthcoming). Joining and belonging to ideological groups: the roles of affiliative and issue uncertainty in self-categorization. Forthcoming PhD thesis, The Australian National University.

Bodenhausen, G. V. and Macrae, C. N. (1998). Stereotype activation and inhibition. In R. S. Wyer (Ed.), *Advances in social cognition* (Vol. 11, pp. 1–52). Mahwah, NJ: Erlbaum.

Bourhis, R. Y. (1994). Power, gender, and intergroup discrimination: some minimal group experiments. In M. P. Zanna and J. M. Olson (Eds.), *The psychology of prejudice: the Ontario symposium* (Vol. 7). Hillsdale, NJ: Erlbaum.

Bourhis, R. Y., Turner, J. C. and Gagnon, A. (1997). Interdependence, social identity and discrimination. In R. Spears, P. Oakes, N. Ellemers and S. A. Haslam (Eds.), *The social psychology of stereotyping and group life*. Oxford, UK and Cambridge, USA: Blackwell.

Branscombe, N. R., Schmitt, M. T. and Harvey, R. D. (1999). Perceiving pervasive discrimination among African Americans: implications for group identification and well-being. *Journal of Personality and Social Psychology, 77,* 135–49.

Brewer, M. B. (1988). A dual process model of impression formation. In T. K. Srull and R. S. Wyer (Eds.), *Advances in social cognition* (Vol. 1, pp. 1–36). Hillsdale, NJ: Erlbaum.

Brewer, M. B. (1991). The social self: on being the same and different at the same time. *Personality and Social Psychology Bulletin, 17,* 475–82.

Brewer, M. B., Dull, V. and Lui, L. (1981). Perception of the elderly: stereotypes as prototypes. *Journal of Personality and Social Psychology, 41,* 656–70.

Brewer, M. B. and Harasty, A. S. (1996). Seeing groups as entities: the role of perceiver motivation. In R. Sorrentino and E. T. Higgins (Eds.), *Handbook of motivation and cognition Vol. 3: The interpersonal context.* (pp. 347–70). New York: Guilford Press.

Brewer, M. B., Weber, J. G. and Carini, B. (1995). Person memory in intergroup contexts: categorization versus individuation. *Journal of Personality and Social Psychology, 69,* 29–40.

Brown, P. M. and Turner, J. C. (2001a). The impact of different background theories on judgements of prototypicality and stereotype content. Manuscript in preparation, University of Canberra.

Brown, P. M. and Turner, J. C. (2001b). Naïve theories and normative fit: explanations, consistency and stereotype content. Manuscript in preparation, University of Canberra.

Brown, R. (1986). *Social psychology: The second edition.* New York: Free Press.

Bruner, J. S. (1957a). On perceptual readiness. *Psychological Review, 64,* 123–52.

Bruner, J. S. (1957b). Going beyond the information given. In H. E. Gruber, K. R. Hammond and R. Jessor (Eds.), *Contemporary approaches to cognition* (pp. 41–69). Cambridge, MA: Harvard University Press.

Bruner, J. S., Goodnow, J. J. and Austin, G. A. (1956). *A study of thinking.* New York: Wiley.

Campbell, D. T. (1956). Enhancement of contrast as a composite habit. *Journal of Abnormal and Social Psychology, 53,* 350–5.

Campbell, D. T. (1958). Common fate, similarity, and other indices of the status of aggregates of persons as social entities. *Behavioural Sciences, 3,* 14–25.

Campbell, D. T. (1967). Stereotypes and the perception of group differences. *American Psychologist, 22,* 817–29.

Cantor, N. and Mischel, W. (1979). Prototypes in person perception. In L. Berkowitz (Ed.), *Advances in Experimental Social Psychology* (Vol. 12, pp. 3–52). New York: Academic Press.

Carlston, D. E. (1994). Associated systems theory: a systematic approach to cognitive representations of persons. In T. K. Srull and R. S. Wyer (Eds.), *Advances in social cognition* (Vol. 7, pp. 1–78). Hillsdale, NJ: Erlbaum.

Castano, E. and Yzerbyt, V. Y. (1998). The highs and lows of group homogeneity. *Behavioural Processes*, 42, 219–38.

Castano, E., Yzerbyt, V. Y., and Bourgignon, D. (2000). We are one and I like it: The impact of group entitativity on group identification. Catholic University of Louvain at Louvain-la-Neuve. Manuscript submitted for publication.

Chapman, L. J. (1967). Illusory correlation in observational report. *Journal of Verbal Learning and Verbal Behavior*, 6, 151–5.

Cheng, P. W. (1997). From covariation to causation: a causal power theory. *Psychological Review*, 104, 367–405.

Chiu, C., Hong, Y. and Dweck, C. S. (1997). Lay dispositionism and implicit theories of personality. *Journal of Personality and Social Psychology*, 73, 19–30.

Claire, T. and Fiske, S. T. (1998). A systemic view of behavioral confirmation: counterpoint to the individualist view. In C. Sedikides, J. Schopler and C. A. Insko (Eds.), *Intergroup cognition and intergroup behavior* (pp. 205–31). Mahwah, NJ: Erlbaum.

Cohen, C. E. (1981). Person categories and social perception: testing some boundaries of the processing effects of prior knowledge. *Journal of Personality and Social Psychology*, 40, 441–52.

Condor, S. (2000). Pride and prejudice: identity management in English people's talk about 'this country'. *Discourse and Society*, 11, 175–205.

Corneille, O. and Judd, C. M. (1999). Accentuation and sensitization effects in the categorization of multi-faceted stimuli. *Journal of Personality and Social Psychology*, 77, 927–41.

Corneille, O., Klein, O., Lambert, S. and Judd, C. M. (2001). Obtaining categorical accentuation with unidimensional physical estimates: the role of familiarity with measurement unit. Manuscript submitted for publication.

Corneille, O., Yzerbyt, V. Y., Rogier, A. and Buidin, G. (2001). Threat and the group attribution error: when threat elicits judgments of extremity and homogeneity. *Personality and Social Psychology Bulletin*, 27, 437–46.

Corter, J. E. and Gluck, M. (1992). Explaining basic categories: features predictability for information. *Psychological Bulletin*, 111, 291–300.

Coull, A. and Yzerbyt, V. Y. (1999). Cognitive resources and stereotype preservation: 'Just gimme a moment'! Manuscript submitted for publication.

Coull, A., Yzerbyt, V. Y., Castano, E., Paladino, P. and Leemans (2001). Dealing with a deviant ingroup member: motivated stereotyping has a cognitive price. Manuscript submitted for publication. Catholic University of Louvain at Louvain-la-Neuve.

Crocker, J. (1981). Judgment of covariation by social perceivers. *Psychological Bulletin*, 90, 272–92.

Dasgupta, N., Banaji, M. R. and Abelson, R. P. (1999). Group entitativity and group perception: associations between physical features and psychological judgment. *Journal of Personality and Social Psychology*, 77, 991–1003.

Dépret, E. and Fiske, S. T. (1999). Perceiving the powerful: intriguing individuals versus threatening groups. *Journal of Experimental Social Psychology*, *35*, 461–80.

Deschamps, J.-C. (1973–1974). L'attribution, la catégorisation sociale et les relations intergroupes. *Bulletin de Psychologie*, *27*, 710–21.

Devine, P. G. (1989). Stereotypes and prejudice: their automatic and controlled components. *Journal of Personality and Social Psychology*, *56*, 5–18.

Devine, P. G. and Elliot, A. J. (1995). Are racial stereotypes *really* fading? The Princeton Trilogy revisited. *Personality and Social Psychology Bulletin*, *21*, 1139–50.

Devine, P. G., Hamilton, D. L. and Ostrom, T. M. (Eds.) (1994). *Social cognition: Contributions to classic issues in social psychology*. San Diego, CA: Academic Press.

Diab, L. N. (1962). National stereotypes and the 'reference group' concept. *Journal of Social Psychology*, *57*, 339–51.

Diab, L. N. (1963). Factors determining group stereotypes. *Journal of Social Psychology*, *61*, 3–10.

Dijksterhuis, A., Spears, R., Postmes, T., Stapel, D. A., Koomen, W., van Knippenberg, A. and Scheepers, D. (1998). Seeing one thing and doing another: contrast effects in automatic behavior. *Journal of Personality and Social Psychology*, *75*, 862–71.

Doise, W., Csepeli, G., Dann, H. D., Gouge, C., Larsen, K. and Ostell, A. (1972). An experimental investigation into the formation of intergroup representations. *European Journal of Social Psychology*, *2*, 202–4.

Doosje, B. and Ellemers, N. (1997). Stereotyping under threat: the role of group identification. In R. Spears, P. Oakes, N. Ellemers and S. Haslam (Eds.), *The social psychology of stereotyping and group life* (pp. 257–72), Oxford, England: Blackwell.

Doosje, B., Ellemers, N. and Spears, R. (1995). Perceived intragroup variability as a function of group status and identification. *Journal of Experimental Social Psychology*, *31*, 410–36.

Doosje, B., Ellemers, N. and Spears, R. (1999). Group commitment and intergroup behaviour. In N. Ellemers, R. Spears and B. Doosje (Eds.) *Social identity: Context, commitment, content.* (pp. 84–106). Oxford: Blackwell.

Doosje, B. and Haslam, S. A. (2000). Exploring the dynamics of reciprocity in intergroup contexts: National judgment and Eurovision. Unpublished manuscript: University of Amsterdam.

Doosje, B., Haslam, S. A., Spears, R., Oakes, P. J. and Koomen, W. (1998). The effect of comparative context on central tendency and variability judgements and the evaluation of group characteristics. *European Journal of Social Psychology*, *28*, 173–84.

Doosje, B., Spears, R. and Koomen, W. (1995). When bad isn't all bad: the strategic use of sample information in generalization and stereotyping. *Journal of Personality and Social Psychology*, *69*, 642–55.

Drury, J. and Reicher, S. D. (in press). Collective action and psychological change: the emergence of new social identities. *British Journal of Social Psychology*.

Dweck, C. S., Chiu, C. and Hong, Y. (1995a). Implicit theories and their role in judgements and reactions: a world from two perspectives. *Psychological Inquiry*, *6*, 267–85.

Dweck, C. S., Chiu, C., and Hong, Y. (1995b). Implicit theories: elaboration and extension of the model. *Psychological Inquiry*, 6, 322–33.

Dweck, C. S., Hong, Y. and Chiu, C. (1993). Implicit theories: individual differences in the likelihood and meaning of dispositional inference. *Personality and Social Psychology Bulletin*, 19, 644–56.

Eagly, A. H. (1987). *Sex differences in social behaviour: A social-role interpretation.* Hillsdale, NJ: Lawrence Erlbaum Associates.

Eagly, A. H. and Steffen, V. J. (1984). Gender stereotypes stem from the distribution of men and women into social roles. *Journal of Personality and Social Psychology*, 46, 735–54.

Eagly, A. H. and Steffen, V. J. (1986). Gender stereotypes, occupational roles, and beliefs about part-time employees. *Psychology of Women Quarterly*, 10, 252–62.

Ehrlich, H. J. and Rinehart, J. W. (1965). A brief report on the methodology of stereotype research. *Social Forces*, 43, 564–75.

Eiser, J. R. and Stroebe, W. (1972). *Categorization and social judgment.* London: Academic Press.

Ellemers, N., Doosje, E. J., van Knippenberg, A. and Wilke, H. (1992). Status protection in high status minorities. *European Journal of Social Psychology*, 22, 123–40.

Ellemers, N., Wilke, H. and van Knippenberg, A. (1993). Effects of the legitimacy of low group or individual status on individual and collective identity enhancement strategies. *Journal of Personality and Social Psychology*, 64, 766–78.

Erber, R. and Fiske, S. T. (1984). Outcome dependency and attention to inconsistent information about others. *Journal of Personality and Social Psychology*, 47, 709–26.

Eysenck, H. J. and Crown, S. (1948). National stereotypes: an experimental and methodological study. *International Journal of Opinion and Attitude Research*, 2, 26–39.

Festinger, L. (1954). A theory of social comparison processes. *Human Relations*, 7, 117–40.

Fiedler, K. (1991). The tricky nature of skewed frequency tables: an information loss account of distinctiveness-based illusory correlations. *Journal of Personality and Social Psychology*, 60, 26–36.

Fiedler, K. (1996). Explaining and simulating judgment biases as an aggregation phenomenon in probabilistic, multiple-cue environments. *Psychological Review*, 103, 193–214.

Fielder, K. and Armbruster, T. (1994). Two halfs may be more than one whole: category-split effects on frequency illusions. *Journal of Personality and Social Psychology*, 66, 633–45.

Fiedler, K., Russer, S. and Gramm, K. (1993). Illusory correlations and memory performance. *Journal of Experimental Social Psychology*, 29, 111–36.

Fiske, S. T. (1998). Stereotyping, prejudice, and discrimination. In D. T. Gilbert, S. T. Fiske and G. Lindzey (Eds.), *The Handbook of Social Psychology* (4th ed., Vol. 2, pp. 357–411). New York: McGraw-Hill.

Fiske, S. T. (2000). Interdependence and the reduction of prejudice. In S. Oskamp (Ed.), *Reducing prejudice and discrimination* (pp. 115–35), Hillsdale, NJ: Erlbaum.

Fiske, S. T. and Dépret, E. (1996). Control, interdependence and power: under-standing social cognition in its social context. *European Review of Social Psychology*, 7, 31–61.

Fiske, S. T., Lin, M. and Neuberg S. L. (1999). The continuum model: ten years later. In S. Chaiken and Trope, Y, (Eds.), *Dual process theories in social psychology* (pp. 231–54). New York: Guilford Press.

Fiske, S. T. and Neuberg, S. L. (1990). A continuum of impression formation, from category-based to individuating processes: influences of information and motivation on attention and interpretation. *Advances in Experimental Social Psychology*, 23, 1–74.

Fiske, S. T., Neuberg, S. L., Beattie, A. E. and Milberg, S. J. (1987). Category-based and attribute-based reactions to others: some informational conditions of stereotyping and individuating processes. *Journal of Experimental Social Psychology*, 23, 399–427.

Fiske, S. T. and Ruscher, J. B. (1993). Negative interdependence and prejudice: whence the affect? In D. M. Mackie and D. L. Hamilton (Eds.), *Affect, cognition, and stereotyping: Interactive processes in group perception* (pp. 239–68). New York: Academic Press.

Fiske, S. T. and Taylor, S. E. (1984). *Social cognition* (First ed.). New York: McGraw-Hill.

Fiske, S. T. and Taylor, S. E. (1991). *Social cognition* (Second ed.). New York: McGraw-Hill.

Ford, T. E. and Stangor, C. (1992). The role of diagnosticity in stereotype for-mation: perceiving group means and variances. *Journal of Personality and Social Psychology*, 63, 356–67.

Fyock, J. and Stangor, C. (1994). The role of memory biases in stereotype main-tenance. *British Journal of Social Psychology*, 33, 331–43.

Gaertner, L. and Insko, C. A. (2000). Intergroup discrimination in the minimal group paradigm: categorization, reciprocation, or fear? *Journal of Personality and Social Psychology*, 79, 77–94.

Gaertner, S. L., Dovidio, J. F., Anastasio, P. A., Bachman, B. A. and Rust, M. C. (1993). Reducing intergroup bias: the common ingroup identity model. In W. Stroebe and M. Hewstone (Eds.), *European Journal of Social Psychology* (Vol. 4, pp. 1–26). Chichester: Wiley and Sons.

Gagnon, A., and Bourhis, R. Y. (1996). Discrimination in the minimal group paradigm: social identity or social interest? *Personality and Social Psychology Bulletin*, 22, 1289–301.

Gelman, S. A. and Wellman, H. M. (1991). Insides and essences: early under-standings of the non-obvious. *Cognition*, 38, 213–44.

Gentner, D. (1983). Structure mapping: a theoretical framework for analogy. *Cognitive Science*, 7, 155–70.

Gentner, D. and Medina, J. (1998). Similarity and the development of rules. *Cognition*, 65, 263–97.

Gerard, H. B. and Hoyt, M. F. (1974). Distinctiveness of social categorization and attitude toward ingroup members. *Journal of Personality and Social Psychology*, 29, 836–42.

Gibson, J. J. (1982). Affordances and behavior. In E. S. Reed and R. K. Jones (Eds.) *Reasons for realism: Selected papers of J. J. Gibson*. Hillsdale, NJ: Erlbaum.

Gigerenzer, G. (1991). How to make cognitive illusions disappear: beyond heuristics and biases. In Stroebe, W. and Hewstone, M. (Eds.), *European Review of Social Psychology*, 2, 83–115.

Gilbert, D. T., Giesler, R. B. and Morris, K. A. (1995). When comparisons arise. *Journal of Personality and Social Psychology*, 69, 227–36.

Gilbert, D.T. and Hixon, J.G. (1991). The trouble of thinking: activation and application of stereotypic beliefs. *Journal of Personality and Social Psychology*, 60, 509–17.

Gilbert, G. M. (1951). Stereotype persistence and change among college students. *Journal of Abnormal and Social Psychology*, 46, 245–54.

Glick, P. and Fiske, S. T. (2001). Ambivalent stereotypes as legitimizing ideologies: differentiating paternalistic and envious prejudice. In J. T. Jost and B. Major (Eds.), *The psychology of legitimacy: Emerging perspectives on ideology, justice, and intergroup relations*. New York: Cambridge University Press.

Goldstone, R. (1994). Influences of categorization on perceptual discrimination. *Journal of Experimental Psychology: General*, 123, 178–200.

Goldstone, R. (1996). Isolated and interrelated concepts. *Memory & Cognition*, 24, 608–28.

Goldstone, R. (1998). Perceptual learning. *Annual Review of Psychology*, 49, 585–612.

Goldstone, R. L. and Barsalou, L. W. (1998). Reuniting perception and conception. *Cognition*, 65, 231–62.

Grice, H. P. (1975). Logic and conversation. In P. Cole and J. L. Morgan (Eds.), *Syntax and semantics: Speech acts* (Vol. 3, pp. 41–58). Orlando, FL: Academic Press.

Guinote, A. and Fiske, S. T. (2000). Outcome dependency affects perceived group variability: evidence for outgroup differentiation. Manuscript submitted for publication.

Guinote, A., Judd, C. M. and Brauer, M. (in press). Effects of power on perceived and objective group variability: evidence that more powerful groups are more variable. *Journal of Personality and Social Psychology*.

Hamilton, D. L. (Ed.) (1981a). *Cognitive processes in stereotyping and intergroup behaviour*. Hillsdale, NJ: Erlbaum.

Hamilton, D. L. (1981b). Illusory correlation as a basis for stereotyping. In D. L. Hamilton (Ed.), *Cognitive processes in stereotyping and intergroup behavior* (pp. 115–44). Hillsdale, NJ: Erlbaum.

Hamilton, D. L. and Rose, T. L. (1980). Illusory correlation and the maintenance of stereotypic beliefs. *Journal of Personality and Social Psychology*, 39, 832–45.

Hamilton, D. L. and Gifford, R. K. (1976). Illusory correlation in intergroup perception: a cognitive basis of stereotypic judgments. *Journal of Experimental Social Psychology*, 12, 392–407.

Hamilton, D. L., Katz, L. B. and Leirer, V. O. (1980). Cognitive representation of personality impressions: organizational processes in first impression formation. *Journal of Personality and Social Psychology*, 39, 1050–63.

Hamilton, D. L. and Sherman, S. J. (1989). Illusory correlations: implications for stereotype theory and research. In D. Bar-Tal, C. F. Graumann, A.W. Kruglanski and W. Stroebe (Eds.), *Stereotypes and Prejudice: Changing Conceptions*. New York: Springer Verlag.

Hamilton, D. L. and Sherman, J. W. (1994). Stereotypes. In R. S. Wyer, Jr. and T. K. Srull (Eds.), *Handbook of Social Cognition* (Second ed. pp. 1–68). Hillsdale, NJ: Erlbaum.

Hamilton, D. L. and Sherman, S. J. (1996). Perceiving persons and groups. *Psychological Review, 103*, 336–55.

Hamilton, D. L., Stroessner, S. J. and Driscoll, D. M. (1994). Social cognition and the study of stereotyping. In Devine, P. G., Hamilton, D. L. and Ostrom, T. M. (Eds.) *Social cognition: Contributions to classic issues in social psychology* (pp. 291–321). New York: Springer Verlag.

Harackiewicz, J. M. and Elliot, A. J. (1995). Life is a roller coaster when you view the world through entity glasses. *Psychological Inquiry, 6*, 298–301.

Harnad, S. (1987). *Categorical perception.* Cambridge University Press.

Haslam, N. (1998). Natural kinds, human kinds, and essentialism. *Social Research, 65*, 291–314.

Haslam, N., Rothschild, L. and Ernst, D. (2000). Essentialists beliefs about social categories. *British Journal of Social Psychology, 39*, 113–27.

Haslam, S. A. (1997). Stereotyping and social influence: foundations of stereotype consensus. In R. Spears, P. J. Oakes, N. Ellemers and S. A. Haslam (Eds.), *The social psychology of stereotyping and group life.* (pp. 119–43). Oxford: Blackwell.

Haslam, S. A. (2001). *Psychology and organizations: The social identity approach.* London: SAGE.

Haslam, S. A., McGarty, C. and Brown, P. M. (1996). The search for differentiated meaning is a precursor to illusory correlation. *Personality and Social Psychology Bulletin, 22*, 611–19.

Haslam, S. A., McGarty, C., Oakes, P. J., Turner, J. C. and Onorato, R. S. (1995). Contextual changes in the prototypicality of extreme and moderate outgroup members. *European Journal of Social Psychology, 25*, 509–30.

Haslam, S. A., Oakes, P. J., McGarty, C., Turner, J. C., Reynolds, K. and Eggins, R. (1996). Stereotyping and social influence: the mediation of stereotype applicability and sharedness by the views of ingroups and outgroup members. *British Journal of Social Psychology, 35*, 369–97.

Haslam, S. A., Oakes, P. J., Reynolds, K. J. and Turner, J. C. (1999). Social identity salience and the emergence of stereotype consensus. *Personality and Social Psychology Bulletin, 25*, 809–18.

Haslam, S. A., Oakes, P. J., Turner, J. C. and McGarty, C. (1995) Social categorization and group homogeneity: changes in the perceived applicability of stereotype content as a function of comparative context and trait favourableness. *British Journal of Social Psychology, 34*, 139–60.

Haslam, S. A., Oakes, P. J., Turner, J. C. and McGarty, C. (1996). Social identity, self-categorization and the perceived homogeneity of ingroups and outgroups: the interaction between social motivation and cognition. In R. M. Sorrentino and E. T. Higgins (Eds.) *Handbook of Motivation and Cognition* (Vol. 3, pp. 182–222). New York: Guilford.

Haslam, S. A., Oakes, P. J., Turner, J. C., McGarty, C. and Reynolds, K. J. (1998). The group as a basis for emergent stereotype consensus. *The European Review of Social Psychology, 8*, 203–329.

Haslam, S. A. and Turner, J. C. (1992). Context-dependent variation in social stereotyping 2: the relationship between frame of reference, self-categorization and accentuation. *European Journal of Social Psychology, 22*, 251–77.

Haslam, S. A. and Turner, J. C. (1995). Context-dependent variation in social stereotyping 3: Extremism as a self-categorical basis for polarized judgement. *European Journal of Social Psychology, 25*, 341–71.

Haslam, S. A., Turner, J. C, Oakes, P. J., McGarty, C. and Hayes, B. K. (1992). Context-dependent variation in social stereotyping 1: the effects of intergroup relations as mediated by social change and frame of reference. *European Journal of Social Psychology, 22*, 3–20.

Haslam, S. A., Turner, J. C., Oakes, P. J., Reynolds, K. J., Eggins, R. A., Nolan, M. and Tweedie, J. (1998). When do stereotypes become really consensual? Investigating the group-based dynamics of the consensualization process. *European Journal of Social Psychology, 28*, 755–76.

Hegarty, P. and Pratto, F. (2001). The effects of social category norms and stereotypes on explanations for intergroup differences. *Journal of Personality and Social Psychology, 80*, 723–35.

Higgins, E. T. (1996). Knowledge activation: accessibility, applicability and salience. In E. T. Higgins and A. W. Kruglanski (Eds.), *Social psychology: Handbook of basic principles* (pp. 133–68). New York: Guilford.

Hilton, D. J. (1995). The social context of reasoning: conversational inference and rational judgment. *Psychological Bulletin, 118*, 248–71.

Hilton, J. L. and von Hippel, W. (1991). Stereotypes. *Annual Review of Psychology, 47*, 237–71.

Hirschfeld, L. A. (1996). *Race in the making: Cognition, culture, and the child's construction of the human kind.* Cambridge, MA: MIT Press.

Hoffman, C. and Hurst, N. (1990). Gender stereotypes: perception or rationalization? *Journal of Personality and Social Psychology, 58*, 197–208.

Hogg, M. A. (1992). *The social psychology of group cohesiveness.* Hemel Hempstead: Harvester Wheatsheaf.

Hogg, M. A., Cooper-Shaw, L. and Holzworth, D. W. (1993). Group prototypicality and depersonalized attraction in small interactive groups. *Personality and Social Psychology Bulletin, 19*, 452–65.

Hogg, M. A. and Turner, J. C. (1987a). Intergroup behaviour, self-stereotyping and the salience of social categories. *British Journal of Social Psychology, 26*, 325–40.

Hogg, M. A. and Turner, J. C. (1987b). Social identity and conformity: a theory of referent informational influence. In W. Doise and S. Moscovici (Eds.), *Current issues in European Social Psychology* (Vol. 2, pp. 139–82). Cambridge University Press.

Hogg, M. A., Turner, J. C. and David(son), B. (1990). Polarized norms and social frames of reference: a test of the self-categorization theory of group polarization. *Basic and Applied Social Psychology, 11*, 77–100.

Hopkins, N. and Cable, I. (in press). Group variability judgements: the context-dependence of stereotypicality and homogeneity judgements. *British Journal of Social Psychology.*

Hornsey, M. J. and Hogg, M. A. (2000). Assimilation and diversity: an integrative model of subgroup relations. *Personality and Social Psychology Review, 4*, 143–56.

Horwitz, M. and Rabbie, J. M. (1982). Individuality and membership in the intergroup system. In H. Tajfel (Ed.), *Social identity and intergroup relations* (pp. 241–74). Cambridge University Press.

Howard, J. M. and Rothbart, M. (1980). Social categorization for ingroup and out-group behavior. *Journal of Personality and Social Psychology*, *38*, 301–10.

Insko, C. A. and Schopler, J. (1998). Differential distrust of groups and individuals. In C. Sedikides, J. Schopler and C. A. Insko (Eds.), *Intergroup cognition and intergroup behavior* (pp. 75–107). Hillsdale, NJ: Erlbaum.

Jennings, D. L., Amabile, T. M. and Ross, L. (1982). Informal covariation assessment: data-based versus theory-based judgments. In D. Kahneman, P. Slovic and A. Tversky (Eds.) *Judgment under uncertainty: Heuristics and biases.* Cambridge University Press.

Jetten, J., Spears, R. and Manstead, A. S. R. (1996). Intergroup norms and intergroup discrimination: distinctive self-categorization and social identity effects. *Journal of Personality and Social Psychology*, *71*, 1222–33.

Jetten, J., Spears, R. and Manstead, A. S. R. (1997). Strength of identification and intergroup differentiation: the influence of group norms. *European Journal of Social Psychology*, *27*, 603–9.

Jetten, J., Spears, R. and Manstead, A. S. R. (1998). Defining dimensions of distinctiveness: group variability makes a difference to differentiation. *Journal of Personality and Social Psychology*, *74*, 1481–92.

Jetten, J., Spears, R. and Manstead, A. S. R. (1999). Group distinctiveness and intergroup discrimination. In N. Ellemers, R. Spears and B. Doosje (Eds.) *Social identity: Context, commitment, content.* (pp. 107–26). Oxford: Blackwell.

Johnston, L. and Hewstone, M. (1992). Cognitive models of stereotype change: III Subtyping and the perceived typicality of disconfirming group members. *Journal of Experimental Social Psychology*, *28*, 360–86.

Johnston, L., Hewstone, M., Pendry, L. and Frankish, C. (1994). Cognitive models of stereotype change: IV Motivational and cognitive influences. *European Journal of Social Psychology*, *24*, 237–65.

Jones, E. E. and Harris, V. A. (1967). The attribution of attitudes. *Journal of Experimental Social Psychology*, *3*, 1–24.

Jones, S. S. and Smith, L. B. (1993). The place of perception in children's concepts. *Cognitive development*, *8*, 113–39.

Jost, J. T. and Banaji, M. R. (1994). The role of stereotyping in system-justification and the production of false consciousness. *British Journal of Social Psychology*, *33*, 1–27.

Judd, C. M. and Park, B. (1993). Definition and assessment of accuracy in social stereotypes. *Psychological Review*, *100*, 109–28.

Judd, C. M., Park, B., Brauer, M., Ryan, S. and Kraus, S. (1995). Stereotypes and ethnocentrism – diverging interethnic perceptions of African-American and White American youth. *Journal of Personality and Social Psychology*, *69*, 460–81.

Jussim, L. (1991). Social perception and social reality: a reflection-construction model. *Psychological Review*, *98*, 54–73.

Kanter, R. (1979). Power failure in management circuits. *Harvard Business Review*, July-August, 65–75.

Karlins, M., Coffman, T. L. and Walters, G. (1969). On the fading of social stereotypes: studies in three generations of college students. *Journal of Personality and Social Psychology*, 13, 1–16.

Katz, D. and Braly, K. (1933). Racial stereotypes of one hundred college students. *Journal of Abnormal and Social Psychology*, 28, 280–90.

Katz, D. and Braly, K. (1935). Racial prejudice and racial stereotypes. *Journal of Abnormal and Social Psychology*, 30, 175–93.

Keil, F. C. (1989). *Concepts, kinds, and cognitive development*. Cambridge, MA: MIT Press.

Kelley, H. H. (1967). Attribution theory in social psychology. In D. Levine (Ed.), *Nebraska Symposium on Motivation*. Lincoln, NE: University.

Khalaf, A. (forthcoming). Stereotyping, typecasting and changing perceptions of mental illness. Forthcoming PhD thesis, The Australian National University.

Klauer, K. C. and Meiser, T. (2000). A source monitoring analysis of illusory correlation. *Personality and Social Psychology Bulletin*, 26, 1074–93.

Klauer, K. C., Ehrenberg, K. and Cataldegirmen, H. (2001). Evaluative and non-evaluative illusory correlations. Unpublished manuscript, University of Bonn.

Krueger, J. (1992). On the overestimation of between-group differences. In M. Hewstone and W. Stroebe (Eds.), *European Review of Social Psychology* (Vol. 3). Chichester: Wiley.

Krueger, J. and Clement, R. W. (1994). Memory-based judgments about multiple categories: a revision and extension of Tajfel's accentuation theory. *Journal of Personality and Social Psychology*, 67, 35–47.

Krueger, J. and Clement, R. W. (1996). Inferring category characteristics from sample characteristics: inductive reasoning and social projection. *Journal of Experimental Psychology: General*, 125, 52–68.

Kunda, Z. (1990). The case for motivated reasoning. *Psychological Bulletin*, 108, 480–98.

Kunda, Z. and Oleson, K. C. (1995). Maintaining stereotypes in the face of disconfirmation: constructing grounds for subtyping deviants. *Journal of Personality and Social Psychology*, 68, 565–80.

Kunda, Z. and Thagard, P. (1996). Forming impressions from stereotypes, traits and behaviors: a parallel-constraint-satisfaction theory. *Psychological Review*, 103, 284–308.

Lala, G. (forthcoming). Virtual communities and social identities: Distinguishing between categories and groups on the Internet. Forthcoming PhD thesis, The Australian National University.

Lea, M., Spears, R. and de Groot, D. (2001). Knowing me, knowing you: effects of visual anonymity on self-categorization, stereotyping and attraction in computer-mediated groups. *Personality and Social Psychology Bulletin*, 27, 526–37.

Lee, Y.-T. and Ottati, V. (1995). Perceived in-group homogeneity as a function of group membership salience and stereotype threat. *Personality and Social Psychology Bulletin*, 21, 610–19.

Levy, S. R. and Dweck, C. S. (1998). Trait-versus process-focused social judgement. *Social Cognition*, 16, 151–72.

Levy, S. R., Stroessner, S. J. and Dweck, C. S. (1998). Stereotype formation and endorsement: the role of implicit theories. *Journal of Personality and Social Psychology*, *74*, 1421–36.

Leyens, J.-P. and Fiske, S. T. (1994). Impression formation: from recitals to symphonie fantastique. In P. G. Devine, D. L. Hamilton and T. M. Ostrom (Eds.), *Social Cognition: Contributions to Classic Issues in Social Psychology* (pp. 39–75). San Diego, CA: Academic Press.

Leyens, J.-P. and Schadron, G. (1980). Porque discriminam mais os grupos que os individuos? Categorizaçao ou pretexto? [Why do groups discriminate more than individuals? Categorization or pretext?] *Psicologia*, *2*, 161–8.

Leyens, J.-P., Yzerbyt, V. Y. and Schadron, G. (1992). Stereotypes and social judgeability. *European Review of Social Psychology*, *3*, 91–120.

Leyens, J.-P., Yzerbyt, V. Y. and Schadron, G. (1994). *Stereotypes and social cognition*. London: SAGE.

Lippmann, W. (1922). *Public opinion*. New York: Harcourt Brace.

Livingston, K. R., Andrews, J. K. and Harnad, S. (1998). Categorical perception effects induced by category learning. *Journal of Experimental Psychology: Learning, Memory, and Cognition*, *24*, 732–53.

Lorenzi-Cioldi, F. (1988). *Individus dominants et groupes dominés*. Grenoble: Presses Universitaires de Grenoble.

Lorenzi-Cioldi, F. (1993). They all look alike but so do we . . . sometimes: perceptions of in-group and out-group homogeneity as a function of sex and context. *British Journal of Social Psychology*, *32*, 111–24.

Machiavelli, N. (1513/1984). *The Prince*. Oxford University Press.

Mackie, D. M., Hamilton, D. L., Susskind, J. and Rosselli, F. (1996). Social psychological foundations of stereotype formation. In C. N. Macrae, C. Stangor and M. Hewstone (Eds.), *Stereotypes and stereotyping* (pp. 41–78). New York: Guilford Press.

Macrae, C. N., Bodenhausen, G., Milne, A. and Jetten J. (1994). Out of mind but back in sight: stereotypes on the rebound. *Journal of Personality and Social Psychology*, *67*, 808–17.

Macrae, C. N., Hewstone, M. and Griffiths, R. J. (1993). Processing load and memory for stereotype-based information. *European Journal of Social Psychology*, *23*, 77–87.

Madon, S., Jussim, L., Keiper, S., Eccles, J., Smith, A. and Palumbo, P. (1998). The accuracy and power of sex, social class, and ethnic stereotypes: a naturalistic study in person perception. *Personality and Social Psychology Bulletin*, *24*, 1304–18.

Malt, B. C. (1994). Water is not H_2O. *Cognitive Psychology*, *27*, 41–70.

Martin, C. L. and Parker, S. (1995). Folk theories about sex and race differences. *Personality and Social Psychology Bulletin*, *21*, 45–57.

McArthur, L. Z. and Friedman, S. A. (1980). Illusory correlation in impression formation: variations in the shared distinctiveness effect as a function of the distinctive person's age, race, and sex. *Personality and Social Psychology Bulletin*, *7*, 615–24.

McCauley, C., Stitt, C. L. and Segal, M. (1980). Stereotyping: from prejudice to prediction. *Psychological Bulletin*, *87*, 195–208.

McConahay, J. B., Hardee, B. B. and Batts, V. (1981). Has racism declined in America? It depends on who is asking and what is being asked. *Journal of Conflict Resolution*, 25, 563–79.

McConnell, A. R., Sherman, S. J. and Hamilton, D. L. (1994a). Illusory correlation in the perception of groups: an extension of the distinctiveness-based account. *Journal of Personality and Social Psychology*, 67, 414–29.

McConnell, A. R., Sherman, S. J. and Hamilton, D. L. (1994b). On-line and memory-based aspects of individual and group target judgments. *Journal of Personality and Social Psychology*, 67, 173–85.

McGarty, C. (1999). *Categorization and social psychology*. London: SAGE.

McGarty, C. and de la Haye, A.-M. (1997). Stereotype formation: beyond illusory correlation. In Spears, R., Oakes, P. J., Ellemers, N. and Haslam, S. A. (Eds.). *The social psychology of stereotyping and group life* (pp. 144–70). Oxford: Blackwell.

McGarty, C., Haslam, S. A., Hutchinson, K. J. and Grace, D. M. (1995). Determinants of perceived consistency: the relationship between group entitativity and the meaningfulness of categories. *British Journal of Social Psychology*, 34, 237–56.

McGarty, C., Haslam, S. A., Turner, J. C. and Oakes, P. J. (1993) Illusory correlation as accentuation of actual intercategory difference: evidence for the effect with minimal stimulus information. *European Journal of Social Psychology*, 23, 391–410.

McGarty, C. and Penny, R. E. C. (1988). Categorization, accentuation, and social judgement. *British Journal of Social Psychology*, 27, 147–57.

McGarty, C. and Turner, J. C. (1992). The effects of categorization on social judgement. *British Journal of Social Psychology*, 31, 253–68.

McGarty, C., Turner, J. C., Hogg, M. A., David(son), B. and Wetherell, M. S. (1992). Group polarization as conformity to the prototypical group member. *British Journal of Social Psychology*, 31, 1–19.

Medin, D. L. (1989). Concepts and conceptual structure. *American Psychologist*, 44, 1469–81.

Medin, D. L., Goldstone, R. L. and Gentner, D. (1993). Respects for similarity. *Psychological Review*, 100, 254–78.

Medin, D. L. and Ortony, A. (1989). Psychological essentialism. In S. Vosniadou and A. Ortony (Eds.), *Similarity and analogical reasoning* (pp. 179–95). New York: Cambridge University Press.

Medin, D. L. and Schaffer, M. M. (1978). Context theory of classification learning. *Psychological Review*, 85, 207–38.

Medin, D. L. and Smith, E. E. (1984). Concepts and concept formation. *Annual Review of Psychology*, 40, 113–38.

Medin, D. L. and Wattenmaker, W. D. (1987). Category cohesiveness, theories, and cognitive archaeology. In U. Neisser (Ed.), *Concepts and conceptual development: Ecological and intellectual factors in categorization* (pp. 25–62). Cambridge University Press.

Meenes, M. (1943). A comparison of racial stereotypes of 1935 and 1942. *Journal of Social Psychology*, 17, 327–36.

Messick, D. M. and Mackie, D. M. (1989). Intergroup relations. In M. R. Rosenzweig and L. W. Porter (Eds.), *Annual review of psychology* (Vol. 40). Palo Alto, CA: Annual Review.

Mulder, M. (1977). *The daily power game.* Leiden, The Netherlands: Martinus Nijoff.

Mullen, B. and Johnson, C. (1990) Distinctiveness-based illusory correlations and stereotyping: a meta-analytic integration. *British Journal of Social Psychology*, 29, 11–28.

Mullen, B. and Johnson, B. (1995). Cognitive representation in ethnophaulisms and illusory correlation in stereotyping. *Personality and Social Psychology Bulletin*, 21, 420–33.

Mummendey, A. and Schreiber, H. J. (1983). Better or just different?: positive social identity by discrimination against or differentiation from outgroups. *European Journal of Social Psychology*, 13, 389–97.

Mummendey, A. and Schreiber, H.-J. (1984). Different just means better: some obvious and some hidden pathways to ingroup favouritism. *British Journal of Social Psychology*, 23, 363–8.

Murphy, G. L. (1993). Theories and concept formation. In I. Van Mechelen, J. Hampton, R. S. Michalski and P. Theuns (Eds.), *Categories and concepts: Theoretical views and inductive data analysis* (pp. 173–200). London, England: Academic Press.

Murphy, G. L. and Medin, D. L. (1985). The role of theories in conceptual coherence. *Psychological Review*, 92, 289–316.

Mussweiler, T., Gabriel, S. and Bodenhausen, G.V. (2000). Shifting social identities as a strategy for deflecting threatening social comparisons. *Journal of Personality and Social Psychology*, 79, 398–409.

Neuberg, S. L. and Fiske, S. T. (1987). Motivational influences on impression formation: outcome dependency, accuracy-driven attention, and individuating processes. *Journal of Personality and Social Psychology*, 53, 431–44.

Ng, S. H. (1981). Power and intergroup discrimination. In H. Tajfel (Ed.), *Social identity and intergroup relations*. Cambridge University Press.

Ng, S. H. (1982). Equity theory and the allocation of rewards between groups. *European Journal of Social Psychology*, 11, 439–44.

Nolan, M. A., Haslam, S. A., Spears, R. and Oakes, P. J. (1999). An examination of resource-based and fit-based theories of stereotyping under cognitive load and fit. *European Journal of Social Psychology*, 29, 641–63.

Norman, W. T. (1963). Toward an adequate taxonomy of personality attributes: replicated factor structures in peer nomination personality ratings. *Journal of Abnormal and Social Psychology*, 66, 574–83.

Oakes, P. J. (1987). The salience of social categories. In J. C. Turner, M. A. Hogg, P. J. Oakes, S. D. Reicher and M. S. Wetherell (Eds.), *Rediscovering the social group: A self-categorization theory*, (pp. 117–41). Oxford: Basil Blackwell.

Oakes, P. J. (1996). The categorization process: cognition and the group in the social psychology of stereotyping. In W. P. Robinson (Ed.), *Social group and identities: Developing the legacy of Henri Tajfel* (pp. 95–119). Oxford, UK: Butterworth-Heinemann.

Oakes, P. J. and Haslam, S. A. (in press). Distortion v. Meaning: categorization on trial for incitement to intergroup hatred. In M. Augoustinos and

K. Reynolds (Eds.), *Social psychological approaches to prejudice and racism.* London: Sage.

Oakes, P. J., Haslam, S. A. and Reynolds, K. J. (1999). Social categorization and social context: is stereotype change a matter of information or meaning? In D. Abrams and M. Hogg (Eds.), *Social identity and social cognition* (pp. 55–79). Oxford, UK: Blackwell.

Oakes, P. J., Haslam, S. A. and Turner, J. C. (1994). *Stereotyping and social reality.* Oxford: Blackwell.

Oakes, P. J., Haslam, S. A. and Turner, J. C. (1998). A consideration of prototypicality from the perspective of self-categorization theory. In J. C. Deschamps, J. F. Morales, D. Paez and H. Paicheler (Eds.), *Current perspectives on social identity and social categorization* (pp. 75–92). Barcelona: Anthropos.

Oakes, P. J. and Reynolds, K. J. (1997). Asking the accuracy question: is measurement the answer? In R. Spears, P. J. Oakes, N. Ellemers and S. A. Haslam (Eds.), *The social psychology of stereotyping and group life* (pp. 51–71). Oxford UK and Cambridge, MT: Blackwell.

Oakes, P. J., Reynolds, K. J., Haslam, S. A. and Turner, J. C. (1999). Part of life's rich tapestry: stereotyping and the politics of intergroup relations. In S. Thye, E. J. Lawler, M. W. Macy and H. A. Walker (Eds.) *Advances in group processes* (Vol. 16, pp. 125–60). Stamford, CT: JAI Press.

Oakes, P. J. and Turner, J. C. (1980). Social categorization and intergroup behavior: does minimal intergroup discrimination make social identity more positive? *European Journal of Social Psychology, 10,* 295–301.

Oakes, P. J. and Turner, J. C. (1990). Is limited information processing capacity the cause of social stereotyping? In W. Stroebe and M. Hewstone (Eds.), *European Review of Social Psychology* (Vol. 1, pp. 111–35). Chichester, UK: Wiley.

Oakes, P. J., Turner, J. C. and Haslam, S. A. (1991). Perceiving people as group members: the role of fit in the salience of social categorizations. *British Journal of Social Psychology, 30,* 125–44.

Onorato, R. S. and Turner, J. C. (1996). *Fluidity in the self-concept: A shift from personal to social identity.* Paper presented in the Symposium 'Self, self-stereotyping and identity', 2nd Meeting of the Society of Australasian Social Psychologists, Canberra, ACT, Australia, May 2–5.

Onorato, R. S. and Turner, J. C. (1997). *Individual differences and social identity: A study of self-categorization processes in the Markus paradigm.* Paper presented at the 3rd Meeting of the Society of Australasian Social Psychologists, Wollongong, NSW, Australia, April 17–20.

Park, B., DeKay, M. L. and Kraus, S. (1994). Aggregating social behavior into person models: perceiver-induced consistency. *Journal of Personality and Social Psychology, 66,* 437–59.

Park, B., Ryan, C. S. and Judd, C. M. (1992). Role of meaningful subgroups in explaining differences in perceived variability for ingroups and outgroups. *Journal of Personality and Social Psychology, 63,* 553–67.

Peeters, G. (1986). Good and evil as softwares of the brain: on psychological 'immediates' underlying the metaphysical 'ultimates'. A contribution from cognitive social psychology and semantic differential research. Ultimate Reality and Meaning. *Interdisciplinary studies in the Philosophy of Understanding, 9,* 210–31.

Peeters, G. and Czapinski, J. (1990). Positive-negative asymmetry in evaluations: the distinction between affective and informational negativity effects. In W. Stroebe and M. Hewstone (Eds.), *European Review of Social Psychology* (Vol. 1, pp. 33–60). New York: Wiley.

Peterson, C. R. (1980). Recognition of noncontingency. *Journal of Personality and Social Psychology*, 38, 727–34.

Prothro, E. T. and Melikian, L. H. (1955). Studies in stereotypes: V. Familiarity and the kernel of truth hypothesis. *Journal of Social Psychology*, 41, 3–10.

Pryor, J. B. (1986). The influence of different encoding sets upon the formation of illusory correlations and group impressions. *Personality and Social Psychology Bulletin*, 12, 216–26.

Rabbie, J. M. and Horwitz, M. (1988). Categories versus groups as explanatory concepts in intergroup relations. *European Journal of Social Psychology*, 18, 117–23.

Rabbie, J. M., Schot, J. C. and Visser, L. (1989). Social identity theory: a conceptual and empirical critique from the perspective of a behavioural interaction model. *European Journal of Social Psychology*, 19, 171–202.

Read, S. J. and Marcus-Newhall, A. (1993). Explanatory coherence in social explanations: a parallel distributed processing account. *Journal of Personality and Social Psychology*, 65, 429–47.

Read, S. J. and Miller, L. C. (1993). Rapist or 'regular guy': explanatory coherence in the construction of mental models of others. *Personality and Social Psychology Bulletin*, 19, 526–41.

Reeder, G. D., Pryor, J. B. and Wojciszke, B. (1992). Trait-behavior relationships in social information processing. In G. R. Semin and K. Fiedler (Eds.), *Language, interaction and social cognition*. London: Sage.

Reicher, S. D. and Hopkins, N. (1996a). Seeking influence through characterising self-categories: an analysis of anti-abortionist rhetoric. *British Journal of Social Psychology*, 35, 297–311.

Reicher, S. D. and Hopkins, N. (1996b). Self-category constructions in political rhetoric: an analysis of Thatcher's and Kinnock's speeches concerning the British Miners' Strike (1984–5). *European Journal of Social Psychology*, 26, 353–72.

Reicher, S. D. and Hopkins, N. (2001). *Self and nation*. London: Sage.

Reicher, S. D., Hopkins, N. and Condor, S. (1997). Stereotype construction as a strategy of influence. In Spears, R., Oakes, P. J., Ellemers, N. and Haslam, S. A. (Eds.). *The social psychology of stereotyping and group life* (pp. 94–118). Oxford: Blackwell.

Reicher, S.D., Spears, R. and Postmes, T. (1995). A social identity model of deindividuation phenomena. *European Review of Social Psychology*, 6, 161–98.

Reynolds, K. J. and Oakes, P. J. (2000). Variability in impression formation: investigating the role of motivation, capacity and the categorization process. *Personality and Social Psychology Bulletin*, 26, 355–73.

Reynolds, K. J., Oakes, P. J., Haslam, S. A., Nolan, M. and Dolnik, L. (2000). Responses to powerlessness: stereotypes as an instrument of social conflict. *Group Dynamics: Theory, Research and Practice* 4, 275–290.

Reynolds, K. J., Turner, J. C. and Haslam, S. A. (2000). When are we better than them and they worse than us? A closer look at social discrimination in positive and negative domains. *Journal of Personality and Social Psychology, 78*, 64–80.

Rogier, A. and Yzerbyt, V. Y. (1999). Social attribution: the role of homogeneity in subjective essentialism. *Swiss Journal of Psychology, 54*, 233–40.

Rojahn, K. and Pettigrew, T. F. (1992). Memory for schema-relevant information: a meta-analytic resolution. *British Journal of Social Psychology, 31*, 81–109.

Rosch, E. (1978). Principles of categorization. In E. Rosch and B. Lloyd (Eds.), *Cognition and categorization* (pp. 28–49). Hillsdale, NJ: Erlbaum.

Rosch, E. and Mervis, C. (1975). Family resemblance: studies in the internal structure of categories. *Cognitive Psychology, 7*, 573–605.

Rosch, E., Mervis, C. B., Grey, W. D., Johnson, D. M. and Boyes-Braem, D. (1976). Basic objects as natural categories. *Cognitive Psychology, 8*, 382–439.

Rosenberg, S. and Sedlak, A. (1972). Structural representations of implicit personality theory. In L. Berkowitz (Ed.), *Advances in experimental social psychology* (Vol. 6, pp. 235–97). New York: Academic Press.

Ross, L., Amabile, T. M. and Steinmetz, J. L. (1977). Social roles, social control, and biases in social-perception processes. *Journal of Personality and Social Psychology, 35*, 485–94.

Rothbart, M. (1981). Memory and social beliefs. In D. Hamilton (Ed.), *Cognitive processes in stereotyping and intergroup relations* (pp. 145–81). Hillsdale, NJ: Erlbaum.

Rothbart, M., Evans, M. and Fulero, S. (1979). Recall of confirming events: memory processes and the maintenance of social stereotypes. *Journal of Experimental Social Psychology, 15*, 343–55.

Rothbart, M. and Hallmark, W. (1988). In-group and out-group differences in the perceived efficacy of coercion and conciliation in resolving social conflict. *Journal of Personality and Social Psychology, 55*, 248–57.

Rothbart, M. and John, O. P. (1985). Social categorization and behavioural episodes: a cognitive analysis of the effects of intergroup contact. *Journal of Social Issues, 41*, 81–104.

Rothbart, M. and Taylor, M. (1992). Category labels and social reality: do we view social categories as natural kinds? In G. Semin and K. Fiedler (Eds.), *Language and social cognition* (pp. 11–36). London: Sage.

Rothgerber, H. (1997). External intergroup threat as an antecedent to perceptions of in-group and out-group homogeneity. *Journal of Personality and Social Psychology, 73*, 1206–11.

Ruscher, J. B. and Fiske, S. T. (1990). Interpersonal competition can cause individuating impression formation. *Journal of Personality and Social Psychology, 58*, 832–42.

Ruscher, J. B., Fiske, S. T., Miki, H. and van Manen, S. (1991). Individuating processes in competition: interpersonal versus intergroup. *Personality and Social Psychology Bulletin, 17*, 595–605.

Sachdev, I. and Bourhis, R. Y. (1985). Social categorization and power differentials in group relations. *European Journal of Social Psychology, 15*, 415–34.

Sachdev, I. and Bourhis, R. Y. (1991). Power and status differentials in minority and majority group relations. *European Journal of Social Psychology, 21*, 1–24.

Sanbonmatsu, D. M., Sherman, S. J. and Hamilton, D. L. (1987). Illusory correlation in the perception of individuals and groups. *Social Cognition*, 5, 1–25.

Sani, F. and Reicher, S. (1998). When consensus fails: an analysis of the schism within the Italian communist party. *European Journal of Social Psychology*, 28, 623–45.

Sani, F. and Reicher, S. (1999). Identity, argument and schism: two longitudinal studies of the split in the Church of England over the ordination of women in the priesthood. *Group Processes and Intergroup Relations*, 2, 279–300.

Schaller, M. and Maass, A. (1989) Illusory correlation and social categorization: toward an integration of motivational and cognitive factors in stereotype formation. *Journal of Personality and Social Psychology*, 56, 709–21.

Scheepers, D., Spears, R., Doosje, B. and Manstead, A. S. R. (2000) *Integrating identity and instrumental approaches to intergroup differentiation: Different contexts, different motives*. Manuscript submitted for publication.

Schopler, J. and Insko, C. A. (1992). The discontinuity effect in interpersonal and intergroup relations: generality and mediation. *European Review of Social Psychology*, 3, 121–51.

Seago, D. W. (1947). Stereotypes: before Pearl Harbour and after. *Journal of Social Psychology*, 23, 55–63.

Sechrist, G. and Stangor, C. (2001). Perceived consensus influences intergroup behavior and stereotype accessibility. *Journal of Personality and Social Psychology*, 80, 645–54.

Sedikides, C., Schopler, J. and Insko, C. A. (1998). *Intergroup cognition and intergroup behavior*. Hillsdale, NJ: Erlbaum.

Sherif, M. (1966a). *Group conflict and co-operation: Their social psychology*. London: Routledge and Kegan Paul.

Sherif, M. (1966b). *In common predicament: Social psychology of intergroup conflict and cooperation*. Boston: Houghton-Mifflin.

Sherif, M., Harvey, O. J., White, B. J., Hood, W. R. and Sherif, C. W. (1961). *Intergroup conflict and cooperation: The Robbers Cave experiment*. Norman: University of Oklahoma Book Exchange.

Simon, B. and Brown, R. (1987). Perceived intragroup homogeneity in minority-majority contexts. *Journal of Personality and Social Psychology*, 53, 703–11.

Sloman, S. A. (1998). Categorical inference is not a tree: the myth of inheritance hierarchies. *Cognitive Psychology*, 35, 1–33.

Sloman, S. A. and Rips, L. J. (1998). Similarity as an explanatory construct. *Cognition*, 65, 87–101.

Smith, E. E. and Medin, D. L. (1981). *Categories and concepts*. Cambridge, MA: Harvard University Press.

Smith, E. R. (1990). The role of exemplars in social judgment. In L. L. Martin and A. Tesser (Eds.), *The construction of social judgments*. Hillsdale, NJ: Erlbaum.

Smith, E. R. (1991). Illusory correlation in a simulated exemplar-based memory. *Journal of Experimental Social Psychology*, 27, 107–23.

Smith, E. R. and de Coster, J. (1998). Knowledge acquisition, accessibility, and use in person perception and stereotyping: simulation with a recurrent connectionist network. *Journal of Personality and Social Psychology*, 74, 21–35.

Smith, E. R. and Zárate, M. A. (1992). Exemplar-based model of social judgment. *Psychological Review*, 99, 3–21.

Snyder, M. E. (1981). On the self-perpetuating nature of social stereotypes. In
    D. L. Hamilton (Ed.), *Cognitive processes in stereotyping and intergroup behavior.*
    Hillsdale, NJ: Erlbaum.
Spears, R. (1995). Isolating the collective self. In A. Oosterwegel and R. Wicklund
    (Eds.). *The self in European and North American culture: Development and pro-
    cesses.* (Nato ASI series, Vol. 84) (pp. 309–22). Amsterdam: Kluwer.
Spears, R. (2000, April). Automatic intergroup behaviour: social identity meets
    social cognition. Keynote address at the Society of Australasian Social
    Psychologists annual meeting, Fremantle, Western Australia.
Spears, R. (2001). The interaction between the individual and the collective
    self: self-categorization in context. In C. Sedikides and M. B. Brewer (Eds).
    Individual self, relational self, and collective self: Partners, opponents or strangers?
    (pp. 171–198). Philadelphia, PA: The Psychology Press.
Spears, R. and Doosje, B. (1996). Categorization and individuation: the effect of
    group identification and encoding set. Unpublished manuscript, University of
    Amsterdam.
Spears, R., Doosje, B. and Ellemers, N. (1997). Self-stereotyping in the face
    of threats to group status and distinctiveness: the role of group identification.
    Personality and Social Psychology Bulletin, 23, 538–53.
Spears, R., Doosje, B. and Ellemers, N. (1999). Commitment and the context
    of social perception. In N. Ellemers, R. Spears and B. Doosje (Eds.) *Social
    identity: Context, commitment, content.* (pp. 59–83). Oxford: Blackwell.
Spears, R. and Haslam, S. A. (1997). Stereotyping and the burden of cognitive
    load. In R. Spears, P. J. Oakes, N. Ellemers and S. A. Haslam (Eds.), *The social
    psychology of stereotyping and group life.* (pp. 171–207). Oxford: Blackwell.
Spears, R., Haslam, S. A. and Jansen, R. (1999). The effect of cognitive load on
    social categorization in the category confusion paradigm. *European Journal of
    Social Psychology, 29,* 621–39.
Spears, R., Jetten, J., Arendt, S., van Norren, M. and Postmes, T. Meaning
    and differentiation in minimal groups: Creative and reflective distinctive-
    ness. Manuscript in preparation, University of Amsterdam/University of
    Queensland.
Spears, R., Jetten, J. and Doosje, B. (2001). The (il)legitimacy of ingroup bias:
    from social reality to social resistance. In J. Jost and B. Major, Eds.) *The psychol-
    ogy of legitimacy: Emerging perspectives on ideology, justice, and intergroup relations.*
    New York: Cambridge University Press.
Spears, R., Jetten, J. and Scheepers, D. (2002). Distinctiveness and the defini-
    tion of collective self: A tripartite model. In A. Tesser, J. V. Wood and D. A.
    Stapel (Eds.). *Psychological perspectives on self and identity* (Vol. 2, pp. 147–171).
    Lexington: APA.
Spears, R. and Lea, M. (1994). Panacea or panopticon: the hidden power in
    computer-mediated communication. *Communication Research, 21,* 427–59.
Spears, R. and Manstead, A. S. R. (1989). The social context of stereotyping and
    differentiation. *European Journal of Social Psychology, 19,* 101–21.
Spears, R., Oakes, P. J., Ellemers, N. and Haslam S. A. (1997). Introduction: the
    social psychology of stereotyping and group life. In R. Spears, P. J. Oakes, N.
    Ellemers and S. A. Haslam (Eds.) *The social psychology of stereotyping and group
    life* (pp.1–19). Oxford: Blackwell.

Spears, R. and Oyen, M. (1992, July). How minimal is the minimal group? *EAESP/SESP Joint Meeting*, Leuven/Louvain-la-Neuve, Belgium.

Spears, R. and van Knippenberg, D. (1997). Cognitive load and illusory correlation. Unpublished manuscript, University of Amsterdam/University of Leiden.

Spears, R., van der Pligt, J. and Eiser, J. R. (1985). Illusory correlation in the perception of group attitudes. *Journal of Personality and Social Psychology*, *48*, 863–75.

Spears, R., van der Pligt, J. and Eiser, J. R. (1986). Generalizing the illusory correlation effect. *Journal of Personality and Social Psychology*, *51*, 1127–34.

Stangor, C. and Jost, J. (1997). Commentary: individual, group and system levels of analysis and their relevance for stereotyping and intergroup relations. In R. Spears, P. J. Oakes, N. Ellemers and S. A. Haslam (Eds.) *The social psychology of stereotyping and group life* (pp. 336–58). Oxford: Blackwell.

Stangor, C. and Lange, J. (1994). Mental representation of social groups: advances in understanding stereotypes and stereotyping. *Advances in experimental social psychology*, *26*, 357–416.

Stangor, C. and McMillan, D. (1992). Memory for expectancy-congruent and expectancy-incongruent information: a review of the social and developmental literatures. *Psychological Bulletin*, *111*, 42–61.

Stangor, C. and Schaller, M. (1996). Stereotypes as individual and collective representations. In C. N. Macrae, C. Stangor and M. Hewstone (Eds.), *Stereotypes and stereotyping* (pp. 3–40). New York: Guilford Press.

Stangor, C. and Sechrist, G. (2000). Social influence and intergroup beliefs: the role of perceived social consensus. In J. Forgas and K. Williams (Eds.), *Social influence*. Philadelphia: Psychology Press.

Stangor, C., Sechrist, G. and Jost, J. (in press). Changing racial beliefs by providing consensus information. *Personality and Social Psychology Bulletin*.

Stapel, D. A., Koomen, W. and van der Pligt, J. (1997). Categories of category accessibility: the impact of trait versus exemplar priming on person judgments. *Journal of Experimental Social Psychology*, *33*, 44–76.

Stern, L. D., Marrs, S., Millar, M. G. and Cole, E. (1984). Processing time and the recall of inconsistent and consistent behaviours in individuals and groups. *Journal of Personality and Social Psychology*, *47*, 253–62.

Stott, C. J. and Drury, J. (2000). Crowds, context and identity: dynamic categorization processes in the 'poll tax riot'. *Human Relations*, *53*, 247–73.

Stott, C. J., Hutchinson, T. P. and Drury, J. (in press). 'Hooligans' abroad? Intergroup dynamics, social identity and participation in collective 'disorder' at the 1998 World Cup Finals. *British Journal of Social Psychology*.

Stott, C. J., and Reicher, S. D. (1998). How conflict escalates: The inter-group dynamics of collective football crowd violence. *Sociology*, *32*, 353–77.

Tajfel, H. (1969). Cognitive aspects of prejudice. *Journal of Social Issues*, *25*, 79–97.

Tajfel, H. (1972). La catégorisation sociale. In S. Moscovici (Ed.), *Introduction à la psychologie sociale* (Vol. 1). Paris: Larousse.

Tajfel, H. (1978a). *Differentiation between social groups: Studies in the social psychology of intergroup relations*. London: Academic Press.

Tafjel, H. (1978b). Interindividual behaviour and intergroup behaviour. In H. Tajfel (Ed.) *Differentiation between social groups*. London: Academic Press.

Tajfel, H. (1981a). *Human groups and social categories*. Cambridge University Press.

Tajfel, H. (1981b). Social stereotypes and social groups. In J. C. Turner and H. Giles (Eds.), *Intergroup behaviour* (pp. 144–67). Oxford: Blackwell; University of Chicago Press.

Tajfel, H. (1982). Social psychology of intergroup relations. In M. R. Rosenzweig and L. W. Porter (Eds.), *Annual Review of Psychology* (Vol. 33, pp. 1–39). Palo Alto, CA: Annual Reviews.

Tajfel, H., Flament, C., Billig, M. G. and Bundy, R. F. (1971). Social categorization and intergroup behaviour. *European Journal of Social Psychology*, *1*, 149–77.

Tajfel, H. and Turner, J. C. (1979). An integrative theory of intergroup conflict. In W. G. Austin and S. Worchel (Eds.), *The social psychology of intergroup relations* (pp. 33–47). Monterey, CA: Brooks/Cole.

Tajfel, H. and Turner, J. C. (1986). The social identity theory of intergroup behaviour. In S. Worchel and W. G. Austin (Eds.), *Psychology of intergroup relations* (pp. 7–24). Chicago, MI: Nelson-Hall.

Tajfel, H. and Wilkes, A. L. (1963). Classification and quantitative judgement. *British Journal of Psychology*, *54*, 101–14.

Taylor, S. E., Fiske, S. T., Etcoff, N. L. and Ruderman, A. J. (1978). Categorical and contextual bases of person memory and stereotyping. *Journal of Personality and Social Psychology*, *36*, 778–93.

Triandis, H. C. and Vassiliou, V. (1967). Frequency of contact and stereotyping. *Journal of Personality and Social Psychology*, *7*, 316–28.

Turner, J. C. (1975). Social comparison and social identity: some prospects for intergroup behaviour. *European Journal of Social Psychology*, *5*, 5–34.

Turner, J. C. (1982). Towards a cognitive redefinition of the social group. In H. Tajfel (Ed.) *Social Identity and Intergroup Relations*, Cambridge University Press.

Turner, J. C. (1985). Social categorization and the self-concept: a social cognitive theory of group behaviour. In E.J. Lawler (Ed.), *Advances in Group Processes: Theory and Research* (Vol. 2, pp. 77–122). Greenwich, CT: JAI Press Inc.

Turner, J. C. (1987a). The analysis of social influence. In J. C. Turner, M. A. Hogg, P. J. Oakes, S. D. Reicher and M. S. Wetherell, *Rediscovering the social group: A self-categorization theory* (pp. 68–88). Oxford: Blackwell.

Turner, J. C. (1987b). A self-categorization theory. In J. C. Turner, M. A. Hogg, P. J. Oakes, S. D. Reicher and M. S. Wetherell, *Rediscovering the social group: A self-categorization theory* (pp. 42–67). Oxford: Blackwell.

Turner, J. C. (1991). *Social influence*. Milton Keynes: Open University Press.

Turner, J. C. (1999). Some current issues in research on social identity and self-categorization theories. In N. Ellemers, R. Spears and B. Doojse (Eds.), *Social identity: Context, commitment, content*. Oxford: Blackwell.

Turner, J. C., Hogg, M. A., Oakes, P. J., Reicher, S. D. and Wetherell, M. S. (1987). *Rediscovering the social group: A self-categorization theory*. Oxford: Blackwell.

Turner, J. C. and Onorato, R. S. (1999). Social identity, personality and the self-concept: a self-categorization perspective. In T. R. Tyler, R. Kramer and O. John (Eds.), *The psychology of the social self* (pp. 11–46). Hillsdale, NJ: Lawrence Erlbaum.

Turner, J. C. and Reynolds, K. J. (in press). The social identity perspective in intergroup relations: theories, themes and controversies. In R. J. Brown and S. Gaertner (Eds.), *Blackwell Handbook in Social Psychology, Vol. 4: Intergroup processes*. Oxford: Blackwell.

Turner, J. C., Oakes, P. J., Haslam, S. A. and McGarty, C. (1994). Self and collective: cognition and social context. *Personality and Social Psychology Bulletin, 20*, 454–63.

Tversky, A. (1977). Features of similarity. *Psychological Review, 84*, 327–52.

Tversky, A. and Kahneman, D. (1973). Availability: a heuristic for judging frequency and probability. *Cognitive Psychology, 4*, 207–32.

Van Knippenberg, A., van Twuyver, M. and Pepels, J. (1994). Factors affecting social categorization processes in memory. *British Journal of Social Psychology, 33*, 419–32.

Van Knippenberg, D. and Spears, R. (2001). The interactive effects of infrequency of occurrence and expectancy on social group representations. *Basic and Applied Social Psychology, 23*, 281–89.

Van Overwalle, F. (1998). Causal explanation as constraint satisfaction: a critique and a feedforward connectionist alternative. *Journal of Personality and Social Psychology, 74*, 312–28.

Van Rijswijk, W. and Ellemers, N. (2000). Stereotypering van meervoudig te categoriseren groepen: De rol van identificatie [Stereotyping of multiply categorizable groups: The role of identification]. In C. Martijn et al. (Eds.) *Fundamentele Sociale Psychologie, 8*, (pp. 1–9). Tilburg University Press.

Vanbeselaere, N. (1991). The impact of in-group and out-group homogeneity/heterogeneity upon intergroup relations. *Basic and Applied Social Psychology, 12*, 291–301.

Verkuyten, M. and Hagendoorn, L. (1998). Prejudice and self-categorization: the variable role of authoritarianism and in-group stereotypes. *Personality and Social Psychology Bulletin, 24*, 99–110.

Vinacke, W. E. (1957). Stereotypes as social concepts. *Journal of Social Psychology, 46*, 229–43.

Wattenmaker, W. D. (1995). Knowledge structures and linear separability: integrating information in object and social categorization. *Cognitive Psychology, 28*, 274–328.

Wegener, I. and Klauer, K.-C. (2000, August). The influence of interpersonal context on the applicability of social categories. Paper presented at the *Second Social Cognition Network Meeting*, Heidelberg, Germany.

Wicklund, R. A. and Gollwitzer, P. M. (1982). *Symbolic self-completion*. Hillsdale, NJ: Erlbaum.

Wilder, D. A. (1978). Reduction of intergroup conflict through individuation of the outgroup. *Journal of Personality and Social Psychology, 36*, 1361–74.

Wilder, D. A. (1986). Social categorization: implications for creation and reduction of intergroup conflicts. In L. Berkowitz (Ed.), *Advances in Experimental Social Psychology* (Vol. 19, pp. 293–355). San Diego, CA: Academic Press.

Wildschut, T., Insko, C. A. and Pinter, B. (in press). The perception of outgroup threat: content and activation of the outgroup schema. Chapter to appear in V. Y. Yzerbyt, C. M. Judd and O. Corneille (Eds.) *The Psychology of Group*

Perception: Contributions to the Study of Homogeneity, Entitivity, and Essentialism. Philadelphia: Psychology Press.

Wisniewski, E. J. and Medin, D. L. (1994). On the interaction of theory and data in concept learning. *Cognitive Science, 18,* 221–81.

Wittenbrink, B., Gist, P. L. and Hilton, J. L. (1997). Structural properties of stereotypic knowledge and their influences on the construal of social situations. *Journal of Personality and Social Psychology, 72,* 526–43.

Wittenbrink, B., Hilton, J. L. and Gist, P. L. (1997). In search of similarity: stereotypes as naïve theories in social categorization. *Social Cognition, 16,* 31–55.

Wittenbrink, B., Park, B. and Judd, C. M. (1998). The role of stereotypic knowledge in the construal of person models. In C. Sedikides, J. Schopler and C. A. Insko (Eds.), *Intergroup cognition and intergroup behaviour* (pp. 177–202). Hillsdale, NJ: Erlbaum.

Wojciszke, B. (1994). Multiple meanings of behavior: construing actions in terms of competence or morality. *Journal of Personality and Social Psychology, 67,* 222–32.

Wojciszke, B., Bazinska, R. and Jaworski, M. (1998). On the dominance of moral categories in impression formation. *Personality and Social Psychology Bulletin, 24,* 1251–63.

Worth, L. T., Allison, S. T. and Messick, D. M. (1987). Impact of a group decision on perception of one's own and others' attitudes. *Journal of Personality and Social Psychology, 53,* 673–82.

Wright, S. C., Taylor, D. M. and Moghaddam, F. M. (1990). Responding to membership in a disadvantaged group: from acceptance to collective protest. *Journal of Personality and Social Psychology, 58,* 994–1003.

Yzerbyt, V. Y. and Buidin, G. (1998). *Subjective essentialism and social categorization.* Unpublished raw data. Catholic University of Louvain, Belgium.

Yzerbyt, V. Y. and Rogier, A. (2001). Blame it on the group: entitativity, subjective essentialism and social attribution. In J. Jost and B. Major (Eds.), *The psychology of legitimacy: Emerging perspectives on ideology, justice, and intergroup relations.* New York: Cambridge University Press.

Yzerbyt, V. Y., Castano, E., Leyens, J.-Ph. and Paladino, P. (2000). The primacy of the ingroup: the interplay of identification and entitativity. In W. Stroebe and M. Hewstone (Eds.), *European Review of Social Psychology* (Vol. 11). Chichester, UK: Wiley.

Yzerbyt, V. Y., Corneille, O. and Estrada, C. (2001). The interplay of naïve theories and entitativity from the outsider and insider perspectives. *Personality and Social Psychology Review, 5,* 141–55.

Yzerbyt, V. Y., Coull, A. and Rocher, S. J. (1999). Fencing off the deviant: the role of cognitive resources in the maintenance of stereotypes. *Journal of Personality and Social Psychology, 77,* 449–62.

Yzerbyt, V. Y., Dardenne, B. and Leyens, J.-Ph. (1998). Social judgeability concerns in impression formation. In V. Y. Yzerbyt, G. Lories and B. Dardenne (Eds.), *Metacognition: Cognitive and social dimensions* (pp. 126–56). London: Sage.

Yzerbyt, V. Y., Rocher, S., McGarty, C. and Haslam, S. A. (1997). Illusory correlation: Perceived entitativity and the formation of social stereotypes. Catholic University of Louvain at Louvain-la-Neuve. Manuscript in preparation.

Yzerbyt, V. Y., Rocher, S. and Schadron, G. (1997). Stereotypes as explanations: a subjective essentialistic view of group perception. In Spears, R., Oakes, P. J., Ellemers, N. and Haslam, S. A. (Eds.), *The social psychology of stereotyping and group life* (pp. 20–50). Oxford: Blackwell.

Yzerbyt, V. Y., Rogier, A. and Fiske, S. (1998). Group entitativity and social attribution: on translating situational constraints into stereotypes. *Personality and Social Psychology Bulletin*, *24*, 1090–104.

Yzerbyt, V. Y., Rogier, A. and Rocher, S. (1998). Subjective essentialism, social attribution and the emergence of stereotypes. *International Review of Social Psychology*, *11*, 115–39.

Yzerbyt, V. Y. and Schadron, G. (1994). Stéréotypes et jugement social. In R. Bourhis and J.-Ph. Leyens (Eds.), *Stéréotypes, discrimination et relations entre groupes* [Stereotypes, discrimination and intergroup relations] (pp. 127–60). Bruxelles: Mardaga.

Yzerbyt, V. Y. and Schadron, G. (1996). *Connaître et juger autrui: Une introduction à la cognition sociale* [Knowing and judging others : An introduction to social cognition]. Grenoble: Presses Universitaires de Grenoble.

Yzerbyt, V. Y., Schadron, G., Leyens, J. -Ph. and Rocher, S. (1994). Social judgeability: the impact of meta-informational cues on the use of stereotypes. *Journal of Personality and Social Psychology*, *66*, 48–55.

Author index

Subject index

accentuation effects, 3, 6, 33, 46–50, 68–9, 112, 122–5, 128, 132, 189–90
attention, 115–16, 134, 142
attribution, *see* explanation
automaticity, 13, 27–8, 71, 139–44

biases, *see* stereotypic distortion

categorization, 2, 3, 14, 16–37, 39, 40, 46–50, 57–8, 73–6, 94–5, 112
category formation, *see* categorization
cognitive load and economy, 3, 4, 7, 115–16, 127, 191–2
cognitive miser view, 3, 4
coherence, 3, 98–9, 108, 193
comparative fit, *see* fit
competition, 117–18
consensus, 5–6, 15, 28–9, 83–4, 88, 160–85, 190, 194, 198–9
constraint relations, 16–19, 109, 187–8
contingency, 90, 193
covariation, 13, 17, 25–6, 27, 29, 30, 38, 187

dependence, 14, 111–26
differentiation, 6, 33, 46–61, 65–6, 127–56
discrimination, 116–17, 155–6, 193–4

entitativity, 12, 35, 41, 45, 196
entity-incremental theory distinction, 45, 78, 80
essentialism, 8, 13, 21, 35, 38–66, 187–8, 195–7
exemplar model of social judgement, 3, 71
expectancies, 14, 49, 50–7, 63, 70–8, 97–9, 118–19, 129, 132, 145–50, 159, 198
explanation, 2–4, 7, 12–14, 16–17, 21, 25, 26, 43, 45, 63–4, 67–8, 87–9, 94–5, 162, 186–99

fit, 21, 40, 58, 67–89, 132, 133, 159, 162–3, 172–3, 188
fundamental attribution error, 42–3

gestalts, 8
group attribution error, 118–22
group homogeneity, 41, 123–4

hierarchies, 33
hypothesis testing, 103–11

identification, 44, 134, 150–1
illusory correlation, 9–11, 32–3, 50–7, 67, 90–110, 135–9, 188, 189
illusory correlation, distinctiveness-based, 9, 10, 50–7, 67, 70, 91, 93, 136, 188
illusory correlation and differentiated meaning, 11, 24–5, 51–7, 91–3, 103–10, 136–9, 155, 160, 193–4
illusory correlation and distinctiveness, 9, 11, 128, 136, 150
illusory correlation, expectancy-based, 9–10, 57, 90–110, 188
illusory correlation, information loss accounts, 11, 51, 93, 136
interdependence, *see* dependence
intergroup relations, 1, 6, 33, 34, 66, 123, 150–2, 174–83, 190–1, 197–8

justification, 16–17, 25, 172, 187

knowledge, enduring nature of, 3, 13, 17–19, 23–5, 27–9, 32, 36, 63–5, 76–85, 134, 144–5, 147, 187, 194–5

labelling, 96–7

meaning, 14, 65–6, 101–10, 128, 189, 192
mechanism-based knowledge, 13, 17, 29–30, 38, 187
meta-contrast, *see* fit